Manage Your Life with Outlook For Dummies®

Cheat Sheet

The Custom Productivity Toolbar

As part of the process of making the Outlook Calendar module the centerpiece of your personal productivity system, I champion the idea of creating a custom Productivity toolbar (shown below in Outlook 2003 as well as Outlook 2007) that you then use in place of the built-in Standard and Advanced toolbars. (See Chapter 6 for details on how you go about creating either of these custom toolbars.)

Outlook 2003 Custom Productivity Toolbar

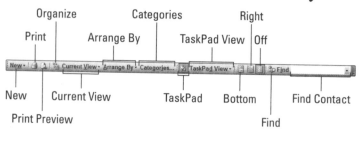

Outlook 2007 Custom Productivity Toolbar

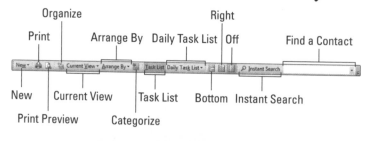

For Dummies: Bestselling Book Series for Beginners

Manage Your Life with Outlook For Dummies®

Cheat Sheet

Essential Outlook Productivity Keyboard Shortcuts

Switching Outlook Modules

Keys to Press	Result in Outlook
Ctrl+1	Makes the Mail module current
Ctrl+2	Makes the Calendar module current
Ctrl+3	Makes the Contacts module current
Ctrl+4	Makes the Tasks module current
Ctrl+5	Makes the Notes module current
Ctrl+6	Displays the Folder List in the Navigation Pane of the current module
Ctrl+7	Displays the Shortcuts in the Navigation Pane of the current module
Ctrl+8	Makes the Journal module current

Creating a New Outlook Item in the Current Module

Keys to Press	Result in Outlook
Ctrl+Shift+M	Opens an Untitled – Message dialog box so you can compose and send out a new e-mail message
Ctrl+Shift+A	Opens an Untitled – Appointment dialog box so you can add a new appointment or event to your calendar
Ctrl+Shift+Q	Opens an Untitled – Meeting dialog box so you can add a new meeting to your calendar and send out meeting requests to all your participants
Ctrl+Shift+C	Opens an Untitled – Contact dialog box so you can add a new contact to your address book
Ctrl+Shift+L	Opens an Untitled – Distribution List dialog box so you can specify the people on your distribution list and add this list to your address book
Ctrl+Shift+K	Opens an Untitled – Task dialog box so you can add a new to-do item to your task list
Ctrl+Shift+U	Opens an Untitled – Task dialog box with a Send button, To field, and Updated Copy and Status Report check boxes so you can send a task request to another co-worker, asking him or her to accept responsibility for the task
Ctrl+Shift+J	Opens an Untitled – Journal so you can add a manual entry to your Journal for an activity that Outlook doesn't automatically track

Copyright © 2008 Wiley Publishing, Inc. All rights reserved. Item 5930-4.

For more information about Wiley Publishing, call 1-800-762-2974.

For Dummies: Bestselling Book Series for Beginners

Manage Your Life with Outlook®

FOR DUMMIES®

Manage Your Life with Outlook® FOR DUMMIES®

by Greg Harvey

WILEY

Wiley Publishing, Inc.

Manage Your Life with Outlook® For Dummies®

Published by
Wiley Publishing, Inc.
111 River Street
Hoboken, NJ 07030-5774

www.wiley.com

Library of Congress Control Number: 2008935816

ISBN: 978-0-471-95930-4

Manufactured in the United States of America

10 9 8 7 6 5 4 3 2 1

WILEY

About the Author

Greg Harvey has authored tons of computer books, the most recent being *Excel Workbook For Dummies* and *Roxio Easy Media Creator 8 For Dummies,* and the most popular being *Excel 2007 For Dummies* and *Excel 2007 All-in-One Desk Reference For Dummies.* He started out training business users on how to use IBM personal computers and their attendant computer software in the rough and tumble days of DOS, WordStar, and Lotus 1-2-3 in the mid-80s of the last century. After working for a number of independent training firms, he went on to teach semester-long courses in spreadsheet and database management software at Golden Gate University in San Francisco.

His love of teaching has translated into an equal love of writing. *For Dummies* books are, of course, his all-time favorites to write because they enable him to write to his favorite audience: the beginner. They also enable him to use humor (a key element to success in the training room) and, most delightful of all, to express an opinion or two about the subject matter at hand.

Greg received his doctorate degree in Humanities in Philosophy and Religion with a concentration in Asian Studies and Comparative Religion last May. Everyone is glad that Greg was finally able to get out of school before he retired.

For the past two years, Greg has been actively researching productivity in the modern workplace and the various ideas and systems developed for improving work/life, especially using Microsoft's Outlook software.

Dedication

To Katie Feltman in great appreciation of her unwavering support for the concept and execution of this book

Author's Acknowledgments

Let me take this opportunity to thank all the people, both at Wiley Publishing, Inc., and at Mind Over Media, Inc., whose dedication and talent combined to get this book out and into your hands in such great shape.

At Wiley Publishing, Inc., I want to thank Andy Cummings and Katie Feltman for their encouragement and help in getting this project under way and their ongoing support every step of the way; Leah Cameron and Paul Levesque for making sure that the project stayed on course and made it into production so that all the talented folks on the production team could create this great final product.

At Mind Over Media, I want to thank Christopher Aiken for his review of the updated manuscript and invaluable input and suggestions on how best to address both the more theoretical and downright practical concerns of personal productivity in the modern workplace.

Publisher's Acknowledgments

We're proud of this book; please send us your comments through our online registration form located at www.dummies.com/register/.

Some of the people who helped bring this book to market include the following:

Acquisitions and Editorial

Senior Project Editor: Paul Levesque

Acquisitions Editor: Katie Feltman

Copy Editors: Virginia Sanders, Susan Christophersen

Technical Editor: Joyce Nielsen

Editorial Manager: Leah Cameron

Editorial Assistant: Amanda Foxworth

Sr. Editorial Assistant: Cherie Case

Cartoons: Rich Tennant
(www.the5thwave.com)

Composition Services

Project Coordinator: Katie Key

Layout and Graphics: Melissa K. Jester, Reuben W. Davis, Christin Swinford, Christine Williams

Proofreaders: Melissa Bronnenberg, Reuben W. Davis, Nancy L. Reinhardt

Indexer: Word Co. Indexing Services

Publishing and Editorial for Technology Dummies

Richard Swadley, Vice President and Executive Group Publisher

Andy Cummings, Vice President and Publisher

Mary Bednarek, Executive Acquisitions Director

Mary C. Corder, Editorial Director

Publishing for Consumer Dummies

Diane Graves Steele, Vice President and Publisher

Composition Services

Gerry Fahey, Vice President of Production Services

Debbie Stailey, Director of Composition Services

Contents at a Glance

Table of Contents

Introduction

. . . .

Make no mistake about it; the subject of this book is enhancing your personal productivity rather than using Microsoft Outlook. As far as this book's concerned, Outlook is merely a means to an end, and that end is simply to bring your professional and personal lives into greater balance. And the full expectation is that this greater balance will bring with it a greater sense of satisfaction and fulfillment to both aspects of your life.

Fortunately, when it comes to enhancing your personal productivity, Outlook can serve you quite well. Beyond its obvious e-mail capabilities, Outlook offers a whole array of tools you can immediately start bringing to bear in your effort to deal more effectively with both your professional and personal obligations. The pages ahead, then, are chock-full of ideas, suggestions, and practical techniques all designed to guide you towards making Outlook the principal toolkit you use in your pursuit of enhanced personal productivity, better work/life balance, and greater happiness.

About This Book

Given that the subject of personal productivity has both its theoretical and practical aspects, so does this book. It consists roughly of one part vision and three parts application. The vision stuff in the first part gives you ideas on the current thinking of what it takes to achieve peak productivity as well as ideas on how to assess your own particular situation. The practical, Outlook-related information in the remainder of the book then gives you the lowdown on how to mold this program to fit your work/life situation so you can actually realize your productivity vision.

This doesn't mean, however, that the book is meant to be read from beginning to end or from cover to cover. Although the chapters are organized in a logical order (progressing from the more theoretical aspects of personal productivity to the downright practical with Outlook), each topic covered in a chapter is really meant to stand pretty much on its own. It's really up to you to figure out where you need to go and what information will be of most help.

How to Use This Book

This book is like a reference in which you start out by looking up the topic you need information about (either in the Table of Contents or the Index), and then you refer directly to the section of interest. I explain most topics conversationally (as though you were in my office). Sometimes, however, my regiment-commander mentality takes over, and I list the steps you need to take to accomplish a particular task in a particular section.

I do recommend you start, at the very least, by perusing the theoretical, assessment-type stuff in the chapters in Part I, even if you think you know exactly where you're coming from and are quite sure where you want and need to go. I say this because framing (or reframing) the problem and possible solutions are often tremendous motivators that can really help get you going and keep you going. This type of fundamental assessment can also prevent you from wasting time on exploring practical, Outlook techniques in chapters in the later parts that really don't address your most pressing and immediate productivity snafus and conundrums.

Foolish Assumptions

The only assumptions I make about you, dear reader (other than you're highly motivated to bring your professional and personal life into better balance), are that you currently use either Microsoft Outlook 2003 or, the latest, Outlook 2007 for taking care of your e-mail and that your computer is running some version of the Windows operating system. And, as a result, you run Outlook every day (whether or not your computer automatically launches the program at its startup) so that Outlook is readily available to you whenever you're at the computer.

As for your experience and skill level with Outlook, it really doesn't matter whether or not you've ever strayed any further than its Inbox or that you have loads of experience using its more advanced features and other modules. The important thing here is that you maintain a willingness to explore aspects of this program that are new to you and to adopt a new perspective towards those aspects with which you're already familiar.

Beyond that, you simply need to be open to developing habits that support and enhance your overall personal productivity. Remember that there are no gold stars for knowing more about Outlook and its hundreds of features. In fact, the only brownie points given are for knowing how to use those Outlook features that actually put you in greater control of your work and life.

How This Book Is Organized

This book is organized in five parts. Each part contains two or more chapters with related content. Each chapter is further divided into loosely related sections that cover the basics of the topic at hand. You should not, however, get too hung up about following along with the structure of the book; ultimately, it doesn't matter at all if you find out how to manage your to-do list in the Tasks module before you find out how to do scheduling in the Calendar. The important thing is that you find the information — and understand it when you find it — when you need to explore a new aspect of personal productivity or use Outlook to achieve it.

In case you're interested, here's a synopsis of what you find in each part that follows.

Part 1: Preparing for Personal Productivity

The four chapters in this part set the stage for using Outlook as your personal information manager. They not only give you basic information on the current thinking on just what it takes to be truly productive in the modern work world, but they also enable you to take a good long look at your situation and come up with your own definition of personal productivity.

Part II: Making Outlook Your Key to Personal Productivity

The two chapters in this part give you an overview of Outlook's complete capabilities as a personal information manager (far beyond just your e-mail and address program). Chapter 5 acquaints (or reacquaints) you with the modular setup of Outlook and how you can use its various features in your quest towards increased productivity. Chapter 6 then gives you suggestions on how you might customize Outlook so that it better serves your productivity goals.

Part III: Taking Control of Your E-Mail Inbox

Increased personal productivity with Outlook starts and ends with taking control of your Outlook e-mail Inbox. The chapters in this part give you the lowdown on exactly how to do this. Chapter 7 shows you how to do a basic Inbox housecleaning and Chapter 8 then goes on to show you how to do ongoing housekeeping to keep your Inbox under your control.

Part IV: Developing Your Outlook Productivity Practices

The first six chapters in this part cover Outlook productivity practices in detail across each of its major modules. The final chapter in this part then gives you suggestions on how to take your Outlook data with you when you're on the go. Together, the practical information in this part is designed to give you everything you need to truly make Outlook your complete personal information manager.

Part V: The Part of Tens

The two chapters in the Part of Tens give you access to two of my top ten lists. Chapter 16 gives you my top ten personal productivity strategies that encapsulate the attitudes that I think are essential for you to cultivate in your quest for increased productivity. Chapter 17 then gives you my top ten Outlook productivity techniques that you can use as a checklist in determining the types of new Outlook habits you should nurture.

Appendixes

The two appendixes give you a guide to more resources on personal productivity along with a tool for assessing your needs and goals. Appendix A offers a list of print and online productivity resources that you can consult for more information on this fascinating subject. Appendix B acts as an assessment tool that you can use to record your vision, aspirations, and near- and long-term objectives for achieving greater personal productivity and better work/life balance.

Conventions Used in This Book

Throughout the text, I give you keyboard shortcuts that you need to learn by heart in order attain top productivity. Most of these shortcuts are key combos that use the Ctrl in combination with other letters, although some use the Shift key as well. With these shortcuts, you need to hold down the Ctrl (and Shift key) as you type the letter.

When it comes to menu commands, this book uses command arrows to lead you from the initial menu, to any submenus, and finally to the command option you ultimately want. For example, if you need to open the File menu to get to the Open command, that instruction would look like this: Choose File⇨Open.

Finally, if you're really observant, you may notice a slight discrepancy between the capitalization of the names of dialog box options (such as headings, option buttons, and check boxes) as they appear in the book and how they actually appear in Outlook on your computer screen. I intentionally use the convention of capitalizing the initial letters of all the main words of a dialog box option to help you differentiate the name of the option from the rest of the text describing its use.

Special Icons

The following icons are strategically placed in the margins to point out stuff you may or may not want to read.

This icon means the paragraph contains nerdy discussions that you may well want to skip (or read when no one else is around).

This icon alerts you to shortcuts or other valuable hints related to the topic at hand.

This icon highlights information to keep in mind if you want to meet with a modicum of success.

This icon indicates some suggestion or hint that you may find really helps you become more productive.

This icon alerts you to information to keep in mind if you want to avert some dire future problems.

This icon flags material that is specific to Outlook 2007, the latest version of the software.

Where to Go from Here

I have a couple of suggestions for where to go from here (after you get a chuckle from the great Rich Tennant cartoons). You may want to go directly to the Part of Tens to check out my top ten lists; in Chapter 16, you find a list for general productivity strategies, and Chapter 17 offers a list with a particular emphasis on Outlook productivity techniques. Otherwise, I suggest you start out by taking a look at the material in Chapter 1 and using its information and suggestions to start devising your very own plan for becoming as productive as you possibly can with Outlook so that you can immediately begin to bring your professional and personal lives into greater harmony.

Part I
Preparing for Personal Productivity

The 5th Wave   By Rich Tennant

"I think the cursor's not moving, Mr. Dundt, because you're using the chalk board eraser instead of a mouse."

In this part . . .

*I*ncreasing your personal productivity to achieve
greater work/life balance is not simply a matter of
acquiring and applying new skills in Outlook. Before that,
you need to do some assessment work. The chapters in this
first part are designed to help you go through the process of
understanding the place from which you're starting as well
as visualize the place you intend to be.

Chapter 1

Planning for Better Balance between Your Work and Personal Life

*B*efore you have any chance of becoming more productive, you really need to take stock of where you're at now regarding keeping your personal life and work in balance.

In this chapter, you begin this process by taking a good long look at your current level of personal productivity on the job and the typical symptoms of imbalance, and from there you imagine how you might improve it so as to create a better equilibrium between work and your personal life.

Next, you get a chance to take a look at the most common reasons people give for not being productive — in other words, all those pitiful excuses that you have for not being able to get it together in the productivity department.

Finally, you get the opportunity to look at some of the ways that Microsoft Outlook can help you become more productive at work and actually help you start making that goal of work/life balance a reality.

"If I Only Had a Life . . ."

One surefire way to tell that your personal life and work aren't in balance is if you don't even think of yourself as really having a personal life. If your work not only takes center stage in your life but leaves little or no room for anyone or anything else, then I think you'd agree that you're in real need of regaining some kind of balance between your office and home. Another clear sign is if you always feel as though both at work and at home you don't have enough time to get all you have to do done, and therefore are decidedly dissatisfied in both environments.

In this age of the knowledge/service worker outfitted with anywhere, anytime Internet access, it can be especially hard to maintain even the smallest semblance of work/life balance.

As someone who's made a living as a self-employed author working principally in a home office setting, I encountered my first major problem with maintaining any real personal life early on in my writing career. It first showed up in the form of extended workdays that were all too soon joined by working weekends. And the moment I got my first laptop computer and realized that my writing could now accompany me on holiday, working vacations immediately took their unrighteous place beside my working weekends and interminable workdays.

And although this unholy alliance may have contributed to my meeting many a book deadline, this came at a high cost to maintaining equilibrium between my professional and personal lives both in terms of personal stress and lost opportunities to unwind from the demands of the job.

Checking out some typical warning signs of work/life imbalance

You may be wondering whether you're really suffering from work/life imbalance or whether the job you currently have is simply a really bad fit. To help you determine whether you should start applying the principles in this book instead of doing an extensive job search online, I've put together the following checklist.

This checklist contains the most common warning signs of the productivity problems that can lead to significant work/life imbalance. If you find that several items in this list apply in your situation, in all probability you need to start implementing steps to regain a sense of equilibrium between your personal and professional life:

  ✔ You feel as though there's never enough time in the day to get all your work done.

- ✔ You regularly work longer than normal hours and/or take work home with you.

- ✔ You feel as though much of any given workday is spent unproductively, laden with ineffective meetings or work interruptions.

- ✔ You're fuzzy about the extent of your job responsibilities and/or the job you thought you were hired to do is not the one you're doing.

- ✔ You feel as though you're trying to do the job of two people.

- ✔ No matter how many hours you put in or how hard you work, you repeatedly leave the office with some important task(s) unfinished.

- ✔ You regularly think about what you couldn't get done at work when you're at home.

- ✔ You often have the vague feeling that you're overlooking or forgetting important tasks that need your attention.

- ✔ You dread dealing with your e-mail.

- ✔ Brief physical interactions with co-workers, telephone calls, and/or incoming e-mail messages become interruptions that take you off task.

- ✔ You often have trouble locating the information you need in order to perform a particular work task and have to spend valuable time searching for it.

- ✔ As a manager, you have trouble successfully tracking the tasks you delegate to members of your team. As a member of a team, you have trouble successfully keeping track of and accomplishing the tasks that are delegated to you.

- ✔ You seldom have time to set your daily or weekly work goals and then lay out and prioritize the objectives necessary to achieve them.

- ✔ You seldom have time to prioritize the tasks you plan to accomplish on any given day or within a given week, and when you *do* get an opportunity to prioritize the tasks you need to accomplish, you often have trouble deciding how they should be ranked.

Work forms such a big part of everyone's life that when clusters of productivity problems such as the ones included in this checklist crop up, more often than not they're bound to end up negatively affecting your personal life in short order. That's why you need to get on the productivity band wagon as soon as you can and nip such problems in the bud. You definitely don't want to wait until they get out of hand and start negatively impacting your health, happiness, and personal relationships.

Making work/life balance your number one priority

When you let your professional and personal lives get out of whack, not only do you find it difficult to maintain your daily well-being but you can also end up regretting, at some point in the future, the toll your work demands took on your personal life.

The real cost of my own work/life imbalance became apparent to me as the result of two separate life-altering incidents: First, at age 40, when I was diagnosed with cancer and then again, at age 49, when my life and business partner of 16 years died suddenly. Both events made me question the amount of time and energy that I had devoted to my professional career at the expense of my personal life. (This included long workdays, working weekends, and taking very few vacations.)

Having to face my own mortality and then the passing of my close partner drove home the notion that you can never get back the time you worked when you should have been playing. It also made it abundantly clear that, when all is said and done, you'll never have to worry about regretting any of the times that you didn't stay longer at the office or work more. On the contrary, you run the real risk of someday being plagued with doubts about the time that you sacrificed your personal life for your work and the time for yourself that you can never get back.

I don't care how great your job is or how rewarding it may be monetarily, the only way to truly avoid any possibility of regret later on is to make sure that your professional and personal lives remain in relative harmony now. In creating such harmony, you not only avoid later disappointment but actually create a level of personal satisfaction that permeates both work and home environments.

Getting your work and life back into balance isn't something that's going to happen all by itself. To get anywhere with it, you have to make creating this type of equilibrium a real priority. In fact, at least for the time being, you have to make it your number one personal and professional goal. One of the best ways to get the ball rolling in this department entails reevaluating your professional objectives, both short- and long-term (a process that I outline in Chapter 2).

Imagining what work/life balance would look like in your life

Before attempting to take any of the steps necessary to become more productive at work and thus bring your work and personal life back into better balance, you can really benefit from taking some time to imagine

just what this balance would look like in your own life. Here are just some of the benefits you might see yourself accruing from creating this balance (please feel free to add your own ideas to this starter list):

- ✔ Normal workdays with no more late nights at the office or bringing work home
- ✔ Weekends off with nary a thought of work
- ✔ More free time to spend with family and friends
- ✔ More energy to devote to personal growth and aspirations
- ✔ Newfound sense of professional accomplishment
- ✔ Rededication to your job and new sense of commitment to your career
- ✔ Greater capacity to deal with the stresses you encounter both at work and at home
- ✔ Heightened level of creativity both at work and at home
- ✔ Whole new sets of professional and personal goals

As some of the items in this list clearly demonstrate, some of these expected benefits are assumed to impact both your personal and professional lives. This makes sense because no matter where you're at or what you're doing, you're really living just one life. As a result, you can anticipate that an increase in your dedication and creativity at work is going to spill over into similar aspects of your personal life.

Before embarking on any of the productivity suggestions I make in later chapters of this book, be sure to take the time to make your own list that catalogs all the benefits you're hoping to see when you bring your work and life into better balance. Your list acts not only as a powerful motivation tool but can also help you better define just what work/life balance means in your situation. You can also use it as a checklist to help you evaluate the progress you're making in terms of achieving this very important equilibrium in your own professional and personal life.

Exploring Common Excuses for Remaining Unproductive

Although you may find the *idea* of feeling fully competent in your job as well as having a real life outside of it to boot very enticing (talk about having your cake and eating it, too), you probably still harbor some doubts about how realistic this is in your particular work situation.

You may be someone who's already tried following a foolproof personal productivity system or two without much enduring success. Heaven forbid, you may even be someone who's gone through a productivity makeover at the hands of a professional organizational life coach or efficiency expert, only to relapse into comfortable chaos and less-than-stellar productivity after the coach had up and gone (and yet long before you had finished paying off his bill).

And even if you don't have any experience (good or bad) with trying to implement somebody else's system for becoming productive, if you're anything like 90 percent of the other people in the working world, you almost certainly harbor some choice excuses about why you're destined to remain organization- and efficiency-challenged despite your best efforts.

Some of these excuses probably stem from doubts you harbor about your own abilities (often known as *self-limiting beliefs*). Many, however, are undoubtedly based on misgivings that you harbor about your job itself and the corporate environment in which you have to perform it.

Before embarking on any steps designed to boost your personal productivity, I think it's useful to review the more common excuses given for remaining unproductive. Here's a short list of excuses that you may have to deal with:

- ✔ I'm just not an organized person.
- ✔ I'm just not good with technology.
- ✔ There's just not enough time in the workday to get it all done.
- ✔ My job involves too many interruptions for me to be truly productive.
- ✔ I just don't do well with self-help systems.

In the sections immediately following, I deal with each of these excuses in more detail.

I'm just not an organized person

Lots of people believe that you're either born a neat freak like immaculate Felix Unger or a total slob like messy Oscar Madison (the mismatched roommates in Neil Simon's Broadway play, *The Odd Couple,* that later became a hit movie and TV series).

Personally, I'm just not convinced there are any "neatness" or "messiness" genes out there for anyone to inherit. It seems more likely to me that, when growing up, you're exposed either to more or to less order, and then your early experience with the relative level of orderliness or disarray in different environments shapes your reactions later in life.

In my case, I'm very uncomfortable with clutter and disorder (especially in my work environment) but nonetheless tend to be a rather disorganized and messy worker. (I seem to have a real knack for creating piles and stacks.) The good news, however, is that I've really made my peace with tidiness. I can now recognize when I really need to get the office organized because the level of disorder is beginning to impede my ability to be really productive. At that point, I proceed to get the place in order straightaway without hesitation or resentment.

Organizing my work environment strictly on this kind of as-needed basis enables me to maintain a high level of productivity without feeling like a neatness drudge. As a result, I no longer bristle at tasks such as filing because I never feel like too much of my work time and energy is spent in tidying up and organizing the place.

In case you consider yourself a dyed-in-the-wool Oscar Madison with little or no hope of becoming the least bit like Felix Unger, you'll be happy to know that there's still hope for you when it comes to achieving high productivity in your work. In fact, there's now a school of thought on personal productivity that actually celebrates a certain degree of chaos in the workplace, maintaining, in short, that one person's mess is another person's order. See Chapter 2 for more on my take on this challenging (crazy?) notion that you can still be productive without being organized, at least in the strictest sense of the word.

I'm just not good with technology

As someone who did corporate computer training for many years, I'm very well acquainted with the "I'm no good with technology" excuse. It's a complaint I heard a lot as business people scrambled to adapt to the wholesale introduction of personal computers into the workplace.

Several factors seem to contribute to the general funk over technology that I sometimes find among many otherwise quite bright and enthusiastic business people:

- **The accelerated rate of change** (in the name of incessant improvement) of the high-tech industry that constantly requires the expense and relearning associated with upgrading your hardware and software.

- **The continuing gap** between the high tech's promise of greater personal productivity and its actual delivery that leaves you wondering whether using all this stuff is really worth it.

- **The ever-increasing portability** of high-tech hardware and omnipresence of high-speed wireless communication that makes it increasingly possible to work anytime, anywhere (commuting, traveling, and even on vacation) and thus harder and harder to keep work and play separate.

Keep in mind that playing the game of eternal catch-up with the tools of your trade can play havoc with your sense of self-worth and competency as a worker. Trying to escape work's longer and longer reach and finally find a time "when the working day is done" can be quite demoralizing and promote early burnout.

Every time I turn around, it's out-of-date!

One of the more vexing aspects of high tech — to everyone but its engineers and programmers — is how hard this industry works at making its own latest and greatest products completely obsolete! It seems as though no sooner do you become competent using a particular version of a computer operating system and the application software upon which your entire job seems to depend than they're replaced with newer, "improved" editions.

Quite often, these new software versions require considerable relearning in order for you to perform the very same work you did just fine using the previous, now-obsolete versions. Not only that, new versions of operating systems and application software sometime require you to make extensive and sometimes expensive upgrades to your existing hardware and other auxiliary software programs.

Perhaps even more demoralizing than having to spend time you don't have relearning the new software and incurring additional upgrade costs is finding out that the installation of this latest and greatest version has introduced incompatibilities into a computer system that was otherwise working just fine.

Still too complex and inflexible

In terms of both flexibility and ease of use, I agree that computer technology continues to promise much more than it can deliver. Despite great strides made to the interface of personal computer operating systems (think Windows Vista) and application software programs (think Microsoft Office) in the last decade or so, computers remain exceedingly complex tools that, more often than not, still work the way they want to rather than the way you want them to.

No matter how you feel about the escalating role of technology in your life, it's not going away any time soon. You can bet your bottom dollar its role is only going to increase both in the workplace and in the home. This is one fate you can't escape and a place where, since you can't beat them, you need seriously consider how best to join them.

The only advice I can come up with for countering the inflexibility and complexity displayed by high tech is to get yourself as well trained in its use as you possibly can. As I hope you discover in this book on using Outlook as your tool for personal productivity, good basic training lets you understand not only how the technology is supposed to be used, but also how you can use it in more creative ways to come up with unique solutions to problems you encounter in getting your particular job done.

It's getting harder and harder to get off the digital leash

Given the phenomenal rise of Wi-Fi (wireless) Internet access for laptop computers, and cellular Internet and e-mail access for mobile phones and other handheld digital devices, it's becoming increasingly difficult for knowledge workers to unplug from the Net. (A *knowledge worker* is someone like you who depends upon technology to get work done.) And because you can now so easily work almost any place you're located, it becomes even more difficult for you to keep your time on and off the job separate.

When the problem is primarily finding ways to work smarter (that is, more efficiently) rather than to work longer hours, simply having constant digital access doesn't really provide much of a boost in terms of personal productivity. More often than not, it simply leads to more resentment as you devote more and more time to job without seeing your work diminish and you lose more and more ground in terms of having a life outside your job.

Not enough time to get it all done

The excuse that there's just not enough time in the day to get everything done is probably not only the one most commonly heard, it's also the one that's the most true. In fact, chances are you're going to have to accept that even when you reach your peak level of personal productivity, you'll face many workdays when you simply won't have enough time to get it all done.

Face it: There are only 24 hours in a day and 7 days in a week, and that's all there's ever going to be. The only way to get more out of your work week is to better manage the time you have. And the best way to manage the time you have is to reach and maintain your peak personal productivity.

Instead of seeing this lack of adequate time as a justification for not trying to reach your peak productivity, I suggest you see this as the perfect rationale for becoming and remaining as productive as you possibly can. For, in doing so, you not only cut down the number of times when you can't get it all done, but you also are in a much better position to manage those very occasions when it's simply not going to happen.

This is because a big part of maintaining peak productivity is knowing how to prioritize pressing obligations in ways that help you reach your current objectives without increasing your stress level. This is, of course, just the skill that you need to make the most of a situation in which there's no way that every obligation is going to get met.

Being able to prioritize in this manner enables you to make intelligent decisions when it comes to separating the tasks you can complete from those you can't. It also helps you deal more effectively with the tasks that spill over into the next day so that you have half a chance to get back on track and not remain behind the eight ball.

I experience too many interruptions to be productive

For many folks, a typical workday is made up of almost entirely of interruptions, one after another. Interruptions to your work come in many forms:

- ✔ Telephone calls
- ✔ E-mail correspondence
- ✔ Instant or text messages
- ✔ Impromptu meetings

Regardless of what form they take, the biggest problem with interruptions such as these is that they're unplanned. Because they're not scheduled, you have a lot less control on how long they'll take you away from the work you need to be doing. Also, after a particular interruption is over, rather than getting directly back to the work you planned to do, you may find yourself naturally responding to matters raised during the interruption instead.

The truth is that, with the obvious exception of interruptions from your managers, you always have a choice not to indulge in your workday interruptions. All you have to do is find the motivation necessary to keep to your stated work objectives and not drop everything you're working on the moment your computer indicates an e-mail's arrived, the phone rings, or a co-worker appears at your cubicle or office doorway. One of the best ways to motivate yourself in this manner is to take inventory of all the time you typically spend in responding to these daily interruptions as well as then getting back to the work you were doing.

Be especially careful not to take small daily interruptions as excuses to get off track and not attend to your other work. When you're not yet at your peak of personal productivity and you're facing more obligations than you're apt to get done in a day, you can all too easily let such interruptions sidetrack you until they reach the point where they become major diversions and additional excuses for not being able to be productive at work.

I just don't do all that well with self-help systems

Another frequent reason for being hesitant about undertaking steps towards personal productivity is that they normally come packaged as part of a complete self-help system (often with a particular productivity coach or guru's name attached to it, such as the FranklinCovey Planning System or Sally McGhee's Productivity Solutions).

If you're anything like so many other people, you're no stranger to self-help systems, perhaps more in the form of diet, physical fitness, and the like than personal productivity. At the outset, as a beginner trying to take in the system, you probably find yourself quite enthusiastic and open to all it appears to offer. As you try out and take on the new routines involved in the process, you may even experience quite rapid and gratifying results.

However, as time goes by, you find your original enthusiasm beginning to wane. You see yourself starting to lose some of your initial interest as the results that came so easily at the outset begin to slow and, in some cases, even cease. It's at this juncture that you may start discovering all the ways that the particular "system" doesn't fit the way you do business or live. Depending upon how heavily you're invested in the system at this point, you may even find yourself questioning its overall efficacy and making the decision to abandon its principles altogether.

The reason I think that so many people experience this type of arc with self-help systems is that they're usually presented as a "one size fits all" deal. This makes them just too demanding and rigid for most people and therefore impossible to maintain as originally packaged over the long haul. In other words, the very strict and narrow progression of steps that they claim as the secret to the success of their system can also often become the source of its own undoing in the eyes of their followers.

Because I'm well aware that "one size" most certainly does not fit all when it comes to personal productivity, in this book I endeavor to present you with many of the best ideas on personal productivity using Microsoft Outlook without pushing anybody's system. (I also give you references for each system so you can get more information if you want it.) My goal throughout is to help you decide under what circumstances a particular technique can help make you more productive. Keep in mind that the most productive knowledge worker is the one who's so comfortable using Outlook as a primary tool for organizing and keeping track of his or her work obligations that the program never becomes the center of attention. The focus instead remains exactly where it needs to: on accomplishing the work objectives required to reach both the short- and long-term goals that you develop.

Outlook and Personal Productivity

To most business folks, the Microsoft Outlook program that comes as part of the Microsoft Office suite of applications represents nothing more than a somewhat satisfactory e-mail program complete with an electronic address book. Of course, when approached from this narrow angle, it's downright impossible to see how one could ever make Outlook the centerpiece of improved job productivity.

Quite frankly, Outlook becomes the keystone in achieving peak personal productivity and true work/life balance only when you approach and use the program as your *Personal Information Manager* — the primary software program you rely on to keep yourself organized and on track. As you discover in Chapters 5 and 6, this means essentially becoming fluent in the use of *all* of Outlook's modules so that you can make full use of the features that you need to truly stay on top of all your professional and, in some cases, personal obligations on a daily basis.

Figures 1-1 and 1-2 show you the Outlook program window for the two program versions (2003 and 2007, respectively) currently in widespread use. As you can see, the opening program windows for both versions are very similar. The biggest difference is that version 2007 displays an additional To-Do Bar along with the standard Navigation Pane, Information Viewer, and Reading Pane.

Navigation Pane

Figure 1-1:
The Outlook
2003
program
window as
it normally
appears
when
you first
launch the
application.

Information Viewer   Reading Pane

Navigation Pane   To-Do Bar

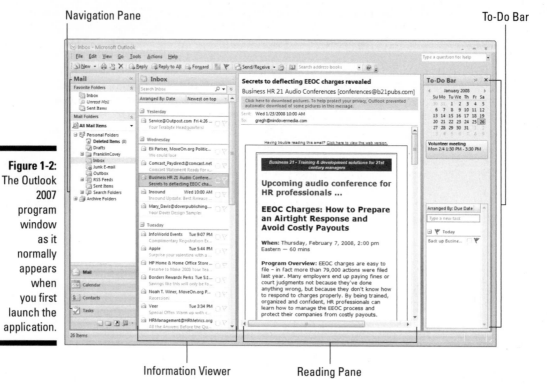

Figure 1-2:
The Outlook 2007 program window as it normally appears when you first launch the application.

Information Viewer   Reading Pane

Looking at these two figures, you can immediately see why so many Outlook users restrict their program use to e-mail alone. After all, it's the Inbox folder in the Mail module that normally appears each time a user launches the application. (You can change this default view to another folder in another module if you want, as you discover in Chapter 5.)

To use Outlook as a true productivity tool, you have to go beyond the Mail module. Looking at the bottom of the Navigation Pane in Figure 1-1 or 1-2, you see a bunch of buttons beneath the Mail button. These additional buttons (only some of which are labeled) are the keys to using Outlook as a full-fledged Personal Information Manager:

✔ **Calendar:** Displays a daily, weekly, or monthly calendar that contains a visual schedule of all your upcoming appointments.

✔ **Contacts:** Displays an address book with cards or listings for all the people and companies you correspond with.

✔ **Tasks:** Displays a Tasks (2003) or To-Do (2007) list that tells you all things you still need to get done in the near future.

✔ **Notes:** Displays all notes to yourself that you add to jog your memory.

- ✓ **Folder List:** Displays a list of the Outlook folders you use in the Navigation Pane.

- ✓ **Shortcuts:** Displays a list of all the shortcuts to the Outlook folders that you use in the Navigation Pane.

- ✓ **Journal:** Displays a timeline that chronicles daily activities such as the e-mail messages you send and documents you open. (Note that the Journal button does not automatically appear in the Navigation Pane until you add the button using the Add or Remove Buttons option on the Configure Button pop-up menu.)

In the chapters in Part II, you find out a whole lot more about accessing and customizing the views of these various modules. In Part IV, you begin your intense training on how to use their particular features to maximize your personal productivity.

Chapter 2

Exploring Accepted Beliefs on Personal Productivity

*I*t's now time to examine the philosophical underpinnings of personal productivity. In this chapter, you get a chance to review the major qualities that most people, both amateur and professional, believe are essential to achieving peak personal productivity.

Before getting into the specific beliefs outlined in this chapter, you may want to take a moment to see how you do with the following true or false statements. Responding to these statements can give you a rough idea of your current viewpoint on what it takes to be productive. So, true or false,

✔ I must be an organized person if you want to become a productive one.

✔ Clutter in my physical environment always makes it harder for me to be productive.

✔ The ability to effectively prioritize my obligations is one of the most important ingredients of organization.

✔ Only workers who know how to manage their time effectively are productive.

✔ Effective planning is a vital component of personal productivity.

✔ The ability to multitask (deal with more than one task at a time) is essential to reaching peak personal productivity.

✔ Maintaining flexibility and remaining resilient are key qualities of a highly productive worker.

✔ Creating and adhering to a workflow diagram is a major factor in reaching peak personal productivity.

✔ Taking the time to set weekly/monthly objectives and goals for yourself is a major factor in maintaining peak personal productivity.

✔ Doing a regular (weekly/monthly) review to ascertain how close you've come to realizing the objectives and goals you've set is a vital part of maintaining peak personal productivity.

So how did you do? How many of these ten statements do you currently think are true and how many do you think are false? If you really, truly believe all ten to be true, then you may have a lot of work ahead in order to reach your peak personal productivity if you don't already possess the qualities being described. Of course, if you're already a highly organized, clutter-free person to whom planning and multitasking come naturally, you may only need a few pointers with using Outlook.

Come back and retake the quiz after you've had a chance to peruse the various sections in the rest of the chapter. Then, compare your original answers with the answers you give after exploring the debate — and there really is a debate! — on the relative importance of organization, time management, lack of clutter, solid planning, stated objectives and goals, and ongoing review in becoming and remaining highly productive. Regardless of whether you change any of your answers, taking the time to keep track of your views will be very valuable when you move on to translating these philosophical beliefs into practices involving Outlook.

When Organization Is King

Organization is one of the most used terms in the discussion on personal productivity. Because of that, it's very important to be very clear on its meaning. For the purposes of this book, *organization* usually refers to the following qualities:

✔ **Orderliness:** The precise arrangement used in presenting collections of information or objects. This arrangement very often entails grouping the information or objects into some sort of hierarchical categories.

✔ **Tidiness:** The relative neatness exhibited by the arrangement applied to like objects.

✔ **Method:** The practice that determines the order in which the information or objects are arranged. (Note that the method applied to create the relative neatness may not be readily apparent.)

✔ **Regulations:** The rules that determine the order by which the information or objects are arranged.

Note that although organization in the context of productivity entails a logical and precise grouping and ordering of the information or objects you work with, the method followed in creating this order does not necessarily ensure greater ease of use.

For example, compare the system of organizing books in your local library with that followed by your neighborhood bookstore. The library organizes its book collections using a version of the famous Dewey Decimal System that categorizes them into a series of classes, divisions, and sections that determine a book's decimal number. And although no one would deny this system is highly logical and precise, outside of people trained in Library Science, the system makes it very difficult for the average person to find what he or she is looking for.

Contrast this to the much more laid-back organizational system used by your local bookstore. In place of the highly complex (scientific?) system of classes, divisions, and sections, most bookstores simply set up broad book categories (fiction, nonfiction, history, sci-fi/fantasy, children's, and so on) and then alphabetize by author the books that fall within a given category. For many people, finding a particular title in a bookstore is much simpler than at the library, provided they can correctly determine the category in which the sought-for title falls and know the name of its primary author.

If, however, you can't figure out the category into which the bookstore help has placed the title you're looking for or don't remember who wrote it, the bookstore's organizational system is no more helpful and transparent than the library's convoluted Dewey Decimal System. As a result, you'll be relying on the bookstore's information desk or kiosk to locate the book just as much as you'd rely upon your library's electronic card catalog.

All this library/bookstore catalog talk brings up an important fact about organization, namely:

> One person's organization can be another person's chaos.

This means that although most everybody agrees that being organized is a key ingredient in being highly productive, few necessarily agree on what actually constitutes "being organized."

For example, the top-down, strictly hierarchical method that Microsoft Windows uses to organize your computer's electronic files may not represent a type of organizational system that you readily understand and are therefore comfortable with. In place of such a rigid, top-down structure, you may naturally favor a more horizontal system that doesn't rely so heavily upon nested sublevels and therefore displays more file information at one time.

Judging from the way that so many Windows users tend to rely on their My Documents folder almost exclusively, stuffing it full of all different types of work files that would be much better off stored in specialized subfolders, lots of people don't find the Windows file hierarchy to be the most natural file organizational method. If you're one of these computer users, I urge you to become more comfortable with the system by finding out how to make appropriate use of it. For a solid introduction to this topic, check out Andy Rathbone's *Windows XP For Dummies,* 2nd Edition or *Windows Vista For Dummies* (both from Wiley Publishing, Inc.).

Examining the relationship of clutter to productivity

Clutter is often portrayed as the companion of disorder. The idea that clutter is the equivalent of chaos is so widespread that people who are "messy" naturally think of themselves as disorganized.

And, of course, you probably know situations where this is definitely the case. No one can deny the disorganization that comes about when someone's a pack rat who collects and collects without ever throwing anything away until he no longer has any idea of what he really has in his collections of stuff and/or he can no longer make use of any particular item without great difficulty.

This extreme is, however, a far cry from the person whose desk contains more than one very strategically placed stack of papers and folders. In such a case, as Eric Abrahamson and David Freedman point out in their book, *A Perfect Mess The Hidden Benefits of Disorder — How Crammed Closets, Cluttered Offices, and On-the-Fly Planning Make the World a Better Place,* (published by Little, Brown and Company) "Mess isn't necessarily an absence of order." Rather, it may simply represent an order that isn't readily apparent to people who played no part in its creation.

In the case of a stack of papers on a desk, immediate usage is what most often determines the underlying order. In practice, this means that the really important papers that you need over and over again remain on top (where you can get to them easily) and the less important (and therefore less used) papers naturally go to the bottom.

It often takes the person who regularly uses the seemingly random pile of papers no time at all to locate a highly desired item in the stack. Therefore, what you and I would otherwise perceive as "clutter" really doesn't have the negative impact usually associated with a mess — at least not for that person. The important thing to keep in mind is that, because the order of the stack remains implicit and not readily apparent to anyone else, its "organization" is of very limited value.

The relative merit of a particular method of organization is a function not only of how well it arranges the items in a collection but also of how well understood and accepted the underlying regulations that produce its orderliness are. For a system of organization to aid in producing peak personal productivity, therefore, it must not only be one that you understand and can keep up with but one that works for your co-workers and, in some cases, clients as well.

Discovering why messy doesn't necessarily mean unproductive

The question remains whether or not messy automatically inhibits peak productivity. The answer to this question is more subtle that you might first guess.

You need to consider a couple of countermanding factors when attempting to answer this question:

- ✔ **Messiness curbs productivity** when your disorder continually forces you to waste time trying to find the things you need to get your work done.

- ✔ **Organization curbs productivity** when tidying and maintaining order occupies so much of your time that you can't make effective use of the resulting orderliness to get your work done.

This ongoing struggle between taking the time to organize your environment and letting it go for a while is fairly easily resolved. Simply take note of which activity is hogging more of your valuable time. If you find yourself continually wasting time searching for items that should be easily located, it's well worth the time it takes to put them in order so that they're at your fingertips next time you need them. If, however, you find yourself fussing over the losing battle of maintaining precise order over your papers, files, and whatnot to the extent that much of your workday is being eaten up playing file clerk, it's clearly time to back off and let some clutter build up (at least, until the disorder once again starts robbing you of more of your time).

When Time Management Is Key

The promise of getting more time in the day to get all your work done is an intriguing one. Time efficiency experts continually promise you "more time" through the attainment of greater efficiency using, of course, their tried-and-true system of time management.

At first glance, this sounds just great. However, have you ever wondered what would happen should you successfully use one of the time-management systems to get everything done and thereby save time in your workday? Wouldn't you then just end up filling all that newly freed time with more work?

This begs the question, "What's the real purpose of time management?" If it's just to make you more efficient so that you can effectively take on and do more work, then it seems like it can't do much to help reduce stress and promote greater work/life balance. Therefore, be very careful not to approach personal productivity merely as increased work efficiency. Simply being more efficient can end up making only the boss happy if you're still as stressed out as before and can't use this efficiency to strike a better balance between your professional and personal lives.

To me, time management isn't a question of attaining greater efficiency in the sense of getting more done in less time. Rather, it's primarily a question of finding good ways to avoid the "time traps" you tend to fall into and which render you less effective, injecting additional stress into your workday.

By avoiding the time traps you're prone to, you become a freer and more capable worker in the sense of being able to make smarter choices regarding what to do with the time you do have. This reduces your stress while at the same time boosting your self-confidence and enhancing your overall happiness and sense of well-being (a key component for achieving work/life balance).

Identifying your time traps

Simply put, a *time trap* is any situation that takes you away from the primary task that you've identified at the time as your top priority. Most, but not all, time traps are unplanned, and their durations are therefore not easily controlled. Many time traps reoccur, even when they're spontaneous and you can't predict the exact timing of their occurrence. For example, you may have a co-worker who likes to drop in on you to discuss work assignments and office politics with some frequency, although you never know for certain when to expect his visit.

Time management experts are almost universal in their condemnation of time traps as a waste of precious work time. And I have to agree that eliminating the bulk of your time traps is essential to reclaiming the time you need in order to be truly productive. Perhaps, the worst feature of time traps is that even when they're of limited duration, you still have to recover from their interruptions by finding your previous place and reengaging fully with the activity that was interrupted.

It's also worth noting that many time management experts consider disorganization to be a colossal time trap (and there, I also have to agree). As a result, they see cleaning up your messes and getting your work environment in top order as an important first step in effectively managing your work time.

Typical time traps include

- ✔ Answering unscheduled telephone calls
- ✔ Reading and/or responding to non-priority e-mail message as soon as your computer notifies you of their arrival
- ✔ Taking part in unplanned visits from co-workers (other than your boss, in which case you really have no choice)
- ✔ Researching extraneous information on the Web
- ✔ Attending to personal appointments and other personal business
- ✔ Wasting time searching for the information you need to complete assigned tasks on time because you did not maintain sufficient order in your work environment

The best way to deal with a time trap is to avoid falling into it altogether. If you find you've fallen into a particular time trap, the next best thing is to pull yourself out of the trap before it ends up wasting significant amounts of your work time and jeopardizing your established schedule.

Of course, you can call a halt to a phone call, end a co-worker's drop-in visit, or suspend work on an e-mail response fairly readily. However, it's not quite so easy to reverse the effects of continued procrastination on a project, make up for a significant lack of planning, or fill in missing and much needed background information (not to mention organize your entire work area).

Despite this fact, provided that you become aware that you've gotten yourself into another time trap, you can always do something to mitigate it before you dig yourself in too deep. And the sooner you become aware, the sooner you can get to work reversing its effects and the less time you'll end up wasting and getting further behind the eight ball.

Mastering moment-by-moment management

In addition to avoiding time traps, good time management is also the product of effective ad hoc or off-the-cuff prioritizing of your work agenda (what I like to call moment-by-moment management). Mastering this skill requires you to identify the paramount needs of the moment as well as to understand the effects that responding to those needs have on the rest of your obligations.

Note that moment-by-moment management, although characterized by the ability to remain flexible so you can continue to respond resourcefully to the demands at hand, rests securely on a foundation of extensive organization, good communication, and effective planning. Without this solid underpinning, instead of formulating effective responses to the exigencies of the moment, you too often end up simply winging it while flying blind (a potentially fatal combination).

Being able to adapt effectively to changing conditions is especially important in being successful in today's fast-paced business world. However, the most significant benefit of moment-to-moment management is the capacity to remain relaxed and unstressed in the face of constant change. This relative composure comes out of a greater sense of control and enhanced self-confidence that results from effectively dealing with shifting priorities. (See "Flowing Like Clouds and Water" later in this chapter, for more on the themes of adaptability and self-assurance.)

Multitasking in the Mix of Personal Productivity

Multitasking is currently all the rage, especially with younger workers who grew up having to deal with a million different distractions — TV, Internet, and cell phones, to name a few — competing for their attention. As a result, some people now actually believe that they can get more work done by dividing their attention among more than one task. (Typing an e-mail response or surfing the Web while talking to a co-worker or client on the phone is a classic example.)

Of course, as anyone who's had a fender bender while talking on his or her cell phone will tell you, how well you can divide your attention between tasks at hand is open to considerable question. The fact is the efficacy of multitasking continues to be found seriously wanting (so much so, in the case of cell phone operation and driving, that some states have banned even hands-free versions of it).

The biggest pitfall with multitasking is that, although you think you're concentrating equally on all the tasks you're undertaking at the same time, you're not. In fact, your brain is actually cheating by going back and forth, giving one and then the other the attention it requires. Like a magician who tricks you with sleight of hand, your brain tricks you with a sleight of attention. This means that you may be paying attention to only one thing at hand at the expense of the others you're undertaking.

Rather than trying to multitask your way to peak productivity, you're much better off doing it by giving your full and undivided attention to just the task at hand. That way you're much more likely to do it right the first time. Not only are you able to do a more thorough job, but you also don't run the risk of losing valuable time redoing some task that you didn't complete or get right the first time.

Harnessing the Power of Goals and Objectives

Setting realistic goals and achievable objectives is another important element in being able to attain and maintain peak personal productivity. To understand their importance in creating and sustaining peak productivity, you to need be clear about the difference between goals and objectives, as well as how they buffer each other.

In short, a *goal* describes the target, end point, or overarching purpose that you have in mind in undertaking a new activity. And *objectives* describe the steps, levels, or stages that you need to reach as a natural part of achieving your goal. Objectives then are subsets of a particular goal. Moreover, objectives are normally set up so they're measurable in some manner that you can use to know when you have achieved them. (This is not usually the case with goals.)

For example, say your goal is to speak Spanish at a basic conversational level. To achieve this goal, you take up some sort of fundamental Spanish course. And this course of study is in all probability divided into groups of related lessons (referred to as units), each of which has its own objective (such as knowing how to identify and correctly use Spanish nouns, pronouns, adjectives, and adverbs, as well as how to use appropriate verb forms).

The lesson quizzes and unit tests that you take as you go through and complete the course measure how well you've met your individual objectives. After completing the entire course, you can then evaluate how close you've come to your initial goal — being able to speak Spanish at a basic conversational level — when you get the opportunity to speak with native Spanish speakers.

When it comes to the goal of achieving a better balance between your professional and personal lives, your objective may be to reach your peak personal productivity. (This is something that's clearly measurable by comparing the amount of work you were able to get done before and after taking the steps specifically designed to increase productivity).

Because attaining peak personal productivity is such a substantial objective, it's probably best to break it up into smaller, more manageable objectives. These would include objectives such as getting your work environment organized, efficiently managing your workday, mastering effective project planning, and setting realistic work goals and objectives that you review and fine-tune as needed. Never one to ignore my own good advice, I'll be breaking larger objectives into more manageable pieces throughout this book.

Exploring the importance of setting goals in achieving peak productivity

Many personal productivity systems consider setting work goals to be an integral part of personal productivity. As the delightful and insightful book, *Does this Clutter Make My Butt Look Fat?: An Easy Plan for Losing Weight and Living More* by Peter Walsh (published by The Free Press), states so well:

> "If your goals aren't clear and your thinking isn't focused, you can't break the habits that stand in your way."

Work goals are so important because, in taking the time to set them, you're in essence evaluating your current performance and saying that it's time to make some sort of change to it. Goals, then, often act as great motivators. Because they help you clarify what's not working or what needs to work better, they offer incentives that help you overcome the inertia of firmly established work habits that, in the vernacular of Dr. Phil, "may not be working so well for you."

Keep in mind that work goals can be both short- and long-term. Short-term goals are normally those that you expect to realize within the current business quarter or sooner. Long-term goals are normally those that you expect to realize somewhere within the current six months or year.

Exploring the importance of establishing achievable objectives

As part of setting your short- and long-term works goals, you naturally have to consider the steps you need to take to bring about their realization. This means laying down the objectives that you need to meet.

When considering the objectives that you feel need to be met, you have to take into account their quantity as well as their relationship to one another. So ask yourself, are the objectives sequential in the sense that you must meet

one objective in the sequence before you can work on another? The easiest way to make sure of this is to approach objectives as the building blocks you deem essential to reach your goal. That way, you can ascertain not only how many are required, but also how they should be sequenced.

The final thing to consider when developing your objectives is how you will go about determining when the objectives are met. By having definite ways to measure when you've attained a particular objective, you have an inkling that the objective is both an achievable one as well as some idea of how to go about achieving it.

When determining the ways you'll be able to measure the achievement of a particular objective, simply fill in the phrase, "As a result of meeting this objective, I'll be able to . . ." The things you fill in may consist of simple statements such as "find all needed client files" or "leave the office at the close of business," as well as quantifiable statements such as "complete my weekly reports by the close of business each Thursday" or "keep my e-mail Inbox empty on a daily basis."

All you need is a good review

Many personal productivity systems call for regular review of how well you've met the objectives you've established for yourself. Taking the time for such progress reviews lets you know how close or far you are from meeting your present goals.

Keep in mind that reviews should also help keep you on target and motivated to reach your goals. Therefore, whenever you do a review, keep it positive. Concentrate first on the progress you've made toward meeting particular objectives before considering what steps you still need to take to complete them.

When doing such reviews, you may want to consider doing a weekly review of the objectives you're working on as part of your short-term goals and a monthly review of the objectives you're working on as part of a long-term goal.

Keep these reviews short and to the point. Simply jot down your overall estimation of your progress, such as 50 percent complete. (Outlook Notes is a perfect way to do this — see Chapter 13 for details.) Then, jot down the tasks that you still need to complete in order to fully meet the objective. (Outlook Tasks is the place to do this — see Chapter 12 for details.)

Flowing Like Clouds and Water

In Japanese Zen Buddhism, novice monks are called *unsui,* which means "clouds and water." The idea here is that clouds and water share the same essence. Clouds form from evaporated water and, in turn, produce rain water when the right weather conditions prevail. In this way, young monks learn to how to remain fluid and assume the proper form of conduct in the Zen monastery according to the prevailing conditions.

Applied to personal productivity, the notion of remaining fluid at all times so that you can adapt quickly and successfully to changing business conditions is becoming ever more important. In the increasingly fast-paced modern workplace, it's often not sufficient to be merely well organized and a real authority on time management to maintain peak personal productivity. You also have to be able to think on your feet so that you can recognize when shifting conditions mandate a change in direction so that you can make the necessary corrections in your planning and scheduling in a timely manner.

Keep in mind that the ability to recognize early on in the game when course corrections are called for is a mark of truly productive worker. This capacity enables you to modify the means by which you reach your goal and thereby saves loads of time that would otherwise be spent pursuing limited or dead-end objectives.

Doing tasks wholeheartedly

In addition to remaining receptive to changes in prevailing business conditions, increased personal productivity also depends heavily upon giving yourself completely over to the tasks at hand.

In Taoist philosophy, you find a similar concept in the Chinese phrase, *wei wuwei.* Although *wei wuwei* literally means "accomplishing without doing," it actually describes a policy of conducting your affairs without a sense of accomplishment. In other words, you give yourself over so totally to what you're doing that your focus remains at all times on the task at hand without any concern for or concentration on the desired end result. By losing yourself in the task, you avoid wasting time and energy judging your progress or fixating on your ultimate success or failure.

The idea here is that you do a much more thorough and efficient job when your attention resides completely on what you're doing. It does not mean, however, that you don't ever do any planning or assessing. You plan before you undertake a task and assess after you've completed it. Nonetheless, once you undertake a task, you don't undermine it by second-guessing your initial planning or evaluating your progress.

Appreciating the true goal of personal productivity

The primary goal of all the productivity methods I've outlined in this chapter (all the way from organization to doing your tasks wholeheartedly) is really the same. Simply put, their purpose is just to enable you to become the most fulfilled person you can be.

Although this book talks a lot about peak performance, efficiency, effectiveness, and so on, you mustn't lose sight of the true prize, which isn't being employee of the month for the next 20 years. The real prize is being the happiest, most self-assured person you can be whether you're hard at work or relaxing at home.

In this view, personal productivity is a secondary issue, a by-product, if you will, of becoming a truly satisfied person. And in order to be truly satisfied, you need to feel as though you're leading a genuinely balanced life, one that honors all your roles in life, both as a worker and as a person with wider interests.

The great thing that adopting productivity methods such as the ones outlined in this chapter can bring you is greater self-assurance and fulfillment in your role as a worker. And if they also can help get you home on time and reduce any lingering angst about the office, then they're also enhancing the balance between your professional and personal lives. This is what I call a win-win situation, indeed.

Chapter 3

Surveying Some Popular Outlook Productivity Systems

*T*his chapter acquaints you with four time management/personal productivity systems whose principles have been especially adapted for Microsoft Outlook users. By taking a cursory look at these systems, you can get a good idea of how broader productivity principles (such as those covered in Chapter 2) are specifically applied to Outlook.

The first system you explore is the one promoted by FranklinCovey, a company perhaps best known for its popular paper calendars and day planners. This company is also famous for coaching all levels of business people on how to become more productive using time management techniques that rely heavily on effective planning.

The second system you examine is the one espoused by productivity maven, David Allen, a highly successful and renowned professional productivity motivator and trainer. Allen's system centers around a five-stage workflow model designed to enable you to prioritize your tasks and act accordingly.

The third system you survey is the one created by corporate productivity trainer, Sally McGhee. McGhee's system is composed of three stages that create what she calls an *integrated management* system — a system designed to lead you to flawless planning and task execution.

The fourth (and final) system you take look at in this chapter is the one championed by "efficiency guru" Michael Linenberger. Linenberger's system for taking control of your workflow concentrates almost exclusively on techniques that promote efficient task and e-mail management.

Getting Cozy with FranklinCovey's Planning System

FranklinCovey is a trusted provider of time management and personal productivity advice. Founded by the merging of Hyrum Smith's Franklin Quest (distributor of the famed Franklin Day Planner) with Stephen R. Covey's Covey Leadership Center in May, 1997, FranklinCovey offers a wide variety of management and assessment tools, training, and personal coaching for businesses of all sizes.

For a complete list of the various types of products and training available from FranklinCovey, visit its Web site at `www.franklincovey.com`.

Understanding Covey's seven habits of highly effective people

In 1989, Stephen Covey published his bestselling self-help book entitled, *The 7 Habits of Highly Effective People: Restoring the Character Ethic* (Tandem Library). This blockbuster explains the seven traits that Covey considers to be the fundamental characteristics of highly successful people, professionally as well as personally.

According to Stephen Covey, decidedly effective people routinely practice the following seven principles:

- **Act Proactive:** They take time to formulate their responses to situations they find themselves in rather than simply making knee-jerk reactions to them.

- **Begin with the End in Mind:** They visualize the desired results and then take the steps necessary to achieve them.

- **Put First Things First:** As the masters of time management and organization, they successfully prioritize their tasks to reach their goals.

- **Think Win/Win:** They seek accords and results that are mutually satisfying to everyone involved rather than simply seeking to triumph at any cost.

- **Seek First to Understand, and Then Be Understood:** They practice "empathic listening" whereby they listen to others with the intention of understanding what others are saying, rather than preparing a reply to it.

- **Synergize:** They practice creative cooperation whereby they remain open to new possibilities, alternatives, and options.

✔ **Sharpen the Saw:** They practice principles of balanced self-renewal that enable them to reenergize themselves physically, mentally, socially, and spiritually.

Examining the importance of planning in Covey's time management system

As you might deduce from Covey's list of the seven habits of highly effective people, his system of time management is very big on planning. In fact, it plays such an important role in his systems that it's probably not an exaggeration to say that, in his estimation, successful time management is a direct byproduct of successful planning.

As the first three principles in his list of habits indicate, this planning can come in the form of responding appropriately to situations at hand, effectively visualizing the outcomes or goals you want to achieve, as well as properly prioritizing tasks that are before you.

Effective planning is then buffered by the other four principles that enable folks to behave ethically and benevolently in their business dealings, practice excellent communication skills, cooperate well, and regularly renew and revitalize themselves.

Keep in mind that, according to FranklinCovey, those who excel at time management are not only are wizzes at setting their priorities but are the ones who use planning tools effectively. They use these planning tools to set goals, to work on those goals, and to relate their professional and personal values and roles to their priorities. In large part, this explains why the company offers such a wide array of paper and electronic scheduling products in addition to training materials and services.

Understanding Covey's Time Management Matrix

In his chapter on organizing your priorities ("Habit 3: Put First Things First: Principles of Personal Management") in *The 7 Habits of Highly Effective People: Restoring the Character Ethic*, Covey introduces his Time Management Matrix (shown in Figure 3-1). You can use this table to analyze your activities and put them into one of four quadrants:

✔ **Quadrant I, Urgent-Important (also known as the Necessity Quadrant):** Activities in this quadrant include problems and projects that must be dealt with on the spot.

✔ **Quadrant II, Not Urgent-Important (also known as the Productivity Quadrant):** Activities in this quadrant enable you to plan effectively.

✔ **Quadrant III, Urgent-Not Important (also known as the Deception Quadrant):** Activities in this quadrant present themselves as critical but actually need to be planned effectively.

✔ **Quadrant IV, Not Urgent-Not Important (also known as the Waste and Excess Quadrant):** The activities in this quadrant aren't really critical but do pass the time.

Covey's Time Management Matrix		
	URGENT	NOT URGENT
IMPORTANT	**I** Crises Pressing Problems Projects with Deadlines	**II** Prevention, Production Capability Planning Relationship Building Management
NOT IMPORTANT	**III** Interruptions, Some Phone Calls Some Meetings Some Reports Most Messages	**IV** Busy Work, Trivia Time Wasters Pleasant Activities

Figure 3-1: Covey's Time Management Matrix with its four quadrants.

The purpose of Covey's Time Management Matrix is not just to identify the quadrant into which your professional and personal activities fall. It's more essential purpose is to encourage you to find ways to spend more of your time doing Quadrant II activities and much less time doing Quadrant III stuff. In fact, the mark of a truly productive person is one who knows how to invest more time in Quadrant II at the expense of time squandered in Quadrant III.

Checking out FranklinCovey PlanPlus software

When you understand how important planning tools are to the FranklinCovey system of time management, you won't be surprised to find out that the company now offers software solutions in addition to its long line of paper day planners and other forms.

FranklinCovey currently offers three versions of PlanPlus, its electronic planning software program: PlanPlus for Outlook, PlanPlus for Windows, and PlanPlus Online (each discussed in the following sections).

PlanPlus for Outlook

PlanPlus for Outlook is really convenient because, as an add-in program, it runs right within Outlook, enabling you to use all of its special features along with all of Outlook's regular features. In Outlook, this add-in program inserts its own pull-down menu and toolbar, and appends specialized folders to the Navigation Pane.

Figure 3-2 shows you the Outlook program window when you click the FranklinCovey folder in the Navigation Pane. Doing so displays the FranklinCovey version of the Outlook Today view in the program's Information Viewer.

PlanPlus   PlanPlus pull-down menu

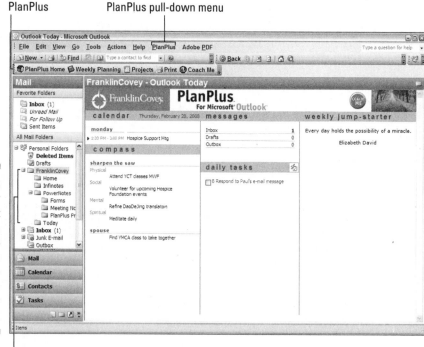

Figure 3-2: PlanPlus for Outlook as it appears in Outlook 2003 when you select the Franklin-Covey folder.

PlanPlus Mail foldus

As you can see in this figure, the FranklinCovey version of Outlook Today is very similar to the regular Outlook Today display (with its Calendar, Tasks, and Messages areas).

What's up with FranklinCovey's big rocks?

You may be just a little puzzled by the appearance of big rocks in the PlanPlus Compass area in verbal form in the Add Big Rock button and graphic form in the rocks icons that precede each task you add. (To open this Compass area, you click the Compass link in the PlanPlus Home in Outlook.) The big rocks idea comes from a Covey training analogy that attempts to convince participants that you can always fill a bucket with more rocks by first putting in the big rocks and *then* filling the remaining spaces between them in with smaller rocks and rubble. If you first fill the bucket with a layer of small rocks, you'll have a hard time filling in the remaining space with big ones. In this analogy, big rocks represent the larger tasks that you want to accomplish in a particular professional or personal role, and the small rocks are the little incidental things that also need to get done. Note that when delineating the "big rock" goals or tasks, Covey wants his trainees and PlanPlus users to link them to a particular professional role (such as manager or co-worker) or to a particular personal role (such as a spouse, parent, or friend) as appropriate. In this way, you end up creating big rock goals for each role that you play that you must then prioritize as you see fit.

In addition to these common areas, PlanPlus adds a Compass and a Weekly Jump Starter area (shown in Figure 3-2). The Compass area is where you can add the physical, social, and spiritual activities that help renew you (listed under the heading, Sharpen the Saw) as well as your major (weekly) goals (referred to as "big rocks") for the various roles that you play (manager, spouse, parent, friend, mentor, and so on). The Weekly Jump Starter contains inspirational quotes and other time management information designed to keep you motivated.

Figure 3-3 shows how the PlanPlus add-in program appears in Outlook when you select the Home folder that appears immediately below the FranklinCovey folder in the Navigation Pane. (Note that you can also select this folder by clicking the PlanPlus Home item on the PlanPlus pull-down menu or the PlanPlus Home button on the PlanPlus toolbar.)

When you select the Home folder, the Outlook 2003 Information Viewer displays the PlanPlus Home, including its own menu buttons, display panels, and e-mail toolbar.

PlanPlus Home gives you immediate access to your monthly calendar, task list, daily schedule, and the e-mail messages in your Outlook (although only the first one or two of the most recent messages can be displayed in the e-mail panel at its default size).

To enlarge the e-mail display panel in the PlanPlus Home so you can read more than just the first message in your Inbox, click the Maximize button — the button on the far right of the e-mail toolbar. (Refer to Figure 3-3.) Then, after reading and dealing with your messages, you can return the e-mail panel to its original size by clicking the Restore button. (This button automatically replaces the Maximize button on the e-mail toolbar.) Note that in its maximized incarnation, the e-mail toolbar appears immediately beneath the menu buttons — Home, Project, Weekly Planning, and Coach Me — at the very top of the Information Viewer.

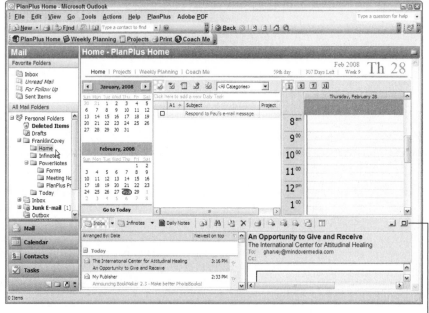

Figure 3-3:
The
PlanPlus
Home as
it appears
in the
Outlook 2003
Information
Viewer
when you
select
the Home
folder.

Maximize button

PlanPlus for Windows

PlanPlus for Windows runs as a separate program under Windows XP or Tablet PC edition or Windows Vista. Figure 3-4 shows the PlanPlus for Windows program window as it appears when you first launch the program. (To launch it, double-click its program icon on the Windows desktop or click the Windows Start button and then choose Start⇨All Programs⇨Franklin Covey⇨FranklinCovey PlanPlus for Windows.)

As you can see in this figure, as a full-fledged application, PlanPlus for Windows has its own pull-down menus; system of toolbars (8 of the total 14 toolbars are automatically displayed); and tabs (Calendar through Notes).

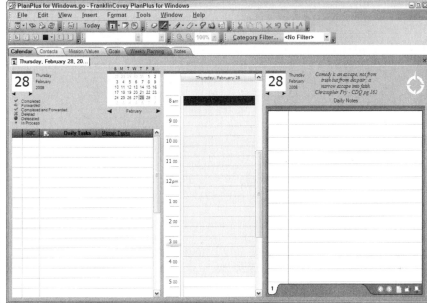

Figure 3-4:
PlanPlus for
Windows
program
window as
it appears
when you
launch this
standalone
program.

Unlike PlanPlus for Outlook, whose Home gives you immediate access to different types of information (calendar, task list, and e-mail) in a single view, PlanPlus for Windows employs a system of tabs that, when clicked, give you access to its various management tools (Calendar, Contacts, Mission/Values, Goals, Weekly Planning, and Notes). In this way, PlanPlus for Windows is more like standard Microsoft Outlook, where you can display each of information modules (Mail, Calendar, Contacts, Tasks, Notes, and Journal) by clicking its button in the Navigation Pane, by selecting its menu item from the Go pull-down menu, or by pressing its shortcut keystroke.

The biggest drawback to using PlanPlus for Windows is that its e-mail functions include only the most rudimentary of features. This means that you will almost definitely still have to use a separate e-mail program such as Outlook Express (when running under Windows XP) or Windows Mail (when running under Vista) to deal with e-mail messages. If you feel as though having to understand and deal with more than one program to manage all your personal information including e-mail may be too much for you, stick with PlanPlus for Outlook or PlanPlus Online if you're tempted at all to adopt the FranklinCovey planning system in some sort of electronic form.

PlanPlus Online

In addition to PlanPlus for Outlook and Windows, FranklinCovey also offers PlanPlus Online. This newest version of the ever-popular PlanPlus program runs in whatever Web browser you use on your personal computer, laptop, PDA, or smart phone.

This means with PlanPlus Online, you can check appointments you keep in your PlanPlus calendar along with the tasks entered in your to-do list from almost any device that can run a Web browser and has Internet access. This ability to check your personal information from any Internet-enabled computer is a real boon to anyone who travels extensively and uses a lot of different types of portable devices (including PDAs, cell phones, and laptop computers) while on the road.

Keep in mind that when you purchase PlanPlus Online, rather than purchasing a software license to a program on a disc or for download, as with PlanPlus for Outlook and PlanPlus for Windows, you're purchasing a monthly subscription service that you can access from any Internet enabled-device. Paying a monthly subscription can make using PlanPlus Online significantly costlier than PlanPlus for Outlook or Windows, when viewed over the long term.

Figure 3-5 shows you the PlanPlus Online initial display screen that appears when you access your account using Microsoft's Web browser, Internet Explorer 7. As you can see in this figure, PlanPlus Online combines Calendar, Tasks, and Note functions in its Home screen (somewhat similar to PlanPlus for Outlook) and also contains a series of tabs (like PlanPlus for Windows) along with a row of buttons immediately below the tabs that enable you to access the different modules included as part of the online program.

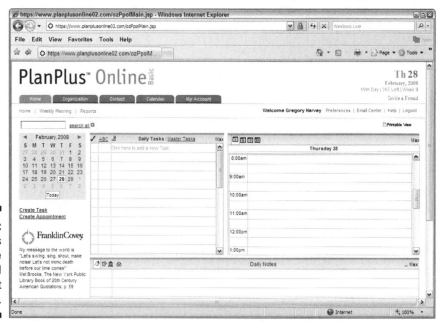

Figure 3-5:
PlanPlus
Online
displayed
in Internet
Explorer 7.

Having Fun with David Allen's Getting Things Done Productivity System

David Allen is a well respected productivity guru in the corporate world. Hailed by *Fast Company* magazine as "one of the world's most influential thinkers on productivity," Allen is the author of a couple of very insightful — not to mention bestselling — books on personal productivity: *Getting Things Done: The Art of Stress-Free Productivity* and *Ready For Anything: 52 Productivity Principles for Work and Life* (both published by Penguin).

Like other experts in the personal productivity field, Allen hasn't stopped at writing self-help books. He also conducts corporate training and seminars. And his company now offers his celebrated productivity system in an electronic form for Outlook called the Getting Things Done (GTD) Outlook Add-In.

For more background information on David Allen as well as to purchase his books or other products, check out his Web site at www.davidco.com.

Looking at the five stages of the Getting Things Done productivity system

David Allen's productivity system, frequently called Getting Things Done after his bestselling title by the same name, is centered on the concept of stress-free productivity. In other words, Allen finds little use for becoming more efficient at work or at home if this efficiency comes at the price of increased stress. (In fact, his emphasis on *stress-free* productivity may be one of the main reasons why he's so well-liked and his ideas are so widely respected in the business world.)

At its most basic, Allen's Getting Things Done productivity system consists of the following five stages:

- ✔ **Collect:** This stage involves using your own preferred tools to accumulate *all* of the stuff in your professional and personal lives that you consider incomplete or requiring some sort of change.

- ✔ **Process:** This stage involves determining the relative importance of all the stuff you identify as incomplete and deciding what steps are required to make them complete.

- ✔ **Organize:** This stage involves deciding where to store all the stuff that you determine still needs completing.

- ✔ **Review:** This stage involves routinely reviewing (Allen usually recommends on a weekly basis) all the stuff that you still identify as incomplete.

✔ **Do:** This stage involves deciding whether or not the stuff you see as incomplete is worth taking up now or at some later time.

As you can see from this list of five stages, Allen sees productivity as fundamentally stemming from a set of planning stages (Collect, Process, Organize, and Review) that are used to help you determine the priority of all incomplete items (Do).

Doing away with your to-do lists!

One of the more radical aspects of Allen's Getting Things Done productivity system is its rejection of the traditional to-do list. According to Allen, traditional to-do lists don't work for two reasons:

✔ A typical workday's fresh input and continuously changing priorities habitually render the items you put on your to-do list impossible to get to and complete.

✔ Anything you put on a to-do list that you don't absolutely have to do on that day reduces the importance of the things you've put on that you really do have to get done.

In place of generating do-do lists, Allen's system calls for placing all reminders of the actions you still need to do either on a calendar (as time-specific appointments, day-specific actions, or day-specific information) or into what he calls Next Actions lists.

Next Actions lists answer the crucial processing questions for every project you undertake. (According to Allen, a *project* is a task that you can't complete with a single action.) Each item you place on a Next Actions list describes a single consecutive action or step that you must complete in the series in order to move along and ultimately finish the project. The most important thing about a Next Action step is that it describes a very specific physical activity that you'll undertake. (Mental planning activities or vague actions like "set up a meeting" don't count.)

After you decide on a Next Action step, you then have three options for handling it:

✔ **Do It:** You perform the action if you estimate that you can complete it within two minutes or less (Allen's two-minute rule).

✔ **Delegate It:** You send it to someone else on the team if you determine that you're not the best person to undertake the action.

✔ **Defer It:** You place it in a Someday or Snooze file if you determine that you need more information to do it or it will take longer than a couple of minutes.

If you find that there's no Next Action step associated with a particular item you come up with for your list, Allen then suggests that you place the item into one of three physical or electronic containers: the trash, a Someday file, or a reference file.

Checking out the Getting Things Done Outlook Add-In

In addition to his bestselling books and ever-popular seminars, David Allen also markets an Outlook add-in program that enables you to better follow his productivity principles when using Outlook as your personal information manager. Developed and supported by an outfit named NetCentrics, this auxiliary program adds Getting Things Done capability to Outlook in the form of a GTD toolbar and several ready-made subfolders in your Outlook Mail Inbox.

Figure 3-6 shows you Outlook 2007 running the Getting Things Done Outlook Add-In. (This add-in program looks the same when running in Outlook 2003.) As you can see in this figure, a GTD toolbar with buttons GTD through Open Project appears directly beneath the Standard toolbar. In addition, you can see that the add-in has created a bunch of subfolders — @Action through Someday — within the Outlook Mail Inbox folder.

Personally, I find the Manage Projects features of the Getting Things Done add-in most useful. You can use these features to quickly record the next actions you've identified in order to complete a particular project as well to track your progress.

How does McGhee's MPS stack up to Allen's GTD?

It's hard not to notice a marked resemblance between the jargon, acronyms, stages, phases, and what-not used by both Sally McGhee's McGhee Productivity Solutions and David Allen's Getting Things Done. Both productivity systems emphasize stages that at some point involve collecting, evaluating, reviewing, and then acting upon the tasks/projects that you've identified as worth doing. Both systems also stress the importance of defining clear-cut sequential actions (dubbed Next Actions in Allen's GTD and Strategic Next Actions in McGhee's MPS) that you need to take to successfully complete your projects, and both offer software add-in programs that help you implement the principles of their productivity systems in Microsoft Outlook. If you find their models appealing and want to use one, you really need to decide which one you find overall simpler to follow and better suited to the particular productivity problems you face.

GTD toolbar

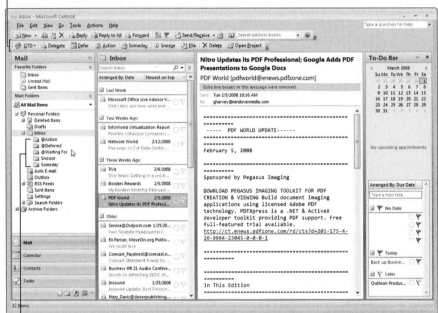

Figure 3-6:
Outlook 2007
running
the Getting
Things Done
add-in.

GTD Inbox subfolders

In addition, the Inbox subfolders created by the Getting Things Done add-in make it a great deal easier to manage your e-mail. As messages come into your Inbox, you quickly process them by simply dragging and dropping them into the appropriate GTD subfolder. Of course, if you drop messages into the Action subfolder, all you have to do is open this subfolder in order to respond to them (assuming that you've determined that you can answer each one in two minutes or less).

Seeking Out Sally McGhee's Productivity Solutions

Sally McGhee is another highly recognized expert in the personal productivity field, having now more than 25 years of experience coaching and training business executives on how to be more productive and achieve better work/life balance. She is the founder and managing partner of McGhee Productivity Solutions (MPS for short) as well as the author of the Microsoft Press book, *Take Back Your Life!: Using Microsoft Outlook to Get Organized and Stay Organized.*

To get more information on the MPS approach to personal productivity, the company's consulting and training services, as well as Sally McGhee's *Take Back Your Life!* title, visit her Web site at www.mcgheeproductivity.com.

Understanding the stages of the McGhee Productivity Solutions (MPS)

Sally McGhee's philosophy on personal productivity is summed up simply in her very astute quote, "Productivity is not about getting more things done. It's about getting the *right* things done."

This emphasis on recognizing the "right" things to do before you undertake them is evident in the stages she singles out in her McGhee Productivity Solutions (MPS):

- ✔ **Identifying Meaningful Objectives:** In this stage, you prioritize things you need to get done and determine how getting them done helps you meet your work and life goals. After spelling out your objectives in this way, you then create a supporting project for each objective that identifies the resources you need in order to meet it.

- ✔ **Creating Strategic Next Actions:** In this stage, you identify and list the sequence of all the actions that you need to take in order to complete the projects and meet the objectives you've set. These next actions count as strategic only if they don't require any additional steps before you undertake them (or are "without dependencies" in the parlance of Sally McGhee).

- ✔ **Scheduling and Completing Strategic Next Actions:** In this stage, you schedule all the strategic next actions you've identified by putting them on your calendar.

- ✔ **Reviewing and Course Correcting:** In this stage, you track your progress on completing the strategic next actions you've identified, evaluate how close you are to realizing your objectives, and make any changes called for by shifting conditions.

Getting to know the Integrated Management System (IMS)

For McGhee, the key to being successful with the McGhee Productivity Solutions cycle involves you creating what she calls the Integrated Management System, or IMS for short. (Is it just me, or are all this jargon and acronyms getting to be a bit too much?)

The McGhee Integrated Management System is composed of the following three systems:

✓ **Collecting System:** This system consists of the physical locations you use to record your actions and where you and other co-workers place tasks and information relevant to your projects. These locations include e-mail, voice mail, and a paper inbox.

✓ **Reference System:** This system consists of the locations where you store all the information needed in order to complete a project as well as any other pertinent information that doesn't require action on your part but to which you may later need to refer. These locations include your address book, Outlook notes, folders you add to the Outlook Folder List, and any other folders on your system or on the Internet in which supporting documents are stored.

✓ **Action System:** This system consists of your meaningful objectives, supporting projects, and Strategic Next Actions. These are normally stored in your Outlook Task List or To-Do List as well as on your Outlook calendar.

Checking out the MPS Take Back Your Life! 4Outlook add-in

To help you implement her productivity system using Outlook, Sally McGhee offers an add-in called the MPS Take Back Your Life! 4Outlook. Developed in collaboration with a company named Standss (South Pacific) Limited, this auxiliary program adds McGhee Productivity Solutions capability to Outlook in the form of a MPS Tack Back Your Life toolbar, a TBYL pull-down menu, and a TBYL folder in the Folders List in the Navigation Pane.

Figure 3-7 shows you Outlook 2003 running the MPS Take Back Your Life! 4Outlook Add-In. (Note that this add-in doesn't appear significantly different when running in Outlook 2007.) When you run this add-in, the MPS Take Back Your Life toolbar appears immediately below the other Outlook toolbars you have open. In addition, this auxiliary program adds its own TBYL folder to your folder list in the Navigation Pane.

Among my favorite features offered by this add-in are the Quick buttons on its MPS Take Back Your Life toolbar. The Quick buttons enable you to quickly process e-mail messages you receive in one of the following three ways:

✓ **Quick Task:** Click this button to create a new task from any e-mail message you receive.

✓ **Quick Calendar:** Click this button to create a new appointment on your Outlook calendar from any e-mail message you receive.

✓ **Quick File:** Click this button to file a copy of any e-mail message you receive in any of the reference folders you maintain.

MPS TBYL pull-down menu

MPS TBYL toolbar

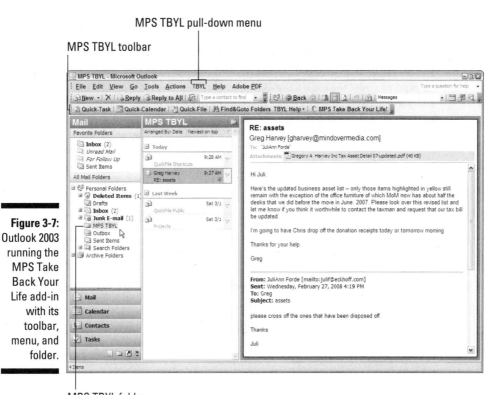

Figure 3-7:
Outlook 2003
running the
MPS Take
Back Your
Life add-in
with its
toolbar,
menu, and
folder.

MPS TBYL folder

Getting in Line with Linenberger's Total Workday Control System

Last but not least is "efficiency guru" Michael Linenberger, the author of *Seize the Workday: Using the Tablet PC to Take Total Control of Your Work and Meeting Day* and *Total Workday Control Using Microsoft Outlook,* 2nd Edition, which was hailed as the number-one bestselling Outlook book on Amazon. com, no less (both books from New Academy Publishers).

Like the other productivity experts highlighted in this chapter, in addition to his books, Linenberger offers a variety of productivity services including training and seminars. For more information on Michael Linenberger and the services his company offers, visit his Web site at www.workdaycontrol.com.

Looking at the eight best practices of task and e-mail management

In place of a complete productivity system on the order of David Allen's or Sally McGhee's, Michael Linenberger's bestselling *Total Workday Control* Outlook book boils successful productivity down to eight simple task and e-mail practices in Microsoft Outlook. These practices can be summarized as follows:

- ✔ Track all your tasks in the Outlook Task List (2003) or To-Do List (2007).

- ✔ Maintain a master task list that's distinct from your daily task lists.

- ✔ Adopt a simple system for prioritizing tasks that stresses the tasks you must get done.

- ✔ In your daily task lists, record only Very Next Actions (think Allen's Next Action and McGhee's Strategic Next Action here) that you need to undertake.

- ✔ Keep your tasks lists up-to-date by performing both daily and weekly planning (similar to doing reviews in both Allen's and McGhee's system).

- ✔ Whenever possible, convert your e-mail messages to tasks.

- ✔ File your e-mail messages into Outlook categories.

- ✔ Effectively delegate the tasks that you're not the best qualified to undertake.

I don't know about you, but I get a certain déjà-vu all-over-again feeling just reading Linenberger's list of best practices. Somehow it seems to contain a hint of David Allen's thinking with a wee bit of Sally McGhee's values thrown in for good measure. Of course, this may be a case of great (productive) minds thinking alike, or maybe it's simply the case that there are only so many ways to emphasize the importance of maintaining to-do lists filled with premeditated next actions?

Checking out the Information Management System Outlook add-in

As you'd expect from any efficiency guru worth his or her salt, Michael Linenberger promotes an Outlook add-in program designed to make it easier for you to implement his best task and e-mail management practices. Called the Information Management System (IMS) for Outlook, this add-in was developed by a company named ClearContext which markets it in partnership with Linenberger's Total Workday Control.

Figure 3-8 shows you Outlook 2007 running the IMS add-in. (Note that this add-in doesn't appear significantly different when running in Outlook 2003.) When you run this add-in, the ClearContext toolbar appears immediately below the other Outlook toolbars you have open. In addition, this auxiliary program adds its own ClearContext pull-down menu and ClearContext Deferred, IMS, and Unsubscribed subfolders to the Inbox folder list in the Navigation Pane.

ClearContext pull-down menu

ClearContext toolbar

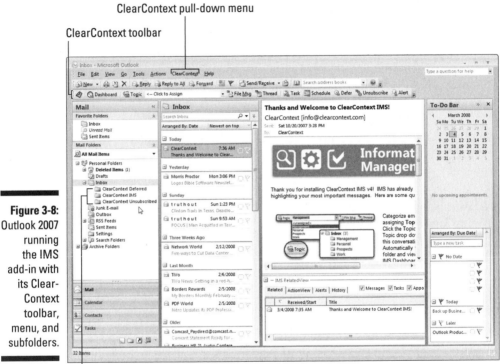

Figure 3-8:
Outlook 2007
running
the IMS
add-in with
its Clear-
Context
toolbar,
menu, and
subfolders.

ClearContext subfolders

After installing the IMS add-in, the program automatically analyzes the e-mail messages you've stored in Outlook to determine which are the most important messages and flags them accordingly. You can then also use its commands to flag a particular message or to modify the priority of a particular contact or to quickly file messages in a particular Inbox folder as well as quickly convert messages to tasks on your Task List or appointments on your Calendar.

In my opinion, one of the niftiest features of the IMS add-in program is its Dashboard view. You can display this view in three ways: by clicking the Dashboard button on the ClearContext toolbar, by clicking the ClearContext IMS folder icon in the Folder list of the Navigation Pane, or by selecting the Dashboard item on the ClearContext pull-down menu.

The IMS Dashboard uses the Outlook Information Viewer to display in a single view various panels listing your currently flagged messages, appointments, and tasks. In addition, the IMS Dashboard contains a Status panel that shows you at a glance the number of flagged messages and appointments you have, along with the number of tasks labeled Overdue, Due Today, and Due Sometime in the Current Week. Having all this information at your fingertips in the IMS Dashboard view can be really helpful in preparing for and planning your workday.

Chapter 4

Defining Personal Productivity on Your Own Terms

. . . .

In This Chapter

▶ Maximizing the use of your very precious and limited time

▶ Prioritizing your tasks and minimizing interruptions

▶ Minimizing your dependence on your memory

▶ Avoiding information overload

▶ Staying prepared for whatever comes

▶ Finding your own formula for personal productivity

. . . .

*P*ersonal productivity isn't magic. It's simply a matter of breaking some very bad work habits and substituting them with some very good productivity practices. And by good, I mean practices that you can actually live with rather than those that would be just great if only you somehow had the time, energy, and inclination to actually follow them.

This chapter surveys the best productivity practices that I've been able to identify in all my research into the personal productivity field (and as part of my experience training and consulting with business folks in companies big and small). As part of this review, I also give you some valuable pointers about how to start cultivating and implementing these great productivity practices into your workday and home life.

Finally, you get the opportunity to assess which of these great productivity practices you need and can actually begin using to get your workday under control and your professional and personal lives into better balance.

Making the Most of Every Moment

You've heard it a thousand times and probably said it yourself almost as many: "There just isn't enough time in the day to get everything done!" So what would you say if I were to tell you that on this one you're right on the money and quite correct? Like it or not, in all but a few situations, there really is *not* enough time in the average workday to get everything you're responsible for done!

The bad news then is that you'll *never* attain 100 percent efficiency and you'll *never* get everything your job calls for completed (not even after reading every word of this little masterpiece). The good news is that that this isn't your fault. Moreover, you can still be a lot more productive and satisfied at work and strike a better balance between work and your personal life despite this reality.

In other words, because you don't have all the time in the world, you have to make the most of the time that you do have. And to paraphrase productivity expert Sally McGhee, author of *Take Back Your Life!* (Microsoft Press), you don't have to worry about not being able to get everything done in a workday provided that you've taken the time to get the right things done.

And what the "right" things are on a given workday depend upon a number of somewhat volatile circumstances:

- ✔ All the things assigned and delegated to you for which you are now responsible (the tasks at hand).
- ✔ The objectives you've set for the day and how they fit into your weekly goals (the task list you've created).
- ✔ Planned interruptions that occur within that workday (weekly team meetings, seminars, research, and so on).
- ✔ The demands your personal obligations make on you while you're still at work (medical appointments, childcare arrangements, jury duty, and so on).
- ✔ Sporadic, unexpected demands made on your time during the workday (unplanned interruptions and crises).

When you look over this list, I wonder if you, like me, get the definite feeling that a great deal of the control during a typical workday is not in your own hands and is, quite frankly, beyond your power to manage (with all apologies to Michael Linenberger, author of *Total Workday Control,* from New Academy Publishers).

Keep in mind that it's precisely because you can control only so much of a typical workday that you want to be as organized and therefore as ready for anything as you can possibly be. By keeping your priorities straight and your work environment as accessible as possible, you're in much better shape to deal with all the inevitable interruptions, both personal and professional, that are bound to come your way.

Establishing your daily priorities

In case no one ever told you, a big part of personal productivity is making decisions. Perhaps nowhere is this truer than in the case of setting your daily and weekly work priorities.

Try this: When you first set foot in your office and are just settling in at your desk, instead of immediately launching into reading your e-mail, making telephone calls, or rifling through your paper inbox, take a few moments to prepare and plan for the day ahead. Begin by opening Outlook and reviewing your daily appointments, noting all the times that are still open. Then, review the things on your task list that you want to get done that day. Finally, make any changes that you deem necessary to your task list and/or calendar.

Because not all the tasks on your to-do list are of equal importance, after establishing which (if any) of the timeslots in your day are open, you need to prioritize them. In prioritizing all the tasks on your to-do list, you can apply a series of ranking criteria by considering the following questions:

- ✔ Do you currently have all the information and supporting materials you need to complete the task? (You need to ask this question before all the others for reasons I get into momentarily.)

- ✔ Does the task have an unmovable deadline, or has it been lingering on your to-do list for some time and has already been postponed one or more times and therefore is technically "overdue" in some sense?

- ✔ Do you think you can complete the task in the timeslots you still have open on today's calendar?

- ✔ Can you break up the task into smaller subtasks that you can complete using timeslots still open on today's calendar (even if they're nonsequential)?

- ✔ Can you readily continue the task over to the next day if you don't have sufficient time to complete it today?

- ✔ Do you need to complete the task before you can move on and complete other related tasks on your to-do list?

- ✔ Do you need to complete the task before your co-workers or other team members can undertake related tasks on their to-do lists as part of the same project?

- ✔ Is this the task you'd most like to remove from your to-do list?

When using these questions to prioritize the items on your to-do list, begin by first establishing whether or not you do have all the information and supporting materials you need to complete the task. If you do, you can then move on to considering other questions in the list.

If you find that don't have all the info and supporting materials you need, then you have to temporarily stop the prioritizing process so that you can note exactly what's missing and where you can get it. You can then later turn these notes into tasks for your to-do list by scheduling a timeslot for it after evaluating the other prominent tasks on your to-do list. (See Chapter 13 for steps on how to document your thoughts in the Outlook Notes module and then convert the notes you make into tasks on your to-do list.)

If you find that several tasks have the same deadline (as in ASAP or yesterday) or have lingered on your to-do list for some time, you can order them by determining how much time you think each will require to complete and then matching them with the timeslots still open on your daily calendar.

When identifying all the timeslots still open on your daily calendar, count those hours you haven't already set aside for some sort of prearranged meeting, appointment, prescheduled task, or needed breaks and lunch. These hours constitute the blocks of time during your workday over which, barring unexpected interruptions, you have total control when it comes to deciding which task to work on.

If you find the open timeslots in your workday broken up into sporadic segments by preset meetings and appointments, you'll probably have to determine how you can split up the larger, high-priority task into smaller subtasks. These subtasks need to be ones that you can either complete within these shorter free timeslots or which are amenable to interruption, allowing you to fairly easily break off for a meeting or other appointment and then resume afterward.

On some rare workdays, you may find you aren't looking at any overdue tasks or tasks with specific deadlines. In that case, you then identify all tasks that are prerequisites for completing other tasks that reside either on your to-do list or which you have reassigned to one of your co-workers or team members.

If you don't find any tasks that are prerequisites of others, you then identify those you'd most like to check off your to-do list. These tasks may be ones that you have to deal with on a daily basis, such as reading and answering e-mail, or simply ones that you know you'll feel better after they're done.

Try to avoid scheduling the tasks you want to get done simply because you find them the easiest to do early in the day when you're fresh and are the most vibrant. Tasks you can almost do with your eyes closed or which really give your spirits a lift are best reserved for low-energy times closer to the end of the workday.

Appling some good old-fashioned 3D decision making

Getting your daily priorities straight is certainly an important contributor to the success of your workday.

When deciding how to proceed with a task on your to-do list that you've identified as high priority, you may want to apply the following 3D model:

- ✔ **Do it:** Break the task down into a series of logical steps. If these steps seem to fit reasonably well within the open timeslots you've allotted the task, go ahead and complete them so you can finally get the task off of your to-do list.

- ✔ **Defer it:** If, in breaking the task down into logical steps, you discover the steps are too numerous and/or too complex to complete in the timeslots you've allotted the task, reschedule the task and substitute another in its place.

- ✔ **Delegate it:** If, in breaking the task down into logical steps, you discover you're not the best-qualified person to complete a number of its steps, entrust them to others on the team you deem better qualified. (Should you find that you're really not the best fit for the vast majority of steps, consider farming out the entire task to someone else better skilled to handle it.)

Anticipating interruptions

The biggest obstacles to keeping to any schedule that you come up with are all the interruptions that seem to spring up at the most inopportune moments in a typical workday. Such interruptions can be planned (a regularly scheduled team meeting, one-time seminar, or weekly training class), or they can be completely unexpected (a sudden office or home emergency, very important telephone call from a client, or high-priority e-mail message from the boss).

The most important thing about an interruption isn't whether it's planned or unanticipated or even how long it lasts and therefore how much time it takes you away from the other high-priority tasks on your to-do list, but rather how seriously it disrupts the rest of your workday once it's over and done with. Therefore, the key to dealing effectively with interruptions is to take every opportunity to minimize their disruption in terms of the rest of your daily schedule.

When dealing with a planned interruption such as a slated meeting or seminar, you're at a decided advantage. You can almost always accommodate the upcoming disruption by purposely not taking on a task or subtask that you know you can't complete before its appointed time or that you can't easily put down and then readily resume after the break.

With an impromptu interruption, you have a lot less time to prepare your response to minimize the effects of the disruption. The best you can do is to quickly mark your place in the task and note down any information that may help you pick up where you leave off after the interruption is over.

To do this, take a moment or two to mark your place and note your comments before you turn your full attention to the new event at hand. In the case of telephone calls or surprise office visits, you can do this by politely asking the other person to give you a second before you're with them.

If you're working on printed matter, use a Post-it note to mark your place and make any comments that'll later help you get back on track. If you're working on an electronic document, do this by creating an Outlook note (see Chapter 13 for details). Also, be sure that you save your document the moment the interruption happens. This means you don't answer the phone or engage in conversation with the person visiting your office before you press the Ctrl+S (Save shortcut) to safeguard your work against the loss of any unsaved changes you made before you were interrupted.

Getting it all down in writing

As any personal productivity expert worth his salt will tell you, one of the more detrimental things to your personal productivity is trying to keep the stuff you have to do in your head. Trying to remember all the tasks, questions, good ideas, and inspirations that suddenly and randomly pop into your head is really taxing (no matter how good your memory is). All too often, it accomplishes little more than adding to your general stress level by making you apprehensive about forgetting something you know really needs to get done or something that's really indispensable to getting something done.

What you need to do instead is give your brain a rest. And the best way to do this is by developing the strict habit of noting every idea that seems like it bears remembering, the moment that idea pops into your head. This includes all tasks you realize you have to do (regardless of when they're due; by the end of the same day or the current fiscal or calendar year), any questions that require answering, along with anything that generally falls into the good idea, intriguing insight, or absolute inspiration category.

This is where using a personal information manager program such as Outlook comes in so handy. In place of a zillion scribbled, indiscriminately placed sticky notes all over your computer monitor, you can safely store all your mental insights as notes in Outlook's Notes module. That way, you not only don't have to worry about being able to read them, but you always know where and how to find them. Moreover, as you discover in Chapter 13, you can easily search Outlook notes, group them into categories, color code them to establish their relative importance, and print them out.

When an idea that pops into your head seems like it might warrant remembering later on, jot it down straight away. Don't waste any of your time assessing whether the thought is really worth noting down. You can easily delete any Outlook note that, on later reading, you find isn't sufficiently weighty to convert into a task on your to-do list or into an appointment on your calendar (see Chapter 13).

Too much information!

Information overload is a real concern to many business people these days. Although called "information" overload, the real problem isn't too much information so much as too much raw data. And, as I'm accustomed to telling the students in all my database management system classes, raw data is not the same as information.

Raw data represents all the facts and figures, pictures, images, statistics, and reports that human beings feel they simply must record and store somewhere. Most of the time, however, the vast bulk of this data is simply trivia that holds no interest and has little value.

It's only when you develop a need for some of the data that its facts, figures, and so on suddenly become meaningful information for you. This need, by the way, may be temporary, so that once you've mined all the pertinent information for its meaning and put this information to appropriate use, it may once again return to the level of mere data (that you take or leave).

The notion that information is only the data that you need at a certain time is a big reason why skillful searching — especially of the electronic kind — is so crucial to successfully managing so-called information overload. It's only by putting on effective blinders (search filters in the case of electronic searching), that you have any hope of successfully navigating the maze of data and reaching the data you regard as pertinent information. Without the benefit of such blinders, you'll either be waylaid by irrelevant data you find en route or overwhelmed by the sheer magnitude of the data you have to comb through.

For this reason, you need to master all the electronic search techniques that your personal computer affords you. This includes performing general searches in the Windows operating system as well as specific searches from particular Outlook modules.

Keeping yourself ready for change

Remember the old Boy Scout motto, "Be Prepared"? For the knowledge worker in modern business, I think this maxim has to be updated to something more like, "Be Prepared for Anything." The pace of modern business and the fluctuations it faces are such that nowadays you not only have to anticipate change as an integral part of your job, but you also have to find a way to welcome it on some level.

And if you can't find a way to actually welcome change into your workplace, you have to at least find a way to accommodate it with some modicum of grace. This is because doing anything less is likely to produce intolerable amounts of stress, regardless of how well you keep up with the pace.

How ready you are as a productive knowledge worker rests squarely upon a number of factors:

- **The degree of mental agility and flexibility** you're able to bring into play. So get as much rest and exercise as possible (both factors really influence your mental agility) and develop attitudes that promote relaxation and openness.
- **The extent of the organization and planning** currently in place supporting your endeavors. So, get organized and stay organized if you possibly can.
- **The depth of knowledge and amount of experience** you're able to bring to bear in problem solving and dealing with the particular challenge or change at hand. So, take every opportunity to hone your skills and get the experience you need.

Finding Your Own Formula for Productivity Success

I think it's essential for you to create your own formula for personal productivity, one that's tailored to the particular set of circumstances and challenges that you face daily, both on the job and at home. Personalizing your productivity plan greatly increases your chances of long-term success because you'll be following a custom blueprint that reflects the unique ways you work and play.

The best way to develop your own formula for personal productivity is to honestly assess your productivity needs and then match these needs to strategies that you can realistically follow. When deciding whether you can successfully follow a specific productivity strategy, you need to consider not only whether you find it effective, but also whether you find that the strategy actually decreases the amount of stress you're under.

To help in developing your own formula for productivity success, I've added a bunch of assessment questionnaires to my productivity Web site at www. harveyproductivity.com. Use these questionnaires to assess the areas of your greatest need. Then, match your needs to the productivity strategies outlined both on this site and described in more detail in the final sections of this chapter.

In extensively researching productivity systems and principles over the last couple of years, I've identified a number of strategies that seem essential to productivity success. They include principles and practices that are designed to boost personal productivity while at the same time reducing stress. These strategies also form the foundation on which I base the Outlook productivity practices detailed in the remainder of this book.

Knowing yourself

"Know yourself" is the adage that appeared above the cave of the ancient Greek Oracle of Delphi along with another bit of relevant wisdom, "Nothing in excess." When applied to personal productivity, "know yourself" simply means that you need be aware of the place you're starting from so that you can figure out how far you have to go as well the easiest and fastest ways to get there.

Comprehending the place you're at is simply a matter of assessing your natural strengths and weaknesses when it comes to being productive. Then you can use this knowledge to devise a plan for making the best possible use of these strengths, especially in overcoming or minimizing the effects of the areas where you're not so strong.

For example, if you know that you're a wiz at organizing your home and work spaces but that prioritizing all the things you have to do in a day isn't currently your strong suit, you can use your natural organizational skills to better determine the most efficient order in which to meet your current obligations. Assuming that all the tasks share the same due date (today), here's what you'd do:

1. **List all your tasks in the detailed view of your Outlook to-do list with the estimated time to complete each task listed in minutes before the description in the Subject column.**

2. **Determine how important each task is and assign it a relative priority (Outlook lets you rate a task Low, Normal, or High) in the Priority column.**

3. **Sort the entire to-do list by Priority in descending order so that now you can see at a glance the high-priority tasks that take the most and least time.**

   See Chapter 12 for step-by-step details on entering and sorting tasks in the Outlook to-do list.

4. **Use this information to decide which high-priority task you have time to tackle and proceed accordingly.**

Considering productivity part of your self-fulfillment

When you get right down to it, the goal of personal productivity is simply greater happiness and fulfillment. Increased efficiency, increased output, recognition as an outstanding employee or parent, or even a much-deserved raise may well be natural byproducts of attaining peak personal productivity (although I can't vouch for the raise) but they're not the goal. And, in fact, all these byproducts contribute to a sense of greater self-esteem and contentment.

By seeing personal productivity in the light of increased work/life balance and making it part and parcel of your personal growth and self-fulfillment, you're actually more likely to succeed at attaining it. In giving personal productivity the priority it deserves, you'll have a powerful incentive to overcome your inertia and make initial changes as well as gain some of the motivation needed to keep making necessary adjustments over the long haul.

Mastering your productivity tools

A master craftsman in any profession is expected to be proficient in the use of the tools of his or her trade. Peak personal productivity for today's knowledge worker demands no less, although the tools of the trade are fast becoming less and less tangible (physical day planners aside).

The very premise of this book is that currently you routinely underutilize Microsoft Outlook by restricting its use primarily to doing your e-mail and, secondarily, perhaps, to maintaining your address book. This limited usage, however, means you're nowhere close to being proficient in using Outlook as it was designed — that is, as a Personal Information Manager (PIM for short) that not only enables you to stay in contact with those you need to stay in contact with, but also enables you to organize and manage your time.

The other assumption of this book is that only when you're able to use Outlook as your complete Personal Information Manager does it become your central personal productivity tool. Mastering all of the Outlook modules and understanding how to adapt their features to your particular needs (which are the stated objectives of this book) should put you well on your way towards attaining a degree of personal productivity that significantly reduces stresses in your life and improves your work/life balance.

Getting yourself organized

The organization of your workspace and work materials isn't the be-all and end-all of personal productivity. Rather, it's the bedrock upon which peak personal productivity sits.

Keeping in mind that being organized often means different things to different people. You still need to be sure that you can put your finger on all the information you need without wasting a bunch of time going through files, folders, and papers. In terms of Outlook, this means being able to quickly find any e-mail messages and address book contacts you may need as well as staying on top of the appointments on your calendar and to-do items on your task list.

Prioritizing your tasks

I say quite a bit about the importance of prioritizing your daily tasks earlier in this chapter, in the "Establishing your daily priorities" section. The only thing worth reiterating here is that being able to determine the most important task at hand is only the first part of the story when it comes to prioritizing.

You also have to be able to determine whether you have the resources and adequate blocks of open time to get this most important task done properly. If you find you have the resources but not the time, you then have to determine how to break the task down into smaller subtasks that do fit within your open time slots.

Keep in mind that many high-priority tasks are complex in nature and require you to subdivide them into simpler subtasks as well as to plan out the logical next steps necessary to complete each. In practical terms, this means that the practice of prioritizing tasks is often tied very closely to planning out the steps required for their execution. This is the reason that, in later chapters, you find me explaining how to prioritize tasks more in the Outlook Task module rather than in the Calendar module.

Always having a plan

Planning sometimes seems like the fool's gold of personal productivity. Although, there's something really satisfying about being able to plan out in detail how to get something done, it's also true that, more often than not, circumstances don't allow you to follow the plan exactly as conceived. For this reason, some knowledge workers become disillusioned with the planning aspect of personal productivity and tend to harbor some rather negative views regarding its overall efficacy.

And while it's true that plans often have to change and projects (especially complex ones) seldom come in exactly on time and right on budget, it's just as true that no significant project, even the late, significantly over-budget ones, ever got off the ground and completed without some kind of planning.

Therefore, my position on planning is to take it seriously, but not too seriously. The idea here is that you shouldn't be overly stressed when your best-laid plans have to change, but you should still have said plans as a solid groundwork from which to make all the necessary adjustments.

Keep in mind that you also have to be prepared to alter your plans as needed and, in rare circumstances, even junk them completely and go back to square one. I know that letting go (particularly of things you've worked really hard on) is a really difficult challenge, but I think it's a challenge that carries with it implications that reach far beyond the boardroom. Life changes whether you like it or not, and the only choice you often get in the matter is how you will respond to those changes.

Focusing on what you can do

The power of positive thinking in determining a good outcome was well documented. I suspect that a large part of burnout, both personal and professional, is due to the inability of a person to focus on what he or she can do about a given situation instead of being fixated on what he or she can't do.

Focusing on what's lacking and not possible is not only generally demoralizing, but it also all too easily leads to a never-ending litany of things that can't be accomplished. It goes without saying that this type of negative thinking is by its very nature stress-inducing. It's probably also true that focusing on what's not happening is the antithesis of productivity and has never made anyone happier with their current situation.

Focusing instead on what it is you can do, even when your options are limited, not only keeps you going, it often leads you down creative paths that you wouldn't have normally traveled.

Sometimes, focusing on options even when the options are quite limited has actually resulted in me coming up with a better, more elegant and efficient solution to a problem at hand (and even greater productivity) than I would have been able to manifest without the limitations. The important point here is that I discovered this more creative solution by keeping a positive attitude focused on what was feasible given the limits of the situation and not by focusing my attention on the limitations themselves.

Staying open to change

Staying open to change is very much a part of keeping the mental agility and flexibility that so often separates a truly productive person from one who is merely getting by. This type of dexterity is also an important component of maintaining that positive attitude that helps you to stay focused on what you can influence rather than on what you're powerless to change.

The people who've had the most positive influence on me, both personally and professionally, are all those who are very nimble mentally and maintain very flexible attitudes when it comes to facing the vicissitudes of life. They understand that change, even the disruptive kind, is an inevitable part of life. They also know that getting stressed over a change, even an unwanted one, is the most counterproductive way to approach the situations that inevitably result from change.

Instead of allowing themselves the luxury of wasting precious energy on fighting change (a losing battle at best), highly productive people do everything they can to channel and direct their energy toward finding solutions and dealing with all the matters that change engenders. In this way, they're able to focus on minimizing the stress that change inevitably creates through attitudes and actions focused squarely on solving the problems at hand.

Avoiding information overload

I already touch upon the challenge that information overload poses to the productivity of the average knowledge worker earlier in this chapter, in the "Too much information!" section. The only thing I want to add here about the topic is to keep in mind that avoiding information overload really isn't a matter of steering clear of data (a clear impossibility in the information age in which you work) but one of steering clear of as much extraneous and trivial data as possible (the all the stuff that you don't consider information).

If you can do that, more often than not it won't matter how much data is out there or how much data comes your way. Provided you can locate and make use of just the small portion of data that is of vital interest to you, you should go a long way toward staying productive without stressing out.

Remember, however, that the data that you consider extraneous can and does change with the task at hand. For example, when you need to compile a report on all the customers in the corporate database who've done significant business with the company for an upcoming ad campaign, data regarding the current status of their account isn't very important. However, when you need to compile a report on all customers in the same company database whose accounts are significantly past due, then the data on the current status of their accounts becomes vital information, and data on their past spending patterns is fairly unimportant.

Developing your interdependence

The final productivity strategy in my top ten is one that's all too easily over-looked. Therefore, keep in mind that although this particular strategy is last on the list, it's definitely not least.

Articles and books on personal productivity and even the gurus creating them very often concentrate almost exclusively on the personal side of things — what an individual knowledge worker needs to know and do in order to be efficient. This imbalance in the coverage can give you the misimpression that personal productivity's all about you (rather than mostly about you).

Even when you do most of your work in isolation, remember that, except in a tiny minority of cases, you're still very much part of a larger team. This larger team is commonly made up of people who are both within the company (such as co-workers and managers) as well as folks outside of it (such as vendors and clients). And if you don't know how to communicate clearly and work efficiently with these people, you have very little hope of attaining peak personal productivity. And even if you do, you're apt to find that this productivity comes at the (high) cost of increased stress.

A large part of any given workday is bound to be devoted to dealing with people on the larger team somehow (more and more often, electronically). Therefore knowing how to deal with them in a truly effective manner is going to help you become and remain more productive by giving you more time that you can allocate to the other 10,000 things you need to do on your own.

To that end, I include detailed coverage in later chapters on how you can use the Outlook Mail and Contacts components to maintain top-notch communication with people on your larger team (see Chapters 9 and 11). I also cover at some length how to make good use of the Calendar and Tasks modules when you need to shift tasks on your calendar or to-do list over to co-workers on your team (see Chapters 10 and 12). To effectively delegate tasks in this way, you have to maintain clear communication with the people who you now expect will get them done. You also have to know how to track these delegated tasks by obtaining all necessary feedback about their progress after you consider them to be "off your desk" and they no longer appear on your calendar or to-do list.

Part II
Making Outlook Your Key to Personal Productivity

The 5th Wave   By Rich Tennant

"I don't care what your e-mail friends in Europe say, you're not having a glass of Chianti with your bologna sandwich."

In this part . . .

*I*f you really want to manage your life with Outlook, you need to know how to use more than just its e-mail and, possibly, address book components. This second part helps you accomplish this task by introducing you to Outlook as a full-fledged personal information manager. It also gives you valuable pointers on how to customize Outlook and use its modular structure to your best advantage.

Chapter 5

Mastering Information Management with Outlook

....

In This Chapter

▶ Understanding what it means to make Outlook your Personal Information Manager

▶ Making friends with Outlook's interface

▶ Taking a quick look at the capabilities of Outlook's various modules

▶ Making effective use of the Task List and Shortcuts

▶ Discovering the Outlook shortcut keys that you need to know by heart

....

*I*f you're anything like most of the professionals I work with, Outlook is one of the programs you use the most often, and at the same time, it's possibly the most underutilized application installed on your work computer. This is because, for many, many knowledge workers, Outlook is merely the program that enables them to "do" their e-mail and, at times, look up vital contact information.

More than a few Outlook users aren't even aware that the program is capable of doing anything useful besides sending and receiving e-mail and storing contact information. Because Outlook always starts up with the display of the Inbox, users naturally spend almost all their time in its Mail module, blissfully unaware of its other capabilities. This rather sad situation is about to change, for in this chapter, I expose you to, as they say, the "full Monty" when it comes to Outlook's functionality and interface (look and feel).

The goal of this chapter is for you to see Outlook as a full-featured personal information management program equipped with all the capabilities you need in order to organize, manage, and track electronic personal information on your computer. Note that to meet this goal, you don't need to become fully familiar with all of Outlook's bells and whistles. You simply need to become familiar with the productivity features that each of its modules offers and know how to work with these modules and blend their features so that your focus remains first and foremost on the task at hand and only secondarily on Outlook itself.

Making Outlook Your Personal Information Manager

In Part I, I have a lot to say about your attitudes and how they affect personal productivity both for better and for worse. Attitude is important here because the first thing you need to do to use Outlook as your Personal Information Manager is to see it and approach it as such. This means that you have to be able to approach Outlook as so much more than an e-mail client with address book functions (even though they're included).

If you're anything like me, making this kind of attitude adjustment is a process that takes some time and comes about only with some experience using the other Outlook modules besides Mail and Contacts on a somewhat regular basis (the kind of experience that you definitely get as a result of following the productivity techniques laid out in this book).

You can start this process of viewing Outlook as a full-fledged Personal Information Manager by taking a quick tour of Outlook's modules. This module tour is designed to get you out of the Mail module and familiar with the others, which I hope you'll soon be using almost as much as Mail.

To take this tour, all you have to do is to follow these easy steps:

1. **Launch Outlook as you normally do.**

   Remember that you can launch Outlook by clicking the Microsoft Office Outlook button in the Quick Launch toolbar on the Windows task bar, or by double-clicking its program icon on the Windows desktop, or by clicking the Windows Start button and then choosing Microsoft Office Outlook at the top of the Start menu.

   When you first launch Outlook, the program automatically opens the Mail module, selecting the Inbox folder and displaying the folder's contents in the Information Viewer and the contents of the currently selected message in the Reading Pane.

2. **In the Navigation Pane on the left, click the Personal Folders icon at the very top of the All Mail Folders section.**

   Doing this displays the Outlook Today view. This is Outlook's snapshot view that lets you see at a glance upcoming appointments on your calendar, tasks on your to-do lists, and unopened messages in your Inbox.

3. **Choose the Go menu from the Outlook menu bar or press Alt+G.**

   Outlook displays Go menu items for selecting the other Outlook modules, as shown in Figure 5-1. Note the shortcut keys associated with each menu option (as I really want you to know these shortcuts by heart).

Navigation Pane

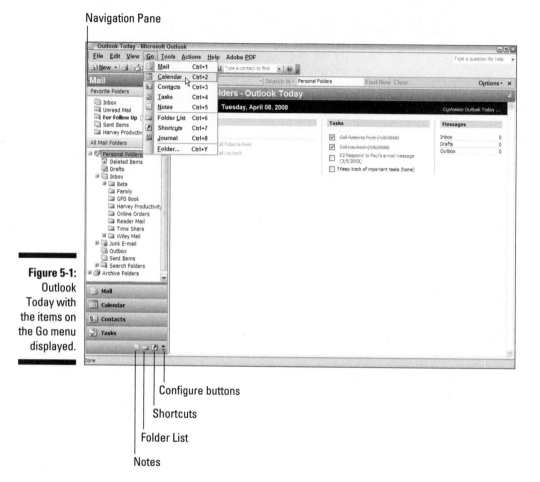

Figure 5-1:
Outlook
Today with
the items on
the Go menu
displayed.

Configure buttons

Shortcuts

Folder List

Notes

4. Choose Calendar from the Go menu.

Outlook displays the Calendar module. Note that the Calendar button in the bottom section of the Navigation Pane is now highlighted. (The Mail button was automatically highlighted in the Navigation Pane when the Mail was displayed, in case you didn't notice.)

5. Click the Contacts button in the Navigation Pane.

Outlook opens the Contacts module. Note that the Contacts button is now highlighted in the Navigation Pane.

6. Click the Tasks button in the Navigation Pane.

Outlook opens the Tasks module. Note that Tasks button is now highlighted in the Navigation Pane.

7. **Press Ctrl+Shift+I.**

   Outlook now opens the Mail module and selects the Inbox folder in the Navigation Pane. Note that if you had just clicked the Mail navigation button or pressed the Ctrl+1 shortcut to return to the Mail module, Outlook would have automatically selected Personal Folders in the Navigation Pane and displayed Outlook Today because this view was the last one you had selected.

That concludes your initial tour of the main modules. As you can see, the Microsoft software engineers include plenty of ways to easily move between these modules. Awareness of this should go a long way towards making you less Inbox dependent and opening you up to the other features that can also make Outlook a first-class Personal Information Manager.

Getting Really Comfy with the Outlook Window

An integral part of my third stress-free productivity strategy, mastering your productivity tools (see Chapter 4), is being able to readily identify the components of each productivity tool in your arsenal. This includes understanding the function of each component as well as its prescribed use.

When applying this specifically to Outlook (the major electronic tool in your productivity arsenal), this translates into being familiar with each of the major command components in the Outlook window as well as its setup of panes, depending upon which of the various modules you select.

Outlook's medley of menus

The most basic command component in Outlook is its *menu* bar — the second bar at the top of the program window immediately beneath the title bar.

The Outlook menu bar contains seven standard menus: File, Edit, View, Go, Tools, Actions, and Help. (*Standard* here means that these same seven menus are available no matter which of the Outlook modules you happen to be in.) As you're undoubtedly aware, you can open a menu by clicking the menu name. You may also know that you can press and release the Alt key and then use an arrow key to highlight the menu name and press Enter, or you can press and hold Alt and type the menu's underlined hotkey. (For example, Alt+T opens the Tools menu because the T in Tools is underlined.)

Keep in mind that even though the menus themselves don't change, depending upon which Outlook module you're in, the menu items they offer you do (with the exception of File and Help). This is the case simply because Outlook performs so many diverse productivity-related tasks that the majority of its menus have to be highly context-sensitive in order to offer you all the options you need.

You can experience the highly context-sensitive nature of Outlook's menus for yourself by following this simple sequence of steps:

1. **With the Mail module displayed in Outlook, press Alt+V to open the View menu.**

   Note the various items on this menu.

2. **Press Alt and then release it without pressing any other key.**

   Doing this closes the View menu, allowing you to switch to the Calendar module in Outlook.

3. **Press Ctrl+2 to switch to the Calendar module and then press Alt+V to open the View menu.**

   Note the appearance of the Day, Work Week, Week, and Month items on the View menu when the Calendar module is selected. Such items are missing from the View menu when the Mail module is current.

4. **Move your mouse pointer over the Actions menu.**

   Doing this closes the View menu while at the same time opening the Actions menu. Note the type of action items available to you with the Calendar module selected.

5. **Press Alt to deselect the menu bar and then press Ctrl+3 to switch to the Contacts module and Alt+A to open the Actions menu.**

   Note the many action items available to you when the Contacts module is current. Also, observe the difference between actions presented here and those presented with the Calendar module selected.

6. **Repeat Step 5, this time pressing Ctrl+4 instead of Ctrl+3.**

   Doing this opens the Actions menu again, this time when the Tasks module is current. Note the rather short list of action items attached to the menu in this module and how they differ from those presented with the Contacts module selected.

7. **Repeat Step 5, this time pressing Ctrl+1 instead of Ctrl+3.**

   Doing this opens the Actions menu when the Mail module is current. Note the completely mail-oriented action items that populate this menu with the Mail module selected.

8. **Press the Alt key one last time to close the open menu.**

I hope this little exercise gives you a taste of how chameleon-like Outlook can be, changing key menu options to suit the particular module you're using at the time. I think this helps reinforce the notion that, as a Personal Information Manager, Outlook really presents you with a collection of various environments. And as you become more and more comfortable moving between modules, you begin to see that each Outlook environment is uniquely designed to help perform a particular group of productivity activities.

Outlook's trio of toolbars

When compared with other Microsoft programs such as Word 2003 and Excel 2003, Outlook appears positively toolbar-challenged. However, don't let the meager number of toolbars fool you, for as with the Outlook menu items the particular buttons on two out of three of the toolbars (the Standard and Advanced) change depending upon which Outlook module you're using at the time (that old context-sensitive thing again).

The three Outlook three toolbars are

- ✔ **Standard:** Contains buttons for creating new entities (messages, appointments, tasks, and so on), printing them, and changing the view, depending upon the current Outlook module.

- ✔ **Advanced:** Contains a specific set of navigation buttons and a limited number of view buttons pertaining to the current Outlook module.

- ✔ **Web:** Contains buttons for navigating Web pages from within Outlook.

Remember that you can always display or hide a particular toolbar in Outlook by choosing View➪Toolbars and then choosing the toolbar name (Standard, Advanced, or Web). You can also display or hide a toolbar by right-clicking anywhere in the menu/toolbar area at the top of the window and then clicking the toolbar name.

The Standard toolbar

The Standard toolbar is the most chameleon-like of the bunch. You can see this clearly by comparing the buttons on the Standard toolbar in Figure 5-2 when the Mail module in Outlook 2003 is selected with those shown in Figure 5-3 when the Calendar module is selected.

Note that if you're running Outlook 2007 on your computer, the Standard toolbar in the Mail and Contacts modules is slightly different. Particularly, the toolbar contains Categorize and Follow Up buttons when you're in the Mail or Contacts module — buttons that don't appear in earlier versions of Outlook. The Categorize button enables you to assign a category to the currently selected e-mail messages or contacts. The Follow Up button enables you to flag currently selected messages or contacts or add reminders so that you'll remember to follow up on them in the near future.

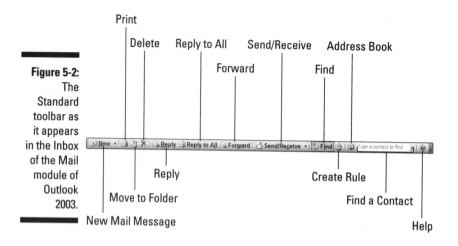

Figure 5-2: The Standard toolbar as it appears in the Inbox of the Mail module of Outlook 2003.

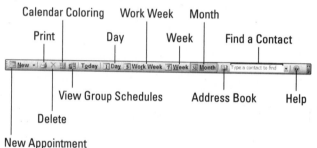

Figure 5-3: The Standard toolbar as it appears in the Calendar module of Outlook 2003.

The two buttons on the Standard toolbar that can save you the most time — and therefore are the ones I want you to pay particular attention to — are the New button at the beginning of the toolbar and the Find a Contact button near the end. You can use the New button to create new entities for all the types of information you track, including new e-mail messages, appointments, contacts, tasks, and notes (especially helpful when you forget the shortcut keys associated with creating them in any module). You can use the text box in the Find a Contact button to locate and open the record for any contact in your address book from any module in Outlook. For example, you can use this button to look up the telephone number for a client with whom you have a telephone appointment right from within the Calendar module.

The Advanced toolbar

The Advanced toolbar is a bit more stable than the Standard toolbar. That being said, as you can see by comparing Figure 5-4 with Figure 5-5, you do find considerable difference in the buttons on the Advanced toolbar when you're in the Calendar module as opposed to the Contacts module.

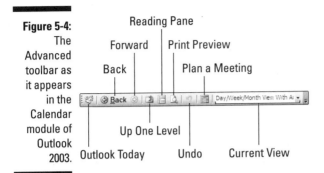

Figure 5-4: The Advanced toolbar as it appears in the Calendar module of Outlook 2003.

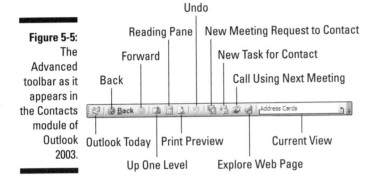

Figure 5-5: The Advanced toolbar as it appears in the Contacts module of Outlook 2003.

The first seven buttons (Outlook Today through Undo) on the Advanced toolbar, however, are the same regardless of which main modules you're in. As such, they're well worth being familiar with:

- **Outlook Today:** Click this button to switch to the Outlook Today view that gives you an overview of your day's appointments, tasks, and unread messages from the current module.

- **Back:** Click this button to return to the view that you previously selected in the current or different module.

- **Forward:** Click this button to go back to the view that was displayed in the module before you clicked the Back button.

- **Up One Level:** Click this button in the Mail module to display the contents of a Mail folder in the level immediately above the current one. (In the Calendar, Contacts, and Tasks modules, clicking this button has the same effect as clicking the Back button.)

- **Reading Pane:** Click this button to display or hide the Reading Pane, which shows the detailed contents of the selected message, appointment, contact, or task when the Mail, Calendar, Contacts, or Tasks module is current. (See "Putting the Reading Pane to best use" later in this chapter.)

✔ **Print Preview:** Click this button to open a Print Preview window that shows how the selected e-mail message or the selected Calendar, Contacts, and Tasks view will appear when printed when the Mail, Calendar, Contacts, or Tasks module is current.

✔ **Undo:** Click this button to undo any action you just completed. It will be as if you had never done it.

In addition to these useful buttons common to all the Outlook modules, you can find some valuable buttons specific to particular modules. For example, when you're in the Calendar module, Outlook adds a Plan a Meeting button to the Advanced toolbar that you can click to open the Plan a Meeting dialog box, where you can set up a meeting and invite others to participate. (See Chapter 10 for details on planning meetings and sending out requests.)

Likewise, when you're in the Contacts module, the Advanced toolbar acquires the following three buttons, which can be very useful and save you time when you need to do something:

✔ **New Meeting Request to Contact:** Opens the Meeting dialog box using the current contact's e-mail address so that you can invite him or her to an upcoming meeting.

✔ **New Task for Contact:** Opens the Task dialog box, where you can assign a new task associated with the current contact.

✔ **Explore Web Page:** Opens the Web page associated with the current contact using your Web browser in a separate program window.

The Web toolbar

The Web toolbar is the most static of the three Outlook toolbars. This toolbar is extremely useful when you need to research online or otherwise refer to some information on the Web and don't want to have to leave Outlook and switch to your Web browser in order to do it.

Figure 5-6 shows how this can work. Here, I've opened the Start page of my productivity Web site from the Mail module in Outlook. To open a page, you simply type in main part of the URL (I used **harveyproducivity.com** in this case) in the Address text box on the Web toolbar.

When you press the Enter key, Outlook opens the Start page of my productivity Web site in a single pane to the right of the Navigation Pane (and automatically adds the rest of the main page address, including the `http://` prefix and the `default.aspx` suffix to the URL in the Address text box).

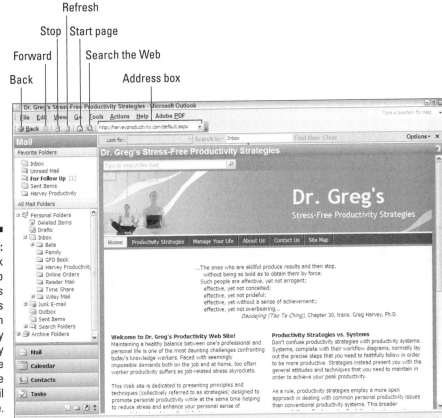

You can then surf the pages of this Web site using the site's internal navigation buttons. Note that you can return to a previously viewed Web page on the site by clicking the Back button on the Outlook Web toolbar and then go back to the currently displayed page from which you made that jump by clicking the toolbar's Forward button. You can also display your Web browser's Home page in the Outlook window by clicking the Web toolbar's Start Page button, or you can use Microsoft's Live Search engine to search the Web by clicking the toolbar's Search the Web button.

If any Web sites contain information to which you regularly need to refer when using a particular Outlook module, don't waste your precious time typing their URLs in the Address text box of the Web toolbar each time you want to open them. Instead, create a new Outlook folder for each Web site you regularly visit and then associate the folder with the Web address before you add it to the Favorite Folders section in Navigation Pane in the Mail module as well as the Shortcuts Navigation mini-pane. (See "Making short work of the Folder List and Shortcuts buttons," later in this chapter, for precise instructions on how you do this.)

Outlook's plethora of panes

It isn't bad enough that Outlook splits up its considerable functions between so many different modules. Outlook also has to go and split up its program window into a bunch of different window panes as well.

And it'll probably come as no surprise to discover that the usage and arrangement of these panes varies from module to module. (Outlook's nothing if not context-sensitive.) The one constant in all the modules is the Navigation Pane. But even here, the groups of links and icons that appear above the standard navigation buttons that switch you between Outlook modules varies according to which module is current.

However, when considering the panes in all four main Outlook modules (Mail, Calendar, Contacts, and Tasks), you can relax by concentrating mainly on the functioning of the Navigation and Reading Panes. In addition, you also need to make yourself familiar with the functioning of the TaskPad in the Calendar module of Outlook 2003 and the To Do Bar (that replaces the TaskPad and appears in all modules) in Outlook 2007.

Putting the Navigation Pane to best use

As its name implies, the primary function of the Navigation Pane is to enable you to switch between Outlook modules as well as between different views in the same module.

You can click the Navigation buttons that appear in the bottom portion of the Navigation Pane in every module to switch to a new module (although I prefer you to use the shortcut keys most of the time — see "The Outlook Shortcut Keys You Need to Know and Use," later in this chapter, for details).

The actual buttons and options that appear in the area above these navigation buttons vary depending upon which Outlook module is active. Each Outlook module divides the area above these buttons into two sections: the top section includes icons that enable you to select the particular module entity you want to work with (be it a favorite folder, calendar, contacts list, to-do list, group of notes, or journal), and the middle section contains options or links for selecting the view to apply in displaying the items that the selected entity contains.

Take the time to become familiar with your choices in the My section — My Calendars, for example, or My Tasks or My Contracts — at the top of the Navigation Pane in each of the Outlook modules you regularly use. As you begin to really use Outlook as your Personal Information Manager, you'll undoubtedly create new entities for particular groups of information whose icons will appear here, and clicking their icons is the fastest way to select and display them in Outlook.

Also, keep in mind that clicking the View Options buttons that appear in the Views section in the middle of the Navigation Pane is by far the fastest way to switch to a new view in the current module. Selecting a view from the Current View drop-down list on the Advanced toolbar is also fine, provided that this toolbar is already displayed in Outlook. (Don't ever waste time redisplaying this toolbar when it's hidden just to use this button.) However, if you're using Outlook 2003, please stay away from selecting a new view using the View menu, as this involves navigating multiple levels of submenus. They shortened the submenus path for selecting a new view considerably in Outlook 2007.

When you know the essential shortcut keys for navigating the Outlook interface (see "The Outlook Shortcut Keys You Need to Know and Use" later in this chapter), you can increase your screen real estate and make working with the individual items in each Outlook module much easier to deal with by routinely hiding the Navigation Pane as you work, redisplaying it only when you need to use its options. Of course, if you keep the Advanced toolbar displayed in Outlook, you'll have to redisplay the Navigation Pane a lot less because you can use the menu attached to its Current View button to change views in the current module.

Putting the Reading Pane to best use

The Reading Pane takes its name from its primary application in the Mail module. Here, where it customarily appears on the right side of the Outlook screen, the Reading Pane displays the contents of the currently selected e-mail message. The value of this pane in enabling you to easily scan and read your e-mail messages in the Mail module goes without question.

However, the Mail module's not the only place in Outlook where the Reading Pane comes in really handy. In other main modules — including the Calendar, Contacts, and Tasks — the Reading Pane displays the details of whatever appointment, contact, or task you select in that module.

You can then use the Reading Pane to get more detailed information about the current item (although you have to open its Appointment dialog box by double-clicking the appointment if you want to change any information). For example, say you're in the Calendar module and your daily calendar has an upcoming telephone appointment with a client. Imagine as well that you've added to the Calendar entry the client's telephone number along with a bunch of notes to remind yourself of the questions you want to ask and get answered, and all that added info doesn't fit in the appointment's AutoPreview. Instead of having to double-click the appointment on the calendar to open its Appointment dialog box to review all this information before making the call, you can simply select the appointment and then turn on the Reading Pane at the bottom of the Information Viewer (Alt+VNB in Outlook 2003 or Alt+VRB in Outlook 2007). This shows you all your notes covering the questions you want answered during the conversation in the Reading Pane that now appears beneath the calendar in the Information Viewer (see Figure 5-7).

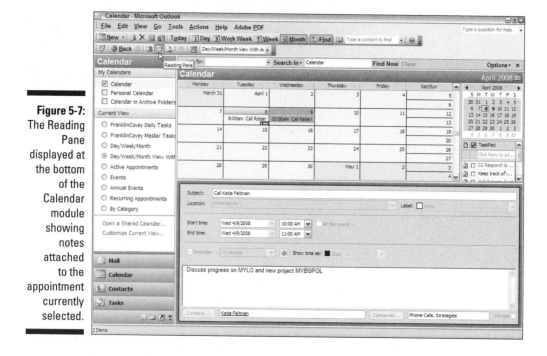

Figure 5-7:
The Reading
Pane
displayed at
the bottom
of the
Calendar
module
showing
notes
attached
to the
appointment
currently
selected.

After you've concluded the conversation with your client, you can then once again hide the Reading Pane in the Calendar module (Alt+VNO in Outlook 2003 or Alt+VRO in Outlook 2007), assuming that you want more of your calendar information displayed in the Outlook screen.

The TaskPad versus the To-Do Bar

There's one more pane with which you need to be on really good terms in Outlook. In versions of the program prior to Outlook 2007, this pane is referred to as the TaskPad, and it appears on the right side of the program window only in the Calendar module. In Outlook 2007, this pane has morphed into the To-Do Bar, which appears on the right side of the program window in each and every Outlook module.

The TaskPad in earlier versions of Outlook displays the Date Navigator (showing a small calendar with the current month and navigation buttons for displaying earlier and later months) above a section displaying the tasks on your to-do list that either have no due dates or have a due date on or before the current date. Note that you can customize the TaskPad from the View⇨TaskPad View submenu so that it displays all tasks, just the overdue tasks, or tasks that are active or complete just for the days you select on the calendar.

The To-Do Bar in Outlook 2007 not only displays the Date Navigator and the most recent tasks on your to-do list, but also a brief list with your three most recent upcoming appointments.

You can also customize the To-Do Bar from the View⇨To-Do Bar submenu so that it contains only the Date Navigator, the three most recent appointments, or tasks on your to-do list. Note that if you do remove the Date Navigator from the To-Do Bar, it automatically appears at the top of the Navigation Pane whenever you're in Outlook's Calendar module.

Using Outlook's Medley of Modules

In this section, I give you a brief overview of the basic functions of each of the eight Outlook modules in terms of how they relate to personal productivity. This survey's intended only to whet your curiosity about how you may be able to fit each module into your quest for greater work/life balance and use its key features to be more productive. You can find loads more detailed information devoted to the personal productivity usage of features in specific modules in later chapters.

The only exception to this "later chapters" strategy of mine is the Folder List and Shortcuts, which, technically speaking, aren't even Outlook modules because they restrict their appearance to the Navigation Pane (although they do rate their own navigation buttons at the bottom of the Navigation Pane and keyboard shortcuts just like the honest-to-goodness Outlook modules do). For detailed information on how to make efficient use of the Folder List and Shortcuts, consult "Making short work of the Folder List and Shortcuts in the Navigation Pane" later in this chapter.

Dispatching any illusions about the functions of the Mail module

I presume that, as a somewhat seasoned Outlook user, you're most familiar with the functioning of the Mail module, specifically its Inbox Mail folder. After all, this is the module and folder in which Outlook automatically opens each and every time you launch the program. And dollars to donuts, you spend most, if not all, of your time in this Mail folder, creating new e-mail to send and reading and answering the messages you receive (when you can get to it and it's not too overwhelming, that is).

And while processing your e-mail is certainly the Mail module's specialty, using it efficiently is obviously not every worker's forte, for how else can you explain the almost universal aversion to e-mail and inability to deal with it effectively? (Jump ahead to Chapters 7 and 8, if this is your main personal productivity bugaboo and you need strategies for getting it under control right away.)

In addition to its considerable role in processing your e-mail correspondence (see Chapter 9), the Mail module also gives you considerable power over organizing it (and this is often the key to getting a handle on your e-mail).

The Mail modules offer you this power through the use of the following special features:

- **Categories:** Categories enable you to organize the e-mail messages that appear in the Information Viewer by the groups to which they're assigned. Viewing the contents of your Inbox by Categories gives you control over which messages are displayed and which are hidden, thus making the contents of your Inbox a whole lot easier to deal with.

- **Folders:** Folders in the All Mail Folders section in the middle of the Mail module's Navigation Pane enable you to store e-mail messages in different custom folders you set up so that you can not only easily find the top priority messages to which you must respond but also those messages that contain particular information to which you need to refer later on. The best thing about using folders to stay on top of incoming messages is that you can often have Outlook automatically move many of these messages out of the general Inbox folder and into the appropriate custom folder through the creation of an e-mail rule. (See Chapter 8 for details.)

- **Favorite Folders:** Favorite folders in the section by the same name at the very top of the Mail module's Navigation Pane enable you to quickly switch between the Mail folders that you maintain. In addition, you can also associate custom folders with particular Web addresses and then use the folders to open their pages in Outlook. (See the "Making short work of the Folder List and Shortcuts in the Navigation Pane" section, later in this chapter, for details.)

Scheduling some time for the Calendar module

The Calendar module enables you to keep track all your appointments in a visual manner. The Information Viewer of the Calendar module therefore takes on the appearance of a printed day planner, with a graphic representation of either your daily, weekly, or monthly schedule. Because it's electronic and not paper, you can switch the Calendar view to the current day, five-day work week, entire seven-day week, and month in the blink of an eye.

The keystrokes for switching to these views in Outlook 2003 are

- **Day:** Alt+1
- **Work Week:** Alt+5

✔ **Week:** Alt+7

✔ **Month:** Alt+= (equal sign)

In Outlook 2007, you switch to these views with the following shortcut keys:

✔ **Day:** Ctrl+Alt+1

✔ **Work Week:** Ctrl+Alt+2

✔ **Week:** Ctrl+Alt+3

✔ **Month:** Ctrl+Alt+4

In versions prior to Outlook 2007, the Calendar module is the only one that can also display tasks on your to-do list alongside your schedule in its TaskPad pane. (In Outlook 2007, your upcoming tasks can appear on the To-Do Bar not only in the Calendar but also in all the other Outlook modules.)

Because the Calendar module enables you combine different views of your appointment calendar with a partial view of your to-do list, it often offers the ideal environment from which to plan your day by enabling you to effectively prioritize your tasks and harmonize them with your standing appointments.

Consider making the Calendar module the heart of your Outlook Personal Information Manager instead of your Inbox in the Mail module. That way, you bring both your current schedule and to-do list (in the To-Do Bar in Outlook 2007 and the TaskPad in earlier versions) into the forefront of your personal productivity while at the same time putting your e-mail in the background (where it clearly belongs). To do this, you simply customize Outlook so that it automatically starts up in the Calendar module when you launch the program instead of the Inbox of the Mail module. (See Chapter 6 for details on how you do this.) Then, you memorize the shortcut keys that I outline later in this chapter in the section entitled, "The Outlook Shortcut Keys You Need to Know and Use" so that you can easily switch over to the Mail module (or any other one you need to access) and deftly return to the Calendar without so much as breaking a sweat.

Getting in touch with the Contacts module

The primary function of the Contacts module is to make it easy for you to keep track of the people that you need to stay in touch with. Although most people track only essential contact information such as name, address, e-mail, and telephone numbers, Contacts enables you to store all sorts of additional, less vital pieces of information about a contact, such as the name of his or her department, manager, assistant, and spouse, as well as his or her title, suffix, nickname, birthday, and anniversary.

And if these additional bits of information in these preset detail fields aren't sufficient, the module enables you add your own custom fields as well as notes about the contact that you can review simply by opening his or her Contact record.

If you're involved in some sort of service profession that relies heavily on good client relations (such as sales, insurance, medicine, and the like), consider adding personal details such as birthday, nickname, and spouse's name for your important clients, along with any other noteworthy items (such as the names of pets, favorite sports, hobbies, and pastimes) on contact records. That way, you can review this information prior to an encounter and use it when appropriate to add a special personal touch that can only enhance and deepen your professional relationship.

In addition to making it possible for you to store information about the notable people in your work and life at large, the Contacts module can facilitate your personal productivity by enabling you to easily review all your activities with them. This feature makes it a breeze to look up an upcoming meeting, an e-mail, or a log of a telephone conversation (provided you note the call as a scheduled appointment or task on your to-do list), saving you loads of precious time that might be lost if you were to blindly shuffle through your Inbox, calendars, or to-do list to find it. All you have to do is double-click the contact's name to open his record and then click the Activities tab (in Outlook 2003) or the Activities button in the Show group of the Contact tab (in Outlook 2007). Outlook then generates a list of all the Outlook activities associated with that person. These include e-mails you've received and sent to this person as well as appointments and tasks involving him. You can then review any of these listed messages, appointments, or tasks in detail simply by double-clicking them.

Understanding the responsibilities of the Tasks module

The function of the Tasks module is fairly self-evident: Tasks keeps track of all the things you have to do; in other words, your obligations, both professional and personal. These can run the gamut from simple tasks such as "Pick up dry cleaning" all the way to complex projects such as "Complete New Product Proposal."

Therefore, it's in the Tasks module that you'll end up doing a lot of your planning work. This is because to be able to accurately record tasks in your to-do list, you just naturally have to determine the following things about them:

✔ **Exact nature of the task:** Is this a simple one-step task or is it a more complex one that would be better split up into lots of smaller, easier-to-accomplish tasks?

✔ **Due date:** Ideally, when should this task be completed, and is it a task that has a drop-dead date attached to it that you can't alter in any way?

✔ **Whether or not it should be delegated:** Are you the best person to perform this task, or is there somebody else on the team better qualified to handle it? And, if you are the one, can you handle the task all by yourself or do you need somebody else's help completing it?

The built-in views that the Outlook Tasks module offers are really valuable in helping evaluate how well you're doing in getting your work load under control and reaching your goal of better work/life balance. You can use the views to quickly filter your to-do list so that only certain tasks appear on the list. This can include just the tasks that are currently active, have due dates coming up in the next week, are currently overdue or assigned to others on the team, or are even now completed. In addition, Outlook supports a Timeline view that shows the tasks on your to-do list on a timeline where you tell at a glance which tasks overlap each other and share the same deadline.

Remarking on the utility of the Notes module

The Notes module gives you the perfect place to jot down and store all the little bits of information that just don't belong anywhere else in Outlook. These can include notes to jog your memory (the electronic equivalent of tying a string around your finger), suggestions for things to work on and ways to improve yourself and your job, and even those wonderful inspirations that come to out of the blue.

The funny thing is that the Notes module is definitely underutilized even by many of those Outlook users who have all kinds of sticky notes plastered all over their computer monitors. This is probably because most users are completely unaware of the benefits of keeping electronic notes (and some aren't even aware that Outlook takes notes), and the program does a good job of hiding this module by reducing its navigation button to a fairly nondescript sticky-note icon in the Navigation Pane. It's also most likely due to the fact that everybody's just in the habit of using physical sticky notes to jot down their stray thoughts.

If you're serious about improving your personal productivity and enhancing your work/life balance with Outlook, I really want you to develop the habit of recording those bits of information that you'd normally jot down on a sticky note as an electronic note in the Outlook Notes module. That way, you not only don't have to worry about losing a note, but you also can quickly search your notes and copy pertinent information to other parts of Outlook and other applications you use.

Recording the uses of the Journal module

The Journal module is probably the least understood module in Outlook, and therefore it ends up being woefully underutilized like the Notes module. This may be because most people think of journaling as something that involves lots of writing. And they don't realize the Outlook Journal can automatically create a log of certain activities that you initiate both within and outside of Outlook. These can include such things as the Microsoft Office documents (including Word documents, Excel worksheets, and PowerPoint presentations) that you create or edit, e-mail you send to or receive from a particular co-worker or client, as well as meeting and task requests that you make and the responses you get back.

Correctly used, the Outlook Journal can not only help you document the dates when certain activities occurred, but it can also help you understand how efficiently you're making use of the bulk of your work time. Because Outlook can do so much of the logging automatically, you have little excuse for not activating the Journal module and using it to be more productive. You certainly can't use the excuse that you don't have the time, because I can help you activate the Journal module and set up the activities you want it to automatically log in literally a matter of a few minutes. (See Chapter 14 for details.)

Making short work of the Folder List and Shortcuts in the Navigation Pane

The Folder List and Shortcuts aren't really Outlook modules as much as mini-panes that appear in the Navigation Pane. These mini-panes appear in the Navigation Pane no matter what module is open as soon as you click their navigation buttons located at the bottom of Navigation Pane (identified respectively by a standard folder icon and an icon with a return arrow pointing to up to the right), or choose their menu items from the Go menu, or press their shortcut keys (Ctrl+6 for Folder List and Ctrl+7 for Shortcuts).

After the Folder List is open in the Navigation Pane, you can open one of its folders and display its contents simply by clicking its folder icon. If the folder is one that contains e-mail, the messages appear in the Information Viewer, and the contents of the selected message show up in the Reading Pane. If the folder is associated with a Web page, Outlook displays that page in the window to the right of the Navigation Pane used by the Information Viewer and Reading Pane when an e-mail folder is selected.

Remember that you can add a custom mail folder to the Folder List by clicking any folder icon in the Navigation Pane and then pressing Ctrl+Shift+E to open the Create New Folder dialog box. Enter the name of the folder in the Name text box and then click the name of the folder in which the new folder is to appear in the Select Where to Place the Folder list box before you click OK.

After the Shortcuts list is open at the top of the Navigation Pane, you can open any of its folders, modules, views, or Web pages simply by clicking the icons.

If your display screen isn't large enough to accommodate more than the four standard navigation buttons (Mail, Calendar, Contacts, and Tasks) but you still want quick-click access to lesser-used modules like Notes and Journal as alternative to using their keyboard shortcuts, be sure to add their folders to your Shortcuts.

Adding and grouping folders in Shortcuts

You can add shortcuts to any folder that appears in your Folder List. This includes both built-in folders that Outlook automatically creates (such as Drafts, Sent Items, Junk E-Mail, and the like) and all the custom folders that you add to your Folder List.

To add an existing folder to Shortcuts, follow these few steps:

1. **Launch Outlook and press Ctrl+7.**

   Outlook displays the Shortcuts list in the Navigation Pane.

2. **Click the Add New Shortcut link in the Navigation Pane.**

   Outlook opens the Add to Navigation Pane dialog box.

3. **Click the name of the folder you want to add to Shortcuts in the list box and then press Enter or click OK.**

   Remember to click the Expand button with a plus sign (+) if the folder you want to add is within another folder in the list.

   Outlook adds the name of the folder to the bottom of the Shortcuts list in the Navigation Pane.

If you end up adding lots of folders to your Outlook Shortcuts, you can help organize them by adding groups to the Shortcuts and then moving the appropriate folders to any of these groups. To do this, you follow these steps:

1. **Launch Outlook and press Ctrl+7.**

   Outlook displays the Shortcuts list in the Navigation Pane.

2. **Click the Add New Group link in the Navigation Pane.**

   Outlook adds a group — provisionally named *New Group* — to the bottom of the Shortcuts.

3. **Replace the New Group name by typing the name you want to give your group and then press Enter.**

   The name of the new group now appears in bold.

4. **To move folders in the general Shortcuts area to the new group, drag and drop their folder icons on the name of the new group.**

5. **To move the new group up in the list of groups in Shortcuts, right-click the group name and choose Move Up from the context menu that appears.**

   Repeat Step 5 as needed until the new group is positioned exactly where you want it in Shortcuts.

Adding folders with Web page links to your Favorite Folders and Shortcuts

Having access to a favorite Web site from within Outlook at the click of an icon comes in real handy. For example, I suggest that you create a folder associated with my productivity Web site that you can then add to your Favorite Folders in the Mail module as well as to your Shortcuts. That way, you can visit the site and get additional information and inspiration on using Outlook as your Personal Information Manager right as you're using the program!

To do this, you follow these simple steps:

1. **Launch Outlook as you normally do.**

   Make sure that you're in the Inbox of the Mail module. If you don't see Mail at the top of the Navigation Pane and the Inbox folder isn't highlighted in this pane, you then need to press Ctrl+Shift+I.

2. **Press Ctrl+Shift+E to open the Create New Folder dialog box and then type** Harvey Productivity **as the new folder name in the Name text box. (See Figure 5-8.)**

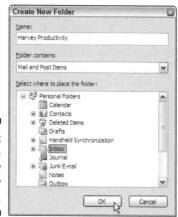

Figure 5-8:
Creating a new Harvey Productivity folder.

3. **Click the Inbox icon in the Select Where to Place the Folder list box and then press Enter or click OK.**

   The Harvey Productivity folder now appears a subfolder of Inbox in the All Mail Folders area of the Navigation Pane.

4. **Right-click the Harvey Productivity folder and then choose Properties from its context menu.**

   Outlook opens the Harvey Productivity Properties dialog box.

5. **Click the Home Page tab and then type** http://www.harveyproductivity. com **in the Address text box.**

6. **Select the Show Home Page by Default for This Folder check box (see Figure 5-9) and then press Enter or click OK.**

   Outlook closes the Harvey Productivity Properties dialog box.

Figure 5-9:
Associating
the Harvey
Productivity
folder with
the Web
site.

7. **Click the Harvey Productivity folder in the Navigation Pane.**

   Outlook should display the Home page of my productivity Web site, and you should start to feel the stress just melting away.

8. **Drag the Harvey Productivity icon up to the Favorite Folders area in the Navigation Pane and drop it wherever you want it to appear. (See Figure 5-10.)**

Now, you're ready to add this folder to your Shortcuts.

9. **Press Ctrl+7 to open your Shortcuts in the Navigation Pane and then click the Add New Shortcut link found there.**

   Outlook opens the Add to Navigation Pane dialog box.

10. **Click the Harvey Productivity folder in the Add to Navigation Pane dialog box (see Figure 5-11) and then press Enter or click OK.**

    Outlook closes the Add to Navigation Pane dialog box and adds a folder named Harvey Productivity to your Shortcuts.

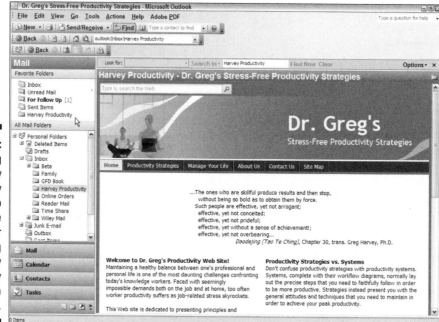

Figure 5-10:
Adding
the Harvey
Productivity
folder to
the Favorite
Folders after
opening
the Harvey
Productivity
Web site in
Outlook.

That's all there is to it — pretty simple once you know the secret. And now that you know the secret, you can go ahead and create custom folders associated with your preferred Web sites and add them to your Favorite Folders and/or Shortcuts.

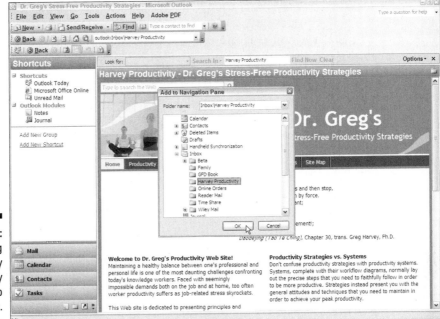

Figure 5-11:
Adding
the Harvey
Productivity
folder to
Shortcuts.

The Outlook Shortcut Keys You Need to Know and Use

In most books on Outlook, the authors present you with a smorgasbord of ways to accomplish a certain task, using either the menus or toolbar buttons or keyboard shortcuts. Such books then leave it to you to decide which of the methods you like best and want to use to get the job done.

However, because the primary focus of this book is work/life balance through personal productivity and not using Outlook, I not going to give you that luxury of user's choice. To save as much time as possible and to put Outlook as far into the background as possible so you can stay focused on being productive, I want you to memorize the following keyboard shortcuts *and* use them consistently. By the way, this doesn't mean that you can never click a Navigation button or use a pull-down menu: It simply means that you need to make using these keyboard shortcuts habitual so that they become your primary means of doing these tasks; the idea here is that you resort to the use of alternative buttons and menus only occasionally when it makes sense in the context of your screen use.

Switching modules and views

So that you can quickly navigate between Outlook modules and open and close important panes, I want you to memorize the following 12 keyboard shortcuts and then rely on them conscientiously as you use Outlook:

- ✔ **Ctrl+1:** Switches to the Mail module.

- ✔ **Ctrl+2:** Switches to the Calendar module.

- ✔ **Ctrl+3:** Switches to the Contacts module.

- ✔ **Ctrl+4:** Switches to the Tasks module.

- ✔ **Ctrl+5:** Switches to the Notes module.

- ✔ **Ctrl+6:** Displays the Folder List in the Navigation Pane in any module.

- ✔ **Ctrl+7:** Displays Shortcuts in the Navigation Pane in any module.

- ✔ **Ctrl+8:** Switches to the Journal module.

- ✔ **Ctrl+Shift+I:** Switches to the Inbox folder in the Mail module.

- ✔ **Ctrl+Y:** Opens the Go to Folder dialog box, where you can select the Mail folder to display in the Mail module.

- ✔ **Alt+F1:** Hides and redisplays the Navigation Pane.

- ✔ **Alt+F2:** Hides and redisplays the To-Do Bar (Outlook 2007 only).

Try to approach these navigation keystroke shortcuts not simply as timesavers but as an integral part of the process of making Outlook your complete Personal Information Manager. And because these shortcuts make the Outlook work environment feel more fluid, they aid you in becoming more flexible. Therefore, it's not likely that you feel as trapped in the Inbox of your Mail module when you're comfortable switching back and forth between modules simply by holding down the Ctrl key and pressing the appropriate number between 1 and 8. Also, note that Outlook never varies the sequence used in the shortcut keys — Mail first, Calendar second, Contacts third, Tasks fourth, Notes fifth, Folder List sixth, Shortcuts seventh, and Journal eighth — either on its Go menu or in the ordering of its navigation buttons in the Navigation Pane.

Creating new Outlook items

To be able to create a new item you need (such as an e-mail message, appointment, contact, task, and so forth) no matter which Outlook module is current, I want you to memorize these six keyboard shortcuts and then rely on them faithfully as you use Outlook:

- **Ctrl+Shift+M:** Opens the Untitled Message window so that you can create a new e-mail in any module other than Mail. (Press Ctrl+N to do this when the Mail module is current.)

- **Ctrl+Shift+A:** Opens the Appointment dialog box so that you can put a new appointment on your calendar in any module other than Calendar. (Press Ctrl+N to do this when the Calendar module is current.)

- **Ctrl+Shift+C:** Opens the Contact dialog box so that you can add a new contact to your address book in any module other than Contacts. (Press Ctrl+N to do this when the Contacts module is current.)

- **Ctrl+Shift+K:** Opens the Task dialog box so that you can add a new task to your to-do list in any module other than Tasks. (Press Ctrl+N to do this when the Tasks module is current.)

- **Ctrl+Shift+N:** Opens a new sticky note dialog box so that you can add a new note in any other module than Notes. (Press Ctrl+N to do this when the Notes module is current.)

- **Ctrl+Shift+J:** Opens the Journal Entry dialog box so that you can add a new entry to your journal in any module other than Journal. (Press Ctrl+N to do this when the Journal module is current.)

To help learn these keystroke shortcuts, remember you press Ctrl+N (for New item) to create a new item for the current module (e-mail message in Mail, appointment in Calendar, contact in Contacts, and task in Tasks). However, when you're not in the Outlook module that automatically generates the item you need to create, keep in mind that you don't have to waste time switching to that module and pressing Ctrl+N. Instead, simply hold down the Ctrl *and* Shift keys as you press the mnemonic letter key assigned to that item (M for Message, A for Appointment, C for Contact, K for tasK, and J for Journal).

Knowing you can be in any Outlook module and still create any Outlook item you need right then and there — and knowing that you can jump instantly to any other module you need to consult — has a freeing effect that's not to be underestimated. Having this ability encourages you to go beyond the confines of the Mail module as it breaks down the psychological walls that somehow tend to grow up between it and the other modules. As such, it represents a big step in truly making Outlook your Personal Information Manager and not simply your e-mail with address book program.

Taking the shortcut keys out for a spin

I suggest that you perform the following exercise to get a feel for these shortcut keys and how they can help you be more comfortable and productive in Outlook as well as to begin training your mind and your fingers in their usage:

1. **Launch Outlook as you normally do.**

   Outlook opens in the Inbox in its Mail module.

2. **Press Ctrl+2.**

   Outlook opens the Calendar module, the second of the main four modules. The Information Viewer depicts the days and weeks in the current monthly calendar.

3. **Press Alt+F1.**

   Outlook hides the Navigation Pane, giving you a better view of the monthly calendar.

4. **Press Ctrl+Shift+M.**

   Outlook opens an Untitled Message dialog box, where you can create a new e-mail and send it right from within the Calendar module.

5. **Press Esc to close the Untitled Message dialog box and then press Ctrl+Shift+C.**

   Outlook opens an Untitled Contact dialog box, where you can enter the information for a new contact to add to your address book.

6. **Press Esc to close the Untitled Contact dialog box and then press Ctrl+Shift+K.**

   Outlook opens an Untitled Task dialog box, where you can enter the information for a new task to add to your to-do list.

7. **Press Esc to close the Untitled Task dialog box and then press Ctrl+Shift+N.**

   Outlook opens a blank sticky note dialog box with today's date and time where you can jot down a note to yourself.

8. **Type** Don't forget to practice using Outlook's shortcut keys **as the text of the note and click the note's Close box.**

9. **Press Ctrl+5.**

   Outlook opens the Notes module, where you see the text of your reminder to practice using these invaluable keystroke shortcuts.

10. **Press Ctrl+6.**

   Outlook opens the Folder List in the Navigation Pane. Note, however, that you're still in the Notes module (no pun intended).

11. **Press Ctrl+7.**

   Outlook replaces the Folder List in the Navigation Pane with Shortcuts.

12. Click Outlook Today at the top of your Shortcuts list in the Navigation Pane.

Outlook opens the Outlook Today. Note, however, that Shortcuts still appears in the Navigation Pane.

13. Press Ctrl+Shift+I.

Outlook opens the Inbox in the Mail module (right back where you started from). Note that your Favorite Folders and All Mail Folders mini-panes have replaced Shortcuts in the Navigation Pane.

Now that you've completed this exercise, you should have a much better idea of how easily you can move from one Outlook module to the next. You should also have a feel for how easy it is to create new Outlook items without having to first move to the particular module known for using the item.

Chapter 6

Giving Outlook a Productivity Makeover

***

In This Chapter

▶ Changing the module in which Outlook starts up

▶ Taking a good look at the options available on the Views menu

▶ Putting the Outlook Today view to best use

▶ Understanding and using categories

▶ Customizing a module's folders, views, and categories using the Organize pane

▶ Configuring the Outlook's Navigation Pane to suit the way you work

***

*E*verybody can use a makeover from time to time, and Outlook is no exception. Part of using Outlook as your primary productivity tool involves looking at the options for customizing it to the way you work.

This chapter covers a bunch of different ways that you can tailor Outlook to the individual ways you work. Understand, however, that the customizing techniques covered here are only suggestions. If you find that a particular technique suits neither your hardware setup nor the way you use a certain module, by all means ignore it.

The only thing that I'm really keen on having you do when customizing Outlook is to find the screen and option setup that makes you the most comfortable — while at same time, productive — for each of the modules you routinely use (and I hope that eventually includes all of them).

Changing the Outlook Startup Module

As seasoned Outlook users, you're perfectly aware that when you launch the program, Outlook automatically opens the Inbox folder in the Mail module. Of course, if the e-mail that fills your Inbox is your great stumbling block to peak productivity, this arrangement may not be such a *good* thing. What you may not know is that you can change which folder opens each time you launch Outlook. This means that you can have another folder in the Mail module as your startup folder (say, Outlook Today) or even make another module such as the Calendar or Tasks module your startup default.

Changing the Outlook startup folder

To change the startup folder that Outlook uses, follow these steps:

1. **Launch Outlook as you normally do and then select Tools⇨Options on the menu bar.**

   Outlook opens the Options dialog box with the first tab selected.

2. **Click the Other tab and then click the Advanced Options button (see Figure 6-1).**

   Outlook opens the Advanced Options dialog box.

3. **Click the Browse button to the right of the Startup in This Folder text box.**

   Outlook opens the Select Folder dialog box, where you can select a new folder within the Mail module, such as Outlook Today or even another module such as Calendar.

4. **Click the icon of the folder you want opened in the Start in This Folder list box (see Figure 6-2) and then press Enter or click OK.**

   If the folder you want opened is hidden because it's a subfolder of another in the list, click its parent's Expand button (+) to display its folder icon.

   After the Select Folder dialog box closes, the new startup folder you just selected appears in the Startup in This Folder text box of the Advanced Options dialog box.

5. **Click the OK button twice — first to close the Advanced Options dialog box and then to close the Options dialog box.**

   Now you're ready to try out the change you made to the startup folder.

6. **Exit Outlook and then relaunch the program, starting it as you normally do.**

   This time, Outlook should open in the new folder or module you selected.

Figure 6-1:
Selecting
the
Advanced
Options
button on
the Other
tab of the
Options
dialog box.

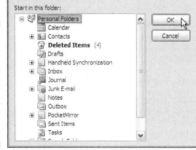

Figure 6-2:
Selecting a
new startup
folder in
the Select
Folder
dialog box.

Assuming that you memorize the essential Outlook shortcut keys that I cover in Chapter 5 for instantly navigating between modules and creating any new item you need, adapting to a different startup module should be a relatively painless process.

When you're considering selecting a new startup module, I suggest you try making the Outlook Calendar module your new home base and see how this works for you. Doing this enables you to glance over both your appointments and tasks for the rest of the day and work week the moment you launch Outlook at the beginning of your workday. That way, you can prepare for the day ahead as you do any last-minute tweaking of your planned activities.

Automatically launching Outlook each time you start your computer

If Outlook isn't already one of the programs that automatically launches each time you boot your personal computer, you should make it one. That way, you'll have your schedule and to-do list right in front of your face. (And if you have the time — and you've digested the techniques for dealing successfully with e-mail in Chapters 7 and 8 — you can go ahead and get your e-mail.)

To have Windows automatically launch Outlook each time you start your computer, follow these steps:

1. **Click the Windows Start button and then position your mouse over the All Programs option.**

   The All Programs submenu appears on-screen.

2. **Right-click the entry labeled Startup in the All Programs submenu and then select the Open option from the contextual menu that appears.**

   Windows opens your Startup dialog box on the desktop.

3. **Re-open the All Programs submenu and then right-click the Microsoft Office Outlook 2003 or the Microsoft Office Outlook 2007 item before you select the Copy option from the contextual menu that appears.**

   Now you're ready to paste the Outlook shortcut into the Startup dialog box.

4. **Click back into the Startup dialog box on the Windows desktop and then press Ctrl+V to paste the Outlook shortcut into this dialog box.**

   The Microsoft Office Outlook 2003 or Microsoft Office Outlook 2007 shortcut appears in the Startup dialog box (see Figure 6-3).

5. **Click the Close button in the Startup dialog box.**

After completing these steps, the next time you restart your computer and every time thereafter, Windows automatically starts up Outlook displaying the folder of the module you've designated as your Start.

Should you no longer want Outlook launched each time you start your computer, re-open the Start dialog box (following Steps 1 and 2 in the procedure) and then click the Microsoft Outlook program icon before you press the Delete key. Next, click the Delete Shortcut button in dialog box to confirm the deletion that Outlook displays before you click the Close button in the Startup dialog box.

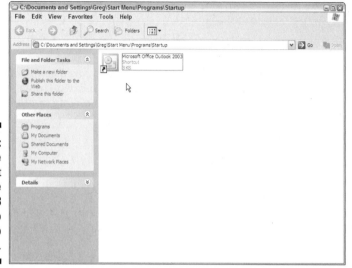

Figure 6-3:
Pasting the
Microsoft
Office
Outlook 2003
shortcut into
the Startup
dialog box.

Customizing the Outlook Toolbars

For many knowledge workers, Outlook's toolbars, at least the Standard and Advanced toolbars, contain a number of buttons that they just never use when working in particular modules. For others, the toolbars in certain modules simply lack buttons that they would love to have available to save them from having to resort to the slower pull-down menus. Even if you're quite content with preset buttons on the Outlook toolbars, you may find that you'd prefer them in a slightly different order.

No matter what your preference, Outlook makes it easy to tailor the contents of the built-in toolbars. And if that isn't enough, you can construct custom toolbars of your own design.

Modifying the contents of a built-in toolbar

Customizing the buttons on one of the three built-in toolbars is pretty easy work (a lot easier than filing all those papers you've accumulated on your desk). To add or remove buttons from a toolbar, follow these steps:

1. **Display the toolbar(s) you want to modify at top of the Outlook program window (View➪Toolbars). If you're modifying buttons on the Standard or Advanced toolbar, select the module that uses the version of the toolbar you want to change.**

   You can't change a toolbar that's hidden, and because the Standard and Advanced toolbars are fairly context-sensitive, making sure you're in the correct module is always your first step in modifying their toolbars.

2. **Right-click somewhere on a displayed Outlook toolbar or menu bar at the top of the program window and then click the Customize option at the bottom of the contextual menu that appears.**

   Outlook opens the Customize dialog box with its Commands tab selected (see Figure 6-4).

3. **To add a new button to a toolbar, click the appropriate category in the Categories list box of the Customize dialog box and then drag its button from the Commands list box up to the toolbar and drop it into the desired position.**

   Outlook indicates where the new button will be inserted on the toolbar with the I-beam that appears at the front of the mouse pointer. If you drop a new button into the wrong position on the toolbar, simply drag and drop it to the correct place.

4. **To remove a button from a toolbar, drag the button until it's some-where off the toolbar and then drop it.**

   Outlook indicates that the button will be deleted when you release the mouse button by displaying an X as the mouse pointer's ScreenTip.

5. **When you finish modifying the toolbars, click the Close button on the Customize dialog box.**

   As soon as you close the Customize dialog box, the buttons on the toolbars become active again and you can try them out for size.

Figure 6-4:
Use the
Commands
tab of the
Customize
dialog box
to add
buttons to
the Outlook
toolbars.

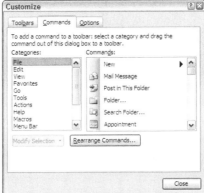

Rearranging buttons on a built-in toolbar

Sometimes, you just want to move the buttons around on a toolbar so that they're in a more convenient location. This is especially true if you're running Outlook on a computer with a relatively small monitor and two of the toolbars share the same row so that not all the buttons can be displayed. In such a case, you will want to move the buttons that you regularly use toward the beginning of each toolbar so that they are always displayed and you don't have to spend time clicking the Toolbar Options button at the end to display a button you want to use.

Outlook provides two ways to reposition buttons on its toolbars. You can drag and drop the button (after opening the Customize dialog box) or you can open the Rearrange Commands dialog box by clicking the Rearrange Commands button at the bottom of the Commands tab of the Customize dialog box (refer to Figure 6-4).

Figure 6-5 shows the Rearrange Commands dialog box after I clicked the Toolbar option button and selected Standard on the adjacent drop-down list. To move a particular button, click to select it in the Controls list box and then click the Move Up or Move Down button until the button is positioned correctly between the other buttons on the toolbar in the Controls list box.

Figure 6-5:
Repositioning buttons on the Outlook Standard toolbar using the Rearrange Commands dialog box.

Note that Outlook doesn't actually move the button on the displayed toolbar until after you close the Rearrange Commands dialog box, which you do after you've moved all your buttons to the correct position and have clicked the dialog box's Close button.

If you make a mess of one of the toolbars, you can restore it to its original "factory" settings by clicking the Toolbars tab in the Customize dialog box and clicking the Reset button. When you click this button, the program displays an alert dialog box asking whether you're sure, and as soon as you press Enter or select OK, Outlook immediately returns the selected toolbar to its pristine condition.

Creating your own toolbars

Rather than fool around with customizing the contents and arrangement of the existing Outlook toolbars, you may find it more advantageous to create a custom toolbar. That way, you can assign buttons with just the commands that you use time and time again in a particular Outlook module.

Keep in mind that even the custom toolbars you create in Outlook are context-sensitive, at least in the sense of not displaying buttons in a module where they can't function. For example, if you create a custom toolbar with the New All Day Event button, this button will appear on the toolbar only when you're in the Calendar module (and can actually add such an event). The button simply drops off the toolbar whenever you switch to any of the other modules.

To create your own custom toolbar for Outlook, follow these steps:

1. **If your custom toolbar is particularly module-specific, select that module in Outlook before you open the Customize dialog box. Otherwise, simply open the Customize dialog box in any Outlook module.**

2. **Click the Toolbars tab in the Customize dialog box and then click the New button (see Figure 6-6).**

   Outlook opens the New Toolbar dialog box.

3. **Replace the provisional name (Custom 1, Custom 2, and so on) with your own descriptive name in the Toolbar Name text box and then press Enter or click OK.**

   Outlook creates a new blank custom toolbar that displays a few letters of the name you assigned.(It will appear next to the Customize dialog box.)

4. **Click the Commands tab of the Customize dialog box and then drag and drop the buttons you want onto the new toolbar in the order you want them to appear.**

   Note that you can reposition any button you add to the new toolbar by dragging it and dropping it into place.

5. **When you finish adding all the buttons you want on your new toolbar and you've arranged them in the preferred order, click the Close button in the Customize dialog box.**

   Outlook closes the Customize dialog box.

6. **Drag the toolbar from the center of the Outlook screen and dock it somewhere at the top of the screen, either on a row that already contains another toolbar or on a new row by itself.**

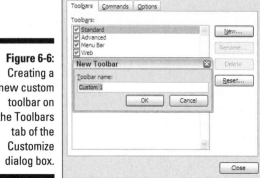

Figure 6-6:
Creating a
new custom
toolbar on
the Toolbars
tab of the
Customize
dialog box.

Keep in mind that custom toolbars are the only ones that you can delete in Outlook. Although Outlook lets you modify the contents of the three built-in toolbars, it doesn't allow you get rid of them. To delete a custom toolbar that you no longer need, select it on the Toolbars tab of the Customize dialog box and then click the Delete button. The program displays an alert dialog box asking you whether you're sure, and, as soon as you press Enter or click OK, it permanently zaps the toolbar (meaning the only way to get it back is to recreate it from scratch).

Checking out a recommended toolbar configuration

If you adopt the Calendar module as the heart of your personal information manager (as I continue to urge you to do), I want to suggest a companion Outlook toolbar configuration. Create a custom Productivity toolbar that combines some of the most useful tools on the Standard and Advanced toolbars in both the Mail and Calendar module with other buttons that can help you be more productive. You can then try using Outlook with only the menu bar and Productivity toolbar displayed, thus giving other panes a little more screen space.

Initially, consider adding the following buttons to this custom Productivity toolbar (to which you can later add buttons for other special features you routinely use). To add each of these buttons, click the name of the category shown in parentheses after the name of the button in following list in the Categories list box on the left side of the Commands tab of the Customize

dialog box. Then, find the button as shown in the following list in the Commands list box on the right and drag its icon up to the Productivity toolbar you're building and drop it into place:

- **New (File):** Enables you to add special items for the current module (as well as standard items for the other modules, in case you forget their shortcut keys).

- **Print (Standard):** Opens the Print dialog box, where you can select the printer and page settings you want to use in printing items in the current module.

- **Print Preview (Advanced):** Opens the Print Preview window so that you can see how a selected item in the current module will print.

- **Organize (Tools):** Opens a special Organize pane at the top of the current module that enables you to customize its look and contents (see "Tailoring the Look of Assorted Outlook Modules with the Organize Pane," later in this chapter, for details).

- **Current View (View):** Enables you to select or define a new view for examining items in the current module.

- **Arrange By (View):** When in the Calendar module, this button enables you to select a new order for your tasks in the TaskPad (Outlook 2003) or To-Do Bar (2007). When in the Mail module, Arrange By lets you select a new order for your e-mail messages. When any other module is current, this button simply disappears from the toolbar.

- **Categories (Edit):** Enables you to assign an existing or new custom category to the selected item in any of the Outlook 2003 modules.

- **Categorize (Edit):** Enables you to assign an existing or new custom category to the selected item in any of the Outlook 2007 modules.

- **TaskPad (View):** Hides and displays the TaskPad in the Calendar module in Outlook 2003.

- **TaskPad View (View):** Enables you to select a new view of the tasks displayed in the TaskPad in the Calendar module of Outlook 2003.

- **Task List (View):** Hides and displays the task list in the To-Do Bar in Outlook 2007.

- **Daily Task List (View):** Enables you to hide, display, and minimize the Tasks pane at the bottom of the Information Viewer in the Calendar module in Outlook 2007.

- **Bottom (View):** Displays the Reading Pane showing details of the selected item in the current module at the bottom of the Information Viewer.

- **Right (View):** Displays the Reading Pane showing details of the selected item in the current module on the right side of the Information Viewer.

✔ **Off (View):** Hides the Reading Pane when it's displayed on the right side or bottom of the Information Viewer.

✔ **Find (Standard):** In Outlook 2003, displays or hides the Look For and Search In combo boxes and associated buttons at the top that enable you to search for particular items in the current Outlook module.

✔ **Instant Search (Tools):** In Outlook 2007, selects the Instant Search combo box at the top of the Information Viewer and positions the cursor in this box so you can search for particular items in the current Outlook module.

✔ **Find a Contact (Standard):** Enables you to open the record for a contact in your address book from any module either by typing his or her name in the text box or selecting the name from its drop-down list.

Figure 6-7 shows the suggested custom Productivity toolbar as it appears in the Calendar module in Outlook 2003 after its Bottom button is clicked. Clicking Bottom here displays the Reading Pane for the appointment selected on the work week calendar at the bottom of the Information Viewer. To hide this Reading Pane, I simply click the Off button on this custom toolbar.

A customized toolbar in Outlook 2003

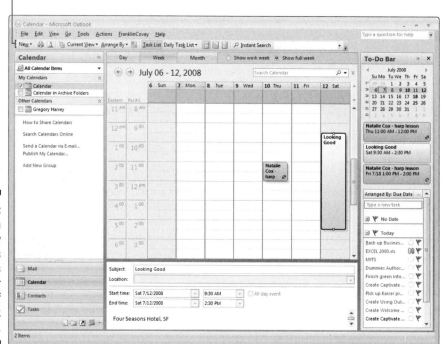

Figure 6-7:
The custom Productivity toolbar as it appears in Calendar module of Outlook 2003.

Figure 6-8 shows the suggested custom Productivity toolbar as it appears in the Calendar module of Outlook 2007 after you click the Normal option on the Daily Task List button's drop-down list. Clicking Normal here displays the Tasks pane at the bottom of the Information Viewer, where daily tasks are listed under the date in the work week calendar with which they're associated. To hide this Tasks pane, I select the Off option from the Daily Task List button's drop-down list.

A customized toolbar in Outlook 2007

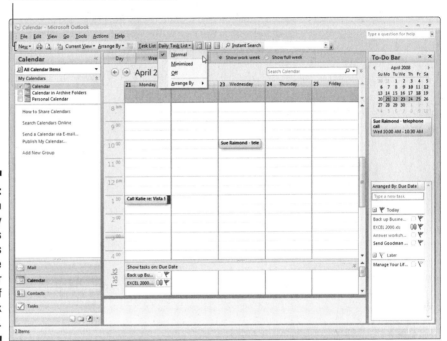

Figure 6-8: The custom Productivity toolbar as it appears in the Calendar module of Outlook 2007.

You can group buttons in your custom Productivity toolbar by demarcating them with vertical bars when the Customize dialog box is displayed. To add a vertical bar to separate a group of buttons on the toolbar, drag the button before which the vertical bar is to appear to the right then release the mouse button to have the vertical bar appear. To remove a vertical bar divider you no longer need, drag the button to the immediate right of the vertical bar to remove; then, drag that button leftward until the vertical bar disappears before you release the mouse button.

Adopting a New Point of View

Just as Outlook supports the use of several specialized modules in its role as a personal information manager, each of the modules (Mail, Calendar, Contacts, Tasks, Notes, and Journal) supports a number of different preset views.

Selecting a new view in a particular Outlook module can do one of three things:

✔ Group the module's data in a different way, modify the order by sorting the data on some field, or both.

✔ Present just a subset of the module's data by filtering the data using some criteria.

✔ Represent the module's data in a completely different manner.

Figures 6-9 through 6-11 demonstrate these three different types of views. Figure 6-9 shows you my Calendar module after selecting By Category option button in the Current View section of the Navigation Pane. In this view, Outlook groups your appointments into groups depending upon the category to which each is assigned, displaying them in a table format (for more on categories in Outlook, see "Setting Up Categories That Are Just Your Type" later in this chapter).

In this view, you can expand or collapse individual categories (assuming that the Show in Groups option is selected on the Arrange By menu) to display as many or few rows of appointments as you need. You can also instantly sort the appointments displayed in the rows of the table by clicking a particular column (field).

Figure 6-10 shows you the same Inbox folder of my Mail module, this time after selecting Last Seven Days as the current view. In the Last Seven Days view, Outlook actually filters the e-mail messages in the Inbox Calendar module so that only messages that I've received in the last full week are now displayed in the Information Viewer. (To see all the messages in your Inbox, you select the Messages or Messages with AutoPreview view instead.). This filtering situation is indicated by the Filter Applied message that appears in the upper-right corner of the Mail module's Information Viewer in parentheses.

Figure 6-11 shows you my tasks in the Tasks module after selecting Task Timeline as the current view. In this view, Outlook doesn't filter or sort the tasks in your to-do list. Instead, the program represents them in a new way that enables you to see at a glance when tasks start, their duration, and how they overlap.

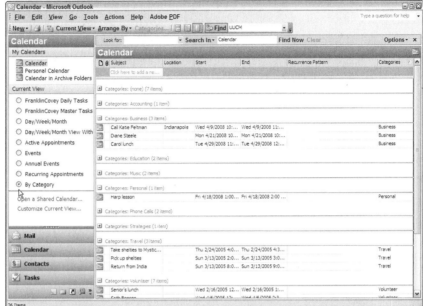

Figure 6-9:
Appoint-
ments in the
Calendar
module after
selecting By
Category as
the current
view.

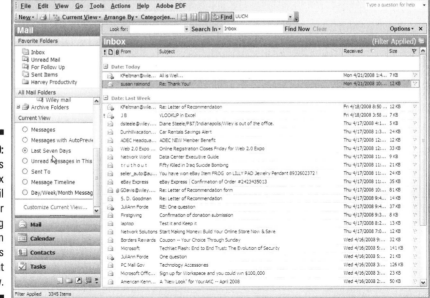

Figure 6-10:
Messages
in the Inbox
of the Mail
module after
selecting
Last Seven
Days as
the current
view.

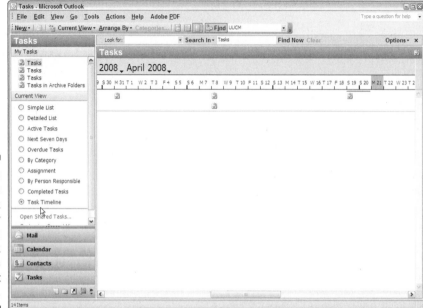

Figure 6-11:
Tasks in
the Task
module after
selecting
Task
Timeline as
the current
view.

Customizing the current view

Although each Outlook module supports several different preset views that
you can use as is, as spelled out in the previous section, you can also easily
customize any of them. To modify a preset view, make that view current in
the module you're using by selecting its name on the drop-down list attached
to the Current View button on your custom Productivity toolbar. Then, click
the Customize Current View item on this same drop-down list to open a
Customize View dialog box named for and containing options tailored to the
view you're modifying.

Figure 6-12 shows you the Customize View: Messages with AutoPreview
dialog box that opens after you select the Customize Current View menu item
when Messages with AutoPreview is your current view.

As you can see in this figure, the Customize View dialog box is full of option
buttons that enable you to modify a wide array of settings for this view
(anything from determining which fields are to be included to deciding the
formatting of the columns containing each field). Note that this customization
can include automatically grouping the messages as well as sorting and
filtering them.

Figure 6-12:
The dialog
box for
custom-
izing the
Messages
with Auto-
Preview
view for the
Inbox of the
Mail
module.

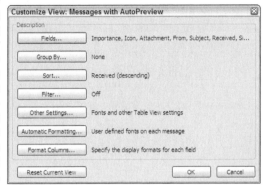

The great thing about customizing an existing view is that it is actually quite easy to change your mind. If, after changing a bunch of different settings for a view, you discover that you really don't want to retain the changes you've made, you can reset the view to its original settings in a flash. All you have to do is to click the Reset Current View button at the bottom of the view's Customize View dialog box to have Outlook restore the view to all its initial settings.

Defining a whole new view

In addition to enabling you to modify the settings of the views that come with Outlook, the program also enables you to create totally new views for a particular module. You can therefore create views unlike any that come with the program as well as ones that use settings similar to other preset views that you want to retain.

Figure 6-13 illustrates a new view that I created for the Outlook Inbox named Day/Week/Month Messages. In this view, the Subject field of incoming mail messages are listed by date on a calendar pad according to the time they are received.

Note that in this figure, the days for the current, seven-day week are displayed by default in the Information Viewer of the Inbox (the equivalent of selecting View➪Week on the Outlook pull-down menus). You can also change this calendar display to show messages for the following dates:

✔ **Day:** Selected in the right pane with the Date Navigators by selecting View➪Day or pressing Alt+1 in Outlook 2003 or Ctrl+Alt+1 in Outlook 2007

✔ **Work Week:** Selected in right pane with the Date Navigators by selecting View➪Work Week or pressing Alt+5 in Outlook 2003 or Ctrl+Alt+2 in Outlook 2007

✔ **Month:** Selected in the right pane with the Date Navigators by selecting View➪Month or pressing Alt+= in Outlook 2003 or Ctrl+Alt+4 in Outlook 2007

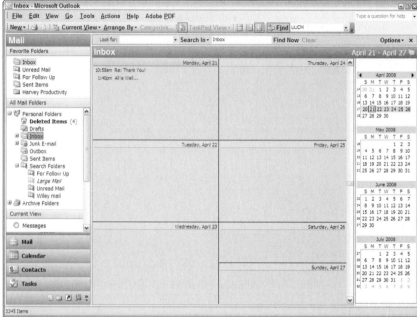

Figure 6-13:
The Inbox
of my Mail
module after
applying
the newly
created
Day/Week/
Month
Messages
view as
the current
view.

To see how easy it is to create new views for Outlook's modules, I want you to follow along with the steps you'd take to create this same custom Day/Week/Month view for the Inbox of your Mail module:

1. **Select the Inbox of the Outlook Mail module, if it's not already current.**

2. **Click the Current View button on your custom Productivity toolbar (or on the Advanced toolbar if you haven't yet created this custom toolbar) and then select Define Views from the button's drop-down list.**

   Outlook opens a Custom View Organizer dialog box similar to the one shown in Figure 6-14.

3. **Click the New button.**

   Outlook opens the Create a New View dialog box. shown in Figure 6-15.

4. **Replace the provisional name, New View, by typing Day/Week/Month Messages in the Name of New View text box.**

5. **Click Day/Week/Month in the Type of View list box.**

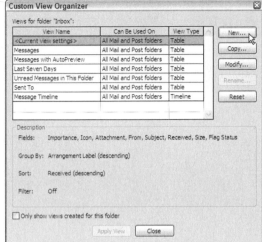

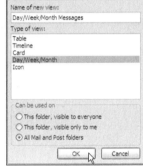

Figure 6-14:
Creating a
new view in
the Custom
View
Organizer
dialog box.

Figure 6-15:
Assigning a
name and
selecting
the settings
for the new
custom view
in the New
View dialog
box.

6. **Click the All Mail and Post Folder option button before you click OK.**

   Outlook closes the Create a New View dialog box while simultaneously opening the Customize View: Day/Week/Month Messages dialog box, where you can make further changes to the new view's settings if you want.

7. **Click OK without changing the Fields, Filters, Other Settings, or Automatic Formatting settings for the Day/Week/Month Messages view.**

   Outlook closes the Customize View: Day/Week/Month Messages dialog box, returning you to the Custom View Organizer dialog box (refer to Figure 6-14) where the new Day/Week/Month Messages view is now listed.

8. **Click the Apply View button.**

   Outlook closes the Custom View Organizer dialog box while applying the new custom Day/Week/Month Messages view you just created to your Inbox (making it look very similar to my Inbox, shown earlier in Figure 6-13).

Keep in mind that when using Outlook 2007, the Day/Week/Month Messages custom view looks a little bit different when Week is selected. Instead of displaying the days of the week in two columns in the Information Viewer from Monday through Sunday as shown in Figure 6-13, Outlook 2007 displays the days of the week seven sequential columns, Sunday through Saturday.

Have It Your Way in Outlook Today

Outlook Today offers what is often known as a dashboard (or an at-a-glance) that gives you a preview of the day by displaying your Calendar, Tasks, and Messages. You switch to this screen by clicking the folder at the very top of the All Mail Folders section of the Navigation Pane. (It's the folder sporting an icon of a little house.)

Depending on the Outlook configuration you use, the folder following this house icon can have either of the following two names:

✔ **Mailbox –** *your name* when you use an Exchange server account

✔ **Personal Folders** when you use a Personal Folders file, or .pst file, to store your messages

When you first install Outlook, the Outlook Today screen displays the current date in the bar at the top of the Information Viewer. Beneath this bar, the main pane contains the following columns:

✔ **Calendar:** This column displays a list of your upcoming appointments for the current week, arranged by the day of the week (Monday through Sunday).

✔ **Tasks:** This column displays a list of the most recent tasks on your to-do list, arranged by due date.

✔ **Messages:** This column displays the number of unopened e-mail messages in your Inbox, the number of draft copies of messages saved in your Drafts folder, and the number of unsent messages still in your Outbox.

Each of the listings displayed in the Calendar and Tasks columns of Outlook Today are hyperlinks that you can click in order to either get more detail about an appointment or task or to modify its settings (by opening its Appointment or Task dialog box).

To display and read the e-mail messages in your Inbox, Drafts, or Outbox folder in the Messages column, click the link associated with the particular folder name in this column.

Making Outlook Today your home base

If you'd like to be able to get a quick overview of the kind of day you're about to face right when you get in the office, make Outlook Today the home base of your personal information manager (rather than the Calendar module).

To make Outlook Today the place that automatically opens each time you launch Outlook, follow these steps:

1. **In the Mail module, click either the Mailbox followed by your name or the Personal Folders folder icon in the Navigation Pane, depending on how Outlook is set up for you.**

   Outlook displays Outlook Today in the Mail module's Information Viewer.

2. **Click the Customize Outlook Today link in the upper-right corner of the Outlook Today screen.**

   Outlook displays the Customize Outlook Today screen in the Information Viewer.

3. **Click the When Starting, Go Directly to Outlook Today check box at the top of the Customize Outlook Today screen and then click the Save Changes button on the right of the Customize Outlook Today title bar.**

   Outlook closes the Customize Outlook Today screen and returns you to Outlook Today.

After following these easy steps to make Outlook Today the startup folder, each time you launch Outlook, the program automatically displays the contents of Outlook Today rather than the contents of your Inbox.

If you really want to make Outlook Today the very first thing you see each morning as soon as you start up your computer, be sure to follow not only the steps for making Outlook Today the program's startup folder (as outlined in these steps) but also the steps for making Outlook an application that automatically launches each time you start your computer, as outlined in the section "Automatically launching Outlook each time you start your computer," earlier in this chapter.

Customizing the appearance of Outlook Today

In addition to making Outlook Today's folder the default for Outlook, you can also easily customize the contents and appearance of its screen. Figure 6-16 shows you the Outlook Today Options screen that appears when you click the Customize Outlook Today button in the upper-right corner of the Outlook Today screen.

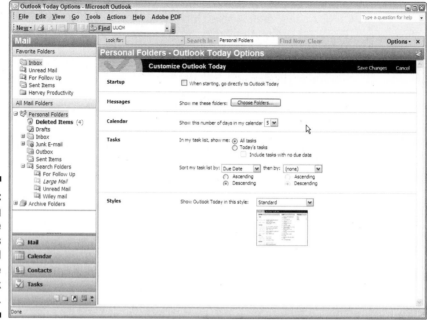

Figure 6-16:
Customizing
the
contents
and
appearance
of Outlook
Today.

As you can see in this figure, the customization options available here are divided into the following four areas:

✔ **Messages:** The Choose Folders button enables you to choose which folders are included in statistics listed in Messages column of Outlook Today by clicking the check boxes in the Select Folder dialog box that this button opens.

✔ **Calendar:** The Show This Number of Days drop-down list enables you to select a new number of days (between 1 and 7) for determining which appointments are to be displayed in the Calendar column.

✔ **Tasks:** The Tasks options enable you to determine which tasks appear in the Tasks column (All Tasks or just Today's Tasks) as well as how these tasks are ordered in the list. By default, Outlook sorts the tasks in descending order (most recent to least recent) by Due Date. To change this sort order, select a new field on the Sort My Task List By and Then By drop-drop list and the Ascending or Descending option button associated with that field. For example, to sort your tasks first by importance and then by due date, select Importance on the Sort My Task List By drop-down list with its Ascending option button and then select Due Date on the Then By drop-down list with its Descending option button.

✔ **Styles:** The Show Outlook in This Style drop-down list enables you to select a new look for the Outlook screen. Select the Standard (Two Column) option to display the Calendar information in the first column of the Outlook Today screen with the Messages information above the Tasks in a single second column. Select the Standard (One Column) option to display all the Outlook Today information in a single vertical column. Select the Summer option to display the Outlook information in the same arrangement as the Standard (Two Column) option but with a light yellow background color, or the Winter option to display the same two-column arrangement with a white background.

When you're finished customizing the Outlook Today options in the Custom Outlook Today screen, be sure to click the Save Changes button to put your changes into effect before you return to the Outlook Today display. You click the Cancel button in the Customize Outlook Today screen only when you decide to abandon your changes and not to put them into effect in Outlook Today.

If you're one of those folks whose work week calendars always seems chock-full of appointments that contain lots of explanatory and detail information, be sure to select one of the two-column arrangements — Standard (Two Column), Summer, or Winter — when you make Outlook Today the default view for Outlook your personal information manager. That way, you'll be much more likely to able to read the text of the daily appointments listed in the Outlook Today screen at a glance.

Setting Up Categories That Are Just Your Type

Outlook enables you to associate any of the items stored in the various Outlook modules (e-mail messages in Mail, contacts in Contacts, appointments in Calendar, and so on) with a particular category. You can then use the category you assign to different Outlook items to group and display them together in a list or search (in the case of Mail), making it a great deal easier to compare and find particular items.

For example, you might want to group together the contact information for all key vendors stored in the Contact module by assigning their contact records to the Suppliers category. Likewise, you can differentiate your business appointments from your personal by assigning the former to the Business category and the latter to Personal in the Calendar module.

Now you can quickly get to the contact information for all your key vendors by clicking the By Category option button in the Current View section of the Contacts Navigation Pane and then collapsing all categories in the grouped list except for Suppliers. You can also easily distinguish the personal from the business appointments you've scheduled by clicking the By Category option button in the Current View section of the Calendar Navigation Pane and then collapsing all other categories in the grouped list except for the Business and Personal.

Using category lists in Outlook 2003

When you install Outlook 2003, the program includes a fair number of preset categories that you can assign to Outlook items right out of the box. To assign one of the categories, select the Outlook item or items you want to assign to that category and then do one of the following:

- Click the Categories button on your customized Productivity toolbar.

- Right-click the selection and then select Categories from the contextual menu that appears.

- Choose Edit⇨Categories from the Outlook menu bar.

Taking any one of these three actions opens the Categories list box (similar to the one shown in Figure 6-17). Here, you click the check box for each category you want to assign to the items you selected in the Available Categories list box. When finished, simply click the OK button.

Figure 6-17: Assigning categories to selected Outlook items in the Categories dialog box.

If you want to create a new category, you have the following choices:

- ✔ Click in the Item(s) Belong to These Categories list box in the Categories text box, type a category name after the semicolon (automatically added when you begin typing), and then click the Add to List button to the immediate right of this list box.

- ✔ Click the Master Category List button at the bottom of the Categories dialog box to open the Master Category List dialog box (refer to Figure 6-17) and then type its name into the New Category list box before you select OK.

Using category lists in Outlook 2007

Outlook 2007 handles categories a little differently from earlier versions of Outlook. This version of Outlook adds color coding to its categories. The different colors then enable you to visually differentiate the groups to which you've assigned various items. That way, you have some visual clues about how your items fit together even before you display some type of group listing of them with a custom Search Folder in the Mail module or a By Category view in some other Outlook module.

Outlook 2007 no longer uses the Master Category list of earlier versions to maintain its categories. This means that all custom categories you add to the Master Category list in earlier versions of Outlook have to be recreated when you upgrade from Outlook 2003 to Outlook 2007. Your custom categories maintained in the Master Category list aren't retained when you install the 2007 version of the program.

In place of a dialog box of category options, Outlook 2007 displays a Categorize drop-down list showing all the colors and names of the current categories when you do any of the following:

- ✔ Click the Categories button on your customized Productivity toolbar.

- ✔ Right-click the selection and then mouse over Categorize from the contextual menu that appears.

- ✔ Click Edit⇨Categorize on the Outlook menu bar.

Figure 6-18 shows how this drop-down list appears on my computer when I click the Categorize button on my customized Productivity toolbar. To assign an existing category to the selected item(s) in the current module, you simply click its color and name on this drop-down list.

Figure 6-18:
Displaying
the
Categorize
drop-down
list in
Outlook
2007.

Note that when assigning categories to your e-mail messages in Mail and appointments in Calendar, Outlook 2007 shows the color assigned to the category. In the case of e-mail messages, the category color appears in the column to the immediate left of the flag column in the Information Viewer. In the case of appointments on the Calendar, the program turns them the color of the category (and displays small color cubes within the appointment when you assign the same appointment to more than one category).

To modify a preset color category by giving them more descriptive names than Red Category, Green Category, and so forth or to create a new custom category in Outlook 2007, you need to select the All Categories menu item near the bottom of the Categorize drop-down list.

When you select All Categories, Outlook 2007 opens a Color Categories dialog box similar to the one shown in Figure 6-19. To rename a present category in this dialog box, click to select the category and then click the Rename button, type in the new name, and press Enter.

To create a new category, click the New button in the Color Categories dialog box to open the Add New Category dialog box. There, enter a descriptive name in the Name box and then select the color you want to associate with it from the Color drop-down list before you click OK.

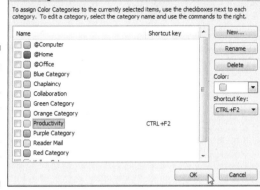

Figure 6-19:
Modifying
a category
in the Color
Categories
dialog box
in Outlook
2007.

Outlook 2007 lets you assign shortcut keys to eleven favorite categories using the key combinations Ctrl+F2 through Ctrl+F12. When you assign one of these shortcut keys to a category, you can assign it to selected items in a module simply by pressing the key combination. To associate a particular combination to a category, select it from the Shortcut Key drop-down list when modifying its settings in the Color Categories dialog box or creating it anew in the Add New Category dialog box.

Tailoring the Look of Assorted Outlook Modules with the Organize Pane

The Organize pane in Outlook offers a great way to organize the information you store in any Outlook module. Depending on which Outlook module is current, the Organize pane can offer any of the following four options:

- ✔ **Using Folders (Mail, Contacts, Tasks, Notes):** Enables you to move the e-mail messages you've selected in the current folder to another mail folder. In the Mail module, this tab also contains a Rules and Alerts button that enables you to modify existing rules and create new ones (see Chapter 8 for details).

- ✔ **Using Colors (Mail):** Enables you to select a particular font color to be used to demarcate messages that are sent only to you or that are sent from specific senders. Also contains an Automatic Formatting button that enables you to modify the font, style, and color automatically assigned to various types of messages.

✔ **Using Categories (Calendar, Contacts, Tasks, Journal):** Enables you to add selected items in a module to a particular existing category as well as create a new category to use.

✔ **Using Views (Mail, Calendar, Contacts, Tasks, Notes, Journal):** Enables you to select a new view for the current module. Also contains a Customize Current View button that enables you to modify the settings for the currently selected view.

Figure 6-20 shows you how the Organize pane appears when the Inbox folder in the Mail module is selected. As you can see in this figure, this Organize pane contains three buttons on the left side of the pane: Using Folders, Using Colors, and Using Views.

Figure 6-20: The Organize pane displayed in the Mail module.

Each of these three buttons is connected to a tab that contains the options you can modify in the body of the pane. In addition, each pane contains its own button in the upper-right corner that you can use to open a dialog box that lets you modify additional related options.

Customizing the Module Buttons in the Navigation Pane

By default, the bottom section of Outlook's Navigation Pane contains large navigation buttons for the big four modules: Mail, Calendar, Contacts, and Tasks. In addition, the very bottom row of this pane also displays smaller navigation buttons (with icons and no labels): the so-called Notes, Folder List, Shortcuts, and Configure Buttons. (The Configure button determines which navigation buttons appear in the Navigation Pane and in what order.)

Because you'll rely mostly on shortcut keys (Ctrl+1 through Ctrl+8, as I outline in Chapter 5) to switch between Outlook modules, you don't need to sacrifice the precious screen space in the Navigation Pane by retaining the four large Mail, Calendar, Contacts, and Tasks buttons. Therefore, I suggest that you reduce these buttons to smaller buttons with icons only in the very bottom row of the pane, right in front of the Notes, Folder List, Shortcuts, and Configure Buttons. To do this, position the mouse pointer on the dotted line at the top of the Mail button and then, when the pointer becomes a double-headed arrow, drag downward until all four buttons are reduced to icons and displayed in the bottom row before you release the mouse. If you later forget what a button does, you can just mouse over the button's icon and read the ScreenTip that appears at the mouse pointer.

Outlook also makes adding or removing navigation buttons from the bottom section of the Navigation Pane easy. For example, if you track your daily activities with the Journal module (see Chapter 14), you may want to add the Journal navigation button to this pane.

To add the Journal navigation button, follow these steps:

1. **Click the Configure Buttons button (the final button on the right — the one with the downward-pointing triangle).**

   Outlook displays a menu of options to the side of the button.

2. **Mouse over the Add or Remove buttons item at the bottom of this menu.**

   A submenu listing each of the six modules plus Folder List and Shortcuts appears.

3. **Click Journal at the bottom of this submenu.**

   Outlook adds the Journal navigation button to the end of the last row of buttons in the Navigation Pane immediately in front of the Configure Buttons button.

If you want to change the order in which the navigation buttons appear in the Navigation Pane, select the Navigation Pane Options item on the menu that appears when you click the Configure Buttons button. Selecting this item opens the Navigation Pane Options dialog box, where you can move selected module buttons by moving them down or up in the order.

Figure 6-21 shows you the Navigation Pane in the Inbox of my Mail module after I added the Journal navigation button and reduced all the big-four module buttons to just their icons. Note how nicely these sized buttons fit on the last row (all eight navigation buttons can be displayed on my smaller laptop screen). Also note that with the big-four navigation buttons minimized, you can now see the Current View section with options buttons for selecting a new Inbox view.

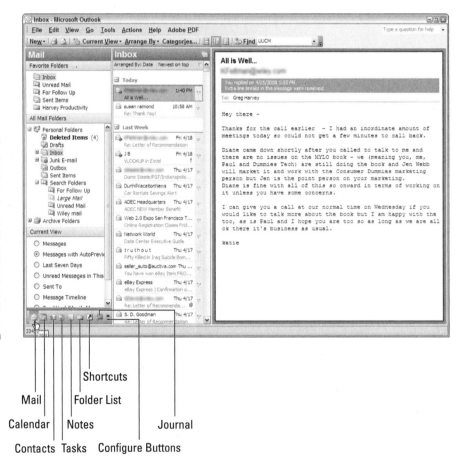

Figure 6-21: The Navigation Pane after displaying all module navigation buttons and minimizing them to a single row of icons.

Adding Outlook Gadgets for Windows Vista

If your computer uses the Microsoft Vista operating system, you're probably already familiar with gadgets, those various little applications that run in the Windows Sidebar on the right side of the Windows desktop. As part of making Outlook into your full-fledged personal information manager, you may want to check out the available Outlook gadgets and at least entertain the possibility of adding one to your system . You could then use the gadget as a means of keeping an eye on Outlook even when you're working in other applications.

I'm particularly fond of the Outlook Info, Mini Inbox, and Outlook Tasks gadgets shown at the top of the Sidebar on my Windows Vista desktop in Figure 6-22.

The Outlook Info gadget enables you to see the number of unread messages in your Inbox along with the three most recent upcoming appointments on your calendar and tasks on your to-do list. The best part of this Outlook gadget is that you can use it to open the Outlook program to check particular messages, appointments, and tasks. Simply click the envelope, calendar, or to-do list icon to open the Mail module (assuming it's still the default module), Calendar, or Tasks module, respectively.

The Mini Inbox gadget enables you to see a few of the most recent e-mail messages in your Inbox. It also contains two bars beneath the list of messages that scroll to display the appointments and tasks on your daily calendar. To read the text of a particular message in a separate pop-up window (without also opening the Outlook program window), click one of the messages listed in the gadget. And to reply to the message, click the Reply button at the top of this dialog box to open the message for your reply.

The Outlook Tasks gadget enables you to scroll through the tasks in your to-do list. You can also add a new task using the gadget's Type a New Task text box or check off as complete any tasks that you finish.

These gadgets (and others like them, created specifically for Outlook) are available online for free download. To check them out and perhaps add one to your Vista Sidebar, follow these steps:

1. **Right-click somewhere in your Vista Sidebar (outside any of the gad**

2. **Click the Get More Gadgets Online link in the lower-right corner of the dialog box.**

   Vista launches your Web browser (Internet Explorer, in most cases) and goes to the Windows Vista Sidebar Web page.

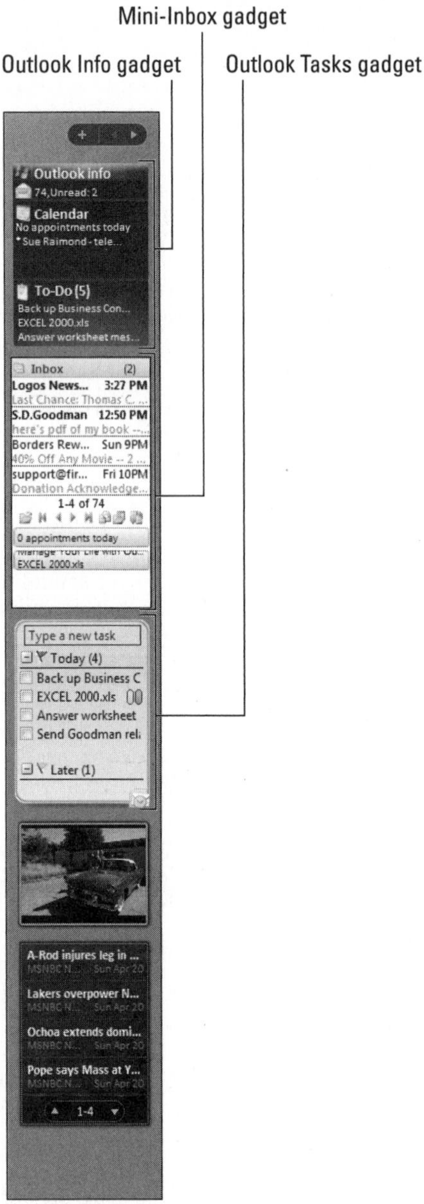

Mini-Inbox gadget

Outlook Info gadget | Outlook Tasks gadget

Figure 6-22:
The
Outlook
Info
gadget
to the
Windows
Vista
Sidebar.

3. **Type** Outlook **in the Find More Gadgets text box near the top of this Web page and then click the Search button.**

A Web page with the Outlook-specific gadgets appears in your Web browser.

4. **Read about the individual Outlook gadgets and if you find one you want to try, click its Download button.**

   To get more information about a particular gadget as well as to read other users' comments about the gadget before downloading it, click the hyperlink attached to its name above the Download button.

   Depending on the gadget you select to download, Vista may display a pop-up warning dialog box that warns you that the gadget is from a third-party vendor and asking whether you still want to install it. If the gadget is from a verified vendor or Microsoft itself and Internet Explorer is your Web browser, the File Download dialog box opens, asking you whether you want to open or save the gadget.

5. **Click the Install, Open, and Run buttons as they appear in the various alert dialog boxes that are displayed as part of the process of downloading and installing the selected gadget.**

   Vista downloads and installs the gadget you selected at the top of the Sidebar on the desktop.

After downloading and installing a gadget on your Sidebar, Vista adds the gadget to your Gadgets dialog box. Having the gadget in that dialog box means that you can always re-install the gadget to the Sidebar without having to download it again if you happen to remove it.

Part III
Taking Control of Your E-Mail Inbox

The 5th Wave   By Rich Tennant

"The new technology has really helped me become organized. I keep my project reports under the PC, budgets under my laptop, and memos under my cell phone."

In this part . . .

The road to increased personal productivity with Outlook begins with housecleaning your e-mail Inbox. This third part starts you on your journey to greater work/life balance by showing you the way to empty that box by organizing your Inbox and then keeping it that way!

Chapter 7

Doing Your Initial E-Mail Inbox Housecleaning

In This Chapter

▶ Getting yourself mentally prepared to empty your e-mail Inbox today!

▶ Archiving older e-mail you want to keep and locating older e-mail you want to dump

▶ Creating the Inbox subfolders you need for the e-mail messages you still need

▶ Rounding up (and organizing) the e-mail messages you still need to deal with

*T*he subject of e-mail is a somewhat controversial one. On the one hand, e-mail can act as a great boon to personal productivity, serving as an efficient communication tool by enabling knowledge workers to stay in touch with each other and save valuable work time by focusing their responses to the specific topics and questions that the messages present.

On the other hand, e-mail can act as a great impediment to personal productivity, serving as a consummate time waster by relentlessly vying for knowledge workers' attention and then forcing them to wade through inordinate amounts of data to separate the spam from the important mail so that they can respond accordingly.

The love/hate relationship that so many knowledge workers seem to have with their e-mail Inboxes is a true reflection of e-mail's dual nature as both a technological boon and the bane of their existence. It also explains why so many workers regard getting a handle on their e-mail as such a crucial first-step in achieving personal productivity at work.

As I see it, effectively dealing with your e-mail is a two-step process. First, you need to do some radical Inbox housecleaning. Second, you need to learn how to perform regular Inbox housekeeping that will keep it that way.

This chapter takes on the first step by leading you through basic strategies for getting rid of all the messages you don't need and won't ever do anything with and then organizing the messages that remain so that you can effectively deal with them.

The next chapter (Chapter 8) then covers how to keep your newly cleared out and spiffed up Inbox organized so that you can stay on top of the new messages that arrive and don't have to perform this type of radical Inbox housecleaning in the future.

Getting Ready to Do Your Inbox Housecleaning

Okay, so you've got what appear to be a million or so messages in your Inbox and you no longer have a clue as to what's really the important stuff and what's the junk you can safely delete. In fact, your Inbox is so stuffed with messages that you don't even want to go any further than the first few hundred that have just come in this morning!

Well, today's your lucky day because regardless of what season the calendar says it is, for you it's Spring Cleaning day (at least as far as e-mail is concerned). So, roll up your sleeves before you sit down and get to work cleaning out that long-neglected Inbox of yours.

Make it your goal that by the end of this workday, your Inbox will be empty of all messages besides those few hundred that come rolling in while you're doing this Inbox housecleaning.

Using the Mailbox Cleanup Feature

The first thing to do in your quest to clean out your Inbox is to use Outlook's own nifty Mailbox Cleanup tool (bet you never heard of that one) to delete old messages you no longer need and to archive those you may have some future use for.

Figure 7-1 shows you the Mailbox Cleanup dialog box as it appears after you open it by choosing Tools➪Mailbox Cleanup (Alt+TX) from the Outlook menu bar.

As you can see in this figure, the Mailbox Cleanup dialog box contains options that enable you to identify messages in your Inbox so that you can then get rid of them:

✔ **View Mailbox Size:** Click this button to open the Folder Size dialog box (see Figure 7-2) that lists the size in kilobytes of all the Mail folders except for Archive Folders. (If your Outlook configuration saves e-mail messages using the .pst file format, then the Folder Size dialog box calculates the size of your Personal Folders.) The Size column in this dialog box shows the folder size without counting the size of the subfolders it contains, whereas the Total Size column shows the folder size including the size of all subfolders.

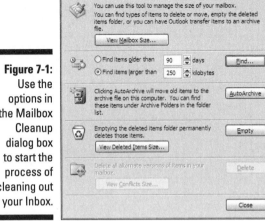

Figure 7-1:
Use the
options in
the Mailbox
Cleanup
dialog box
to start the
process of
cleaning out
your Inbox.

✔ **Find Items Older Than:** Click this option button to identify all the items in your Mail folders that are older than the number of days listed in the associated text box (90 by default). After you set the number of days, click the Find button to display the results in the Advanced Find dialog box.

✔ **Find Items Larger Than:** Click this option button to identify all the messages in your Mail folders that are larger than the number of kilobytes listed in the associated text box (250 by default). After you set the size, click the Find button to display the results in the Advanced Find dialog box.

✔ **AutoArchive:** Click this button to move the older messages out of your regular Mail folders and place them into your Archive folders (thus clearing your Inbox of a lot of mail without actually deleting it from your computer).

✔ **View Deleted Items Size:** Click this button to open the Folder Size dialog box showing the size in kilobytes of all the messages marked for removal in your Deleted Items folder. Then, after closing this dialog box, click the Empty button to permanently remove these messages from your computer (thus freeing some hard drive space).

✔ **View Conflict Size:** Click this button to open the Folder Size dialog box showing the size in kilobytes of all the messages marked that are duplicates of another message and therefore placed in your Conflicts folder. Then, after closing this dialog box, click the Delete button to permanently remove these messages from your computer (thus freeing some hard drive space).

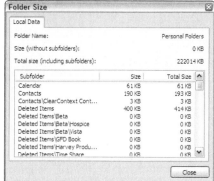

Figure 7-2:
Using the
options in
the Folder
Size dialog
box to view
the current
sizes of
various
Outlook
folders.

Rounding Up and Deleting Unneeded Messages

Very often, if you haven't looked at or done anything with an e-mail message for some time, by default the message becomes junk e-mail — chances are, you'll never have the time to open it again. If this is your situation, you can use it to good advantage for the initial housecleaning of your e-mail Inbox.

Rather than archive older messages you'll probably never look at again, you can just round them up and get rid of them. That way, you kill two birds with one stone: You get them not only out of your Inbox but off your hard drive as well.

To round up and delete older e-mail, you can use the Mailbox Cleanup feature as follows:

1. **Choose Tools⇨Mailbox Cleanup from the Outlook menu bar (or press Alt+TX).**

   Outlook displays the Mailbox Cleanup dialog box. (Refer to Figure 7-1.)

2. **Click the Find Items Older Than option button and then type in the number of days in the associated text box or select the number with its spinner buttons and then click the Find button.**

   Outlook opens the Advanced Find dialog box (similar to the one shown in Figure 7-3) containing the messages in your Personal Folders that are older than the number of days you specified in the Mailbox Cleanup dialog box.

Figure 7-3:
E-mail
messages
older than
90 days are
listed in
the Results
pane of the
Advanced
Find
dialog box.

3. **Select all the messages listed in the Results pane of the Advanced Dialog box by clicking the first message and then pressing Ctrl+A. Next, choose Edit⇨Move to Folder from the dialog box's menu bar or press Ctrl+Shift+V.**

   Outlook opens the Move Items dialog box, similar to the one shown in Figure 7-4.

4. **Click the Deleted Items recycle bin folder icon in the Move the Selected Items to the Folder list box and then click the OK button or press Enter.**

   Outlook moves the selected items into the Deleted Items folder. Note, however, that even though Outlook has indeed moved the selected messages to the Deleted Items dialog box, they remain listed in the Results pane of the Advanced Find dialog box.

5. **Click the Close button in the top-right corner of the Advanced Find dialog box.**

   Before permanently deleting the messages you've moved into the Deleted Items folder, you may want to check some out to make sure that they don't contain information you'd be really sorry to lose forever.

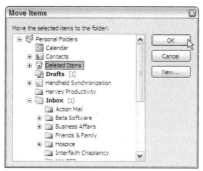

Figure 7-4:
Moving
e-mail
messages
older than
90 days to
the Deleted
Items folder.

6. (Optional) Click the Deleted Items trash bin icon in the Navigation Pane and then click each message you want to double-check before deleting so that you can look over its contents in the Reading Pane.

If you find messages in the Deleted Items folder that you in fact *do* need to keep, you need to move them to appropriate subfolders of the Inbox before permanently deleting the rest.

7. (Optional) Select the message or messages you don't want permanently deleted and then move them to the appropriate Inbox subfolder by dragging and dropping them on that subfolder's icon in the Navigation Pane.

Only after you're sure that *every* message in your Deleted Items folder is spam clogging your Inbox and taking up valuable drive space, and you therefore want to vaporize them all, proceed to Step 8.

8. Choose Tools⇨Empty "Deleted Items" Folder from the Outlook menu bar or press Alt+TY and then click Yes in the alert dialog box asking for confirmation to permanently delete them.

Outlook deletes all the messages in the Deleted Items folder, thus completely emptying the Mail module's Information Viewer, which now displays the message, "There are no items to show in this view."

Archiving Messages in Your Inbox

Running Outlook's AutoArchive feature on your Inbox in the Mail module is great for reducing the number of older messages the Inbox contains without actually deleting messages from your hard drive. When Outlook archives messages, it merely moves them from your active Mail folders to Archive folders. That way, you don't have to worry about inadvertently getting rid of messages that, to your dismay, you find you need to refer back to at some later date.

To use AutoArchive to move older messages out of your Inbox and into your Archive folders, follow these steps:

1. **Launch Outlook if it's not already running and then click File⇨Archive on the Outlook menu bar or press Alt+FR.**

   Outlook opens the Archive dialog box similar to the one shown in Figure 7-5. By default, Outlook archives everything in your Personal Folders (including appointments on your calendar, names in your contact list, notes, and journal entries) as well as the e-mail contained in your Inbox, Drafts, and Deleted Items mail folders.

   To have Outlook archive only the e-mail messages in your Inbox (and all its subfolders) that are older than the specific date you set, you need to select just the Inbox folder as outlined in Step 2.

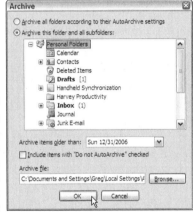

Figure 7-5:
Modifying the archive settings in the Archive dialog box.

2. **Make sure that the Archive This Folder and All Subfolders option button is selected and then click the Inbox folder icon in this list box to select it.**

   Next, you need to select the cutoff date. All e-mail messages with dates before this cutoff date are moved and stored in your Archive folder, whereas those messages with dates on or after this cutoff date remain in your Inbox.

3. **Click the Archive Items Older Than option's drop-down button and then use the date picker with its drop-down mini calendar to select the new cutoff date: First, click the Back or Forward buttons displayed at the top of the mini calendar (the triangles pointing to the left and right, respectively, of the name of the current month and year) until the calendar for the new cutoff month and year is displayed below; then click the precise cutoff date on this mini calendar.**

As soon as you click the cutoff date, Outlook closes the drop-down mini calendar and lists the day of the week plus the complete date in the Archive Items Older Than drop-down list box. Now you're ready to archive your e-mail messages using the settings you've selected in the Archive dialog box.

4. Click the OK button or press Enter.

Outlook displays an Archiving message on the Status bar of its program window showing each of the messages that it is moving to the various subfolders within your Archive folders (mirroring those in your Inbox).

If you ever need access to some of the e-mail messages that you've moved to the Archive folder in this manner, you can look through or search your archived messages and restore any of them to active duty by following these simple steps:

1. Choose File⇨Open⇨Outlook Data File from the Outlook menu bar (or press Alt+FOF).

Outlook displays the Open Outlook Data File dialog box, similar to the one shown in Figure 7-6.

2. Click to select the name of your archive file (`archive.pst` if Outlook stores its data in a `.pst` file) and then click OK or press Enter.

Outlook opens the archive file, adding the folders and subfolders to the Archive Folders in All Mail Folders sections of the Navigation Pane. To display actual archived e-mail messages you have moved out of your Inbox folder, you need to select the Inbox subfolder under Archived Folders.

3. Click the Expand button (the one with the plus sign) in front of the Archive Folders icon in the Navigation Pane and then click the Inbox folder icon underneath it.

Outlook displays the messages archived from your Inbox folder arranged by date with the oldest messages on top. You can then peruse or search them to find the ones you're interested in.

Figure 7-6:
Opening the file containing the messages you've archived in the Open Outlook Data File dialog box.

If you locate messages in an archive folder containing information to which you need ready access, you can move these messages out of the archive Inbox folder or subfolder into your active Inbox or appropriate subfolder. Select the messages in the Information Viewer and then drag and drop them onto the active Inbox folder icon or one of its subfolders in the Navigation Pane.

Organizing the Messages You Need to Keep

After deleting all the spam messages in your Inbox and moving all the old messages you don't need to access any time soon to your archive folder, you're ready to tackle the last big job in cleaning out your e-mail Inbox. Namely, you need to organize the remaining e-mail messages by putting them into appropriate subfolders of the Inbox.

Grouping the e-mail messages you still need to respond to or refer to into Inbox subfolders offers several advantages:

- With subfolders, you're usually facing much smaller and easier-to-deal-with groups of e-mail messages (say, hundreds rather than thousands).

- Subfolders tell you immediately where to find the e-mail you still need to respond to in some manner.

- A subfolder containing only the e-mail you need to respond to is much easier to prioritize, thus enabling you to more accurately estimate the total processing time so that you can better accommodate your busy schedule.

- Subfolders containing just the different types of e-mail you use for reference make finding the information you need at any given moment faster and easier.

- Subfolders can be tailored precisely to the type of business you conduct and the kinds of e-mail you generally receive.

These benefits not only make dealing with your e-mail less intimidating overall but also make it possible to dispense with said e-mail in a lot less time. And although these benefits may not go as far as making you love dealing with e-mail, they can't help but make processing e-mail a lot more manageable and, therefore, a lot less distasteful and stressful.

Creating Inbox subfolders for wanted e-mail

The first step in organizing your wanted e-mail messages is to create all the Inbox subfolders needed to store them. The process for creating a new Mail folder within your Inbox is a simple one. The process for deciding exactly which subfolders you need to create is a bit more involved.

Here are the steps for creating a new Inbox subfolder:

1. **Launch Outlook as you normally do and be sure that the Inbox of the Mail module is selected in the Navigation Pane.**

   Selecting the Inbox before you open the Create New Folder dialog box saves you time because Outlook automatically creates the new mail folder right inside your Inbox folder.

2. **Press Ctrl+Shift+E or File⇨New⇨Folder on the menu bar.**

   Outlook opens the Create New Folder dialog box with the Inbox selected in the Select Where to Place This Folder list box.

3. **Type the name you want to give your new folder into the Name text box and then click OK or press Enter.**

   When naming the new subfolder, keep in mind that Outlook automatically alphabetizes the Inbox subfolders. If the order is important to you, you need to name your new folders appropriately.

Now that you know the process for creating an Inbox subfolder, all you have to do is come up with folders for all the categories of e-mail messages that you receive and want to store until the messages are old enough to remove from active service by archiving.

In deciding upon the folders you need to create, be sure that you create an Inbox subfolder for the messages that you need to respond to in some manner but don't have to process (and for pointers on the most efficient way to go about this, see Chapter 8). After that, you need to consider the categories of the particular types of e-mail that you need to keep around for reference purposes.

In my primary job as a *For Dummies* author, I need subfolders in which to store the reader feedback I get. I also need subfolders for correspondence on beta software programs I participate in as well as correspondence with the various editors I deal with. Sometimes I also need Inbox subfolders for particular book projects that I'm working on (this book being the most recent example).

In my job on the side as a hospice volunteer and Interfaith Chaplaincy student, I need folders for correspondence concerning hospice and my ministerial studies. In addition, I need to maintain a few subfolders for personal and business orders and correspondence (especially online orders).

Figure 7-7 shows my expanded Inbox with a partial list of the subfolders I maintain, both for e-mail that still requires action as well as the messages that I need to keep active for reference purposes.

Inbox subfolders created for storing active messages

Figure 7-7:
Expanded Inbox in the Navigation Pane of my Outlook showing the list of the subfolders I use for organizing e-mail.

And here's a list of all the main category Inbox subfolders I maintain, with a brief description of the contents of each:

- ✔ **Action Mail:** This folder contains all the messages that require a response but that I don't have time to deal with at present. The most common response is to reply to each message, although the response can end up being to forward the message to someone else better suited to deal with it.

- ✔ **Beta Software:** This folder contains all the messages regarding software beta testing that I'm involved in at this time. These messages are stored in their own subfolders named for the various software manufacturers. Currently, this Beta Software folder contains Adobe and Microsoft subfolders.

- ✔ **Business Affairs:** This folder contains messages concerning business transactions, vendors, and service providers with whom my business conducts business. It contains various subfolders for each business entity.

✔ **Friends & Family:** This folder contains all personal messages from friends and family members. I divide the main folder into subfolders bearing the names of friends and family members.

✔ **Hospice:** This folder contains all the messages concerning my involvement with hospice and palliative care. It contains subfolders for the various organizations to which I belong as well as the hospice with which I volunteer.

✔ **Interfaith Chaplaincy:** This folder contains all the messages concerning my involvement with interfaith chaplaincy.

✔ **MYLOFD:** Stands for *Manage Your Life with Outlook For Dummies*. This folder contains all the messages concerning the various phases of this book project.

✔ **Personal Affairs:** This folder contains messages concerning personal transactions, vendors, and service providers.

✔ **Reader Feedback:** This folder contains messages from readers of my various books to which I've replied but which aren't yet old enough to archive.

✔ **Wiley Publishing:** This folder contains all the messages from various editors. It contains a bunch of its own subfolders with the name of each editor I deal with.

When creating your own folders, you need to think about the major and minor categories of e-mail messages you deal with. One way to help this thought process along is to consider all the paper folders you maintain and how they're organized. Another way is to consider the keywords and various criteria that you'd use if you were to search for the different categories of e-mail that you need to store (something that you'll find out about in the very next section of this chapter and, I hope, doing shortly).

Be sure to put every message to which you haven't yet replied but that definitely needs a response into your equivalent of my Action Mail Inbox subfolder. Then, after you've replied to the message or forwarded a copy of it to someone else for a reply, you can move that message into the appropriate category subfolder. That way, you always know where to look for *all* the mail that you still have to deal with and for which you still have to schedule time. See Chapter 8 for hints on how to go about prioritizing the e-mail that you put into your equivalent of this folder as well as hints on scheduling time to respond to them all.

Rounding up and moving e-mail messages into their respective Inbox subfolders

The second step in organizing the e-mail messages that you want to store is to round them up so that you can then move them into the appropriate Inbox subfolders. The easiest way to do this is to conduct e-mail searches that find most of or all the messages that fall into a single category and therefore need to be moved into a particular Inbox subfolder you've created.

Performing basic e-mail searches

Outlook enables you to conduct basic searches using the Find bar that appears at the top of the Information Viewer when you press Ctrl+E (sEarch) or when you click the Find button on your Outlook 2003 custom Productivity toolbar (the Instant Search button in your Outlook 2007 Productivity toolbar).

Basic searches from the Find bar are perfect for finding groups of messages that share certain keywords. For example, if you maintain an Inbox subfolder for a particular project or client, you can probably locate the messages in the Inbox that need to be moved to that subfolder by entering the project or client name in the Look For text box.

The great thing about the basic search in Outlook is how comprehensive such a search is. When you conduct a basic search, Outlook looks for matches to the keywords you enter in the Look For text box in all the fields of the e-mail message. This means that the program will find a message if the project or client name is mentioned in the message's From field or Subject field or even in the body of the message itself.

After you enter your keywords into the Look For text box on the Outlook 2003 Find bar, you still need to click the Find Now button to start the search and display matching messages in the Information Viewer. In Outlook 2007, however, because of its new Instant Search feature, Outlook begins trying to find matches for the keywords you enter — and begins displaying matching messages in the Information Viewer — as you type the words in its text box.

Figure 7-8 shows you the results of a basic search I conducted in my Inbox to round up all e-mail messages I've recently received from Microsoft regarding various software products and initiatives. To find all these messages so that I can move them into the appropriate Inbox subfolders, all I had to do was enter Microsoft into the Look For text box of the Find bar and then click its Find Now button.

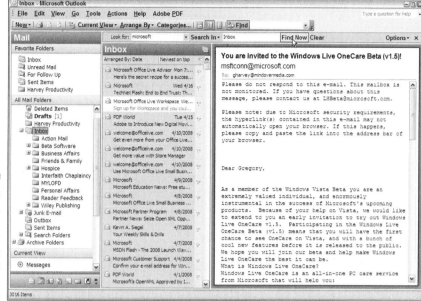

Figure 7-8:
Performing
a basic
search from
the Outlook
2003
Find bar.

Keep in mind that, by default, during a basic search Outlook searches only the Inbox folder for the keywords you enter into the Look For text box of the Find bar. This is just fine when you're rounding up groups of messages so that you can move them to one of your Inbox subfolders. However, when you're searching for a particular e-message within one of your Inbox subfolders in Outlook 2003, you have to remember to change the Search In option so that Outlook either searches all Mail folders or just the subfolder you think contains the message (In Outlook 2007, you don't have to worry because the program automatically searches all subfolders). To have Outlook search all Mail folders, choose the All Mail Folders option from the Search In drop-down list. To search just a particular Inbox subfolder, choose the Choose Folders option from this drop-down list and then click the check box for that subfolder in the Folders list box of the Select Folder(s) dialog box before you click OK or press Enter.

Finding related e-mail messages

Sometimes you may want to round up all back-and-forth correspondence related to a particular e-mail message in your Inbox so that you can store all the related messages and replies in the same Inbox subfolder.

You can gather this correspondence very easily by conducting a search for all related e-mail messages. When you conduct this type of search, Outlook searches not only your Inbox folder but also your Sent Items and Draft folder, enabling it to root out all pertinent messages written to and received from clients, co-workers, and vendors.

To search for e-mail related to a particular message, follow these steps:

1. **Click a message that you've received in your Inbox or have stored in one of your Inbox subfolders for which you want to find all your replies.**

   Outlook selects the message in the Information Viewer and displays its contents in the Reading Pane.

2. **Right-click the message in the Information Viewer.**

   Outlook displays a drop-down contextual menu for the selected message.

3. **Choose the Find All option from the drop-down contextual menu and then click the Related Messages option on the continuation menu that appears to right of the Find All item.**

   Outlook displays the Advanced Find dialog box; its Results pane at the bottom lists all the messages and replies related to selected message.

4. **To move these related messages into a particular Inbox subfolder, select the messages in the Results pane of the Advanced Find dialog box and then press Ctrl+Shift+V or click Edit⇨Move to Folder from the Advanced Find dialog box's menu bar.**

   Outlook displays the Move Items dialog box.

5. **In the Move the Selected Items to the Folder list box, click the name of the Inbox subfolder where the related messages are to be stored and then click OK or press Enter.**

   Outlook moves the selected messages to the subfolder you selected (without removing them from the Results pane of the Advanced Find dialog box).

6. **Click the Close box in the top-right corner of the Advanced Find dialog box to close it.**

Performing advanced e-mail searches

Outlook's Advanced Search feature is another very helpful tool when it comes to rounding up the e-mail messages you want to move out of the Inbox. This type of search enables you to locate groups of messages by conducting more targeted keyword searches than are possible with a basic search. The Advanced Search feature also allows you to conduct searches using multiple criteria targeting attributes well beyond just keywords.

Figure 7-9 shows you the Messages tab of the Advanced Find dialog box that appears when you press Ctrl+Shift+F (Find) or choose Tools⇨Find⇨Advanced Find from the Outlook 2003 menu bar (Tools⇨Instant Search⇨Advanced Find from the Outlook 2007 menu bar).

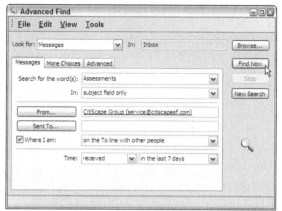

Figure 7-9:
Using the
options
on the
Messages
tab of the
Advanced
Find
dialog box
to round up
particular
messages.

You can use the options on the Messages tab of the Advanced Find dialog box to perform a targeted text search of your e-messages that can also include other conditions.

The Messages tab contains the following options for conducting an advanced text search of your e-mail messages:

- **Search For the Word(s):** Enter the text you want Outlook to search for in this field's drop-down text box.

- **In:** By default, Outlook searches only the Subject field for the text you specify in the Search For the Word(s) field described previously. Select the Subject Field and Message Body option on the In field's drop-down list to have Outlook also search for the text in the body of the message. Select the Frequently-Used Text Fields option to have Outlook search numerous fields for the text (including To, From, Subject, and the body of the message).

- **From:** Use this field to have Outlook search for messages from particular people. When you click the From button, Outlook opens the Select Names dialog box, where you can type the name(s) of the senders in the Type Name or Select From List text box (be sure to separate multiple names with semicolons) or select them from the list box below by clicking the names and then clicking the From button before you select OK.

- **Sent To:** Use this field to have Outlook search for messages you've sent to particular people. When you click the Sent To button, Outlook opens the Select Names dialog box, where you can type the name(s) of the recipients in the Type Name or Select From List text box (again, separate multiple names with semicolons) or select them from the list box below by clicking the names and then clicking the Sent To button before you select OK.

✔ **Where I Am:** Select this check box to have Outlook search messages where your name appears alone in the To field (by selecting the Only Person on the To Line option in the associated drop-down list), in the To field along with the names of other recipients (by selecting the On the To Line with Other People option), or in the CC field along with the names of other recipients (by selecting the On the CC Line with Other People).

✔ **Time:** Use the two Time drop-down list boxes to specify the timeframe that you want Outlook to use when conducting the text search of your messages. Specify the significance of the time by clicking the Received, Sent, Due, Expires, Created, or Modified option in the first Time drop-down list box. Next, specify the period by clicking the Anytime, Yesterday, Today, In the Last 7 Days, Last Week, This Week, Last Month, or This Month option in the second Time drop-down list.

Figure 7-10 shows you the options that appear on the More Choices tab of the Advanced Find dialog box. These options enable you to conduct the search using a smorgasbord of criteria besides the text entered in the body and various fields of the messages. These additional criteria include the following:

✔ **Categories:** Click this button to open the Categories dialog box, where you can click the check boxes for all the categories you want included in the search.

✔ **Only Items That Are:** Select this check box and use its related drop-down list box to specify that Outlook find only messages marked either as Unread or Read.

✔ **Only Items With:** Select this check box and use its related drop-down list box to specify that Outlook find only messages with One or More Attachments or with No Attachments.

✔ **Whose Importance Is:** Select this check box and use its related drop-down list box to specify that Outlook find only messages whose importance is marked as Normal, High, or Low.

✔ **Only Items Which:** Select this check box and use its related drop-down list box to specify that Outlook find only messages that have been marked with a particular type of flag (including distinct colors ranging from red to purple, any colored flag, any completed flag, or having been flagged by someone else) or have no flag.

✔ **Match Case:** Select this check box to have Outlook use exact case matching for the text you specified in the Search For the Word(s) field on the Messages tab of the Advanced Find dialog box.

✔ **Size (Kilobytes):** Use this option's drop-down list box and the related text boxes to specify the size range (in kilobytes) of the messages to find. Select the condition — Equals (Approximately), Between, Less Than, or Greater Than — in the drop-down list box and then specify the number of kilobytes in the text box to the right. (You enter values in both text boxes when you select the Between option.) For example, to have Outlook find messages smaller than 25K, you select Less Than in the drop-down list box and then type **25** in the text to its immediate right.

Figure 7-10:
The More
Choices
tab of the
Advanced
Find
dialog box.

Figure 7-11 shows you the options on the Advanced tab of the Advanced Find dialog box. These options enable you to carry out very precise searches using multiple criteria directed toward particular message fields.

The options offered on the Advanced tab include the following:

✔ **Field:** Use this drop-down list to specify the field to search in the e-mail messages by selecting one of the following categories: Frequently-Used Fields, Address Fields, Date/Time Fields, All Mail Fields, or All Post Fields in Outlook 2003. In Outlook 2007, you have several other choices including, All Document Fields, All Contact Fields, All Appointment Fields, All Task Fields, All Journal Fields, and All Notes Fields.

✔ **Condition:** The options available on the Condition drop-down list depend on the type of field you select from the Field drop-down list to its immediate left. If you specify a text field, these options include Contains, Is (Exactly), Doesn't Contain, Is Empty, and Is Not Empty. If you specify a date field, these options include Anytime, Yesterday, Today, Tomorrow, In the Last 7 Days, In the Next 7 Days, Last Week, This Week, Next Week, Last Month, This Month, Next Month, On, On or After, On or Before, Between, Exists, and Does Not Exist.

✔ **Value:** Specify the text or value that matching messages must have (or not have) to meet the condition you specified in the Condition drop-down list box in the field you specified in the Field drop-down list box.

✔ **Add to List:** Click this button to add the field criterion you just created using the Field, Condition, and Value fields to the Find Items That Match These Criteria list box. Keep in mind that when you add multiple field criteria to this list box, all the conditions must be met in order for Outlook to display the message in the Results pane of the Advanced dialog box when you finally conduct the search by clicking the Find Now button.

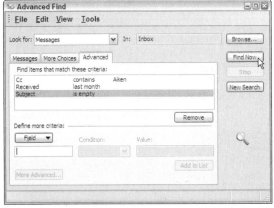

Figure 7-11:
The
Advanced
tab of the
Advanced
Find
dialog box.

Moving groups of messages into the appropriate Inbox subfolder

After you've located a group of messages you need to move, you have a choice in how you move them:

✔ **Drag and Drop:** If the Inbox subfolder into which you want to move the messages is displayed in the Navigation Pane of the Mail module, you can move the messages by selecting them in the Information viewer and then dropping the selection on the subfolder icon in the Navigation Pane.

✔ **Move to Folder:** If the Inbox subfolder into which you want to move the messages isn't displayed in the Navigation Pane, or you need to move messages listed in the Results pane of the Advanced Search dialog box, use the Move to Folder command (press Ctrl+Shift+V).

All you have to do to move the messages in the Move Items dialog box (refer to Figure 7-4) is to click the subfolder in the Move the Selected Items to the Folder list box (remembering that you may have to click an Expand button — with the plus sign — to display the subfolder you want to use) and then click OK or press Enter.

Sometimes, instead of moving a reply out of the Sent Items folder into an Inbox subfolder, you may want to just send a copy of the reply to that subfolder. To retain the original reply messages in the Sent Items folder and place a copy in one of your Inbox subfolders, select the messages and then choose Edit⇨Copy to Folder on the Outlook menu bar. Doing this opens the Copy Items dialog box, where you click the subfolder you've chosen as the new home for the copies to go in the Copy Selected Items to the Folder list box before you click OK or press Enter.

Living with an Empty Inbox

Congratulations on your nice clean, empty Inbox that should now look just like my Inbox shown in Figure 7-12 — unless some groups of new messages snuck in while you were finishing moving your last messages to their rightful subfolders! Doesn't it feel really good and downright liberating to have an empty Inbox (even if it's only a very transitory situation)?

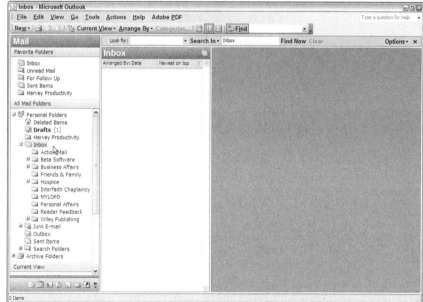

Figure 7-12: Experiencing the liberating, albeit momentary, feeling of having an empty Inbox!

An empty Inbox can, however, also feel scary, especially if you're not used to seeing it in that condition and you're afraid you'll forget about all those messages that are now conveniently hidden in your equivalent of my Action Mail subfolder (creating that that old "out of sight, out of mind" conundrum).

This is where good Inbox maintenance habits become critical. It's not sufficient simply to hide away your e-mail in a bunch of subfolders. (That's not much different from hiding all your stuff in closets and under the bed when company comes over at home.) You also have to develop habits that help you prioritize and tackle the messages that you put there.

Moreover, as much fun as doing this Inbox housecleaning has been [:(], you can't expect to spend this much time in the future cleaning out accumulated e-mail messages and hope to achieve anything close to stress-free productivity. But your Inbox will fill up again as bad as or worse than before if you just let it go.

To keep your Inbox lean and under control, you have to put Outlook to work for you, automatically routing as many incoming e-mail messages as electronically possible to their correct locations. In addition, you have to develop some new habits that lead you to tag messages as soon as they come in with categories and priorities. The idea is to that make dealing with them appropriately and then rounding them up and moving them to their appointed Inbox subfolders as easy as child's play. All the information you need for learning to live happily ever after with an empty Inbox with only the lightest Inbox housekeeping lies right ahead of you in Chapter 8.

Chapter 8

Doing Your Ongoing E-Mail Inbox Housekeeping

. . . .

In This Chapter

▶ Implementing strategies for keeping your Inbox nearly empty

▶ Prioritizing and scheduling the action e-mail you can't get to right away

▶ Using rules to automatically organize more routine e-mail messages

▶ Using AutoArchive to routinely clean out old messages and keep your Inbox manageable

▶ Backing up your Outlook data files so that all this e-mail organizing is not in vain

. . . .

*I*n the last chapter, you took the first step in gaining mastery over your wayward e-mail by performing a much-needed, initial Inbox housecleaning. In this chapter, you find out how to take the second step — the one that enables you to maintain nearly the same level of control over your Inbox as part of the process of increasing your personal productivity with Outlook.

To help you achieve this goal, this chapter explores strategies designed specifically for dealing effectively with new e-mail on an ongoing basis. Adopting these strategies — when combined with developing some new habits regarding when and how you respond to e-mail — can go a long way in making sure that your Inbox doesn't again become a forbidding part of Outlook that you dread to face.

In evaluating these strategies and creating these new habits, you have to take into consideration exactly how you've organized your Inbox subfolders for storing active e-mail using the information covered in the previous chapter. (See Chapter 7 for details if you haven't yet gone through this process.) You may also find modifying some of your e-mail default settings advantageous — and it wouldn't hurt to create some additional rules for automatically managing your e-mail messages.

And finally, to make sure that all your hard housekeeping work is not in vain, you need to learn how to back up your Outlook data files and then actually get into the habit of backing the stuff up!

Keeping Your Inbox Spick-and-Span

Now that you've followed the plan outlined in the previous chapter and you've got your e-mail Inbox empty or nearly empty, you have to work hard to keep it that way. The first order of business is to evaluate strategies for actually achieving this goal. Then, you're ready to develop some new habits that help you implement these strategies and make them the normal way of "doing your e-mail."

Looking at various strategies for effectively dealing with new e-mail

David Allen and Sally McGhee, two noted productivity experts who counsel knowledge workers who have committed to using Outlook as their Personal Information Manager, have developed a very similar strategy for dealing with new e-mail — a strategy that complements their respective personal productivity systems.

Allen and McGhee both argue that one's first order of business when dealing with e-mail is to determine whether a particular e-mail message you receive is "actionable." That is, can you respond appropriately to the e-mail message within two minutes? If you can, you go ahead and deal with the message right after reading it. If not, you put off dealing with it until a later time or forward it to someone else who will deal with it for you.

To accommodate this two-minute actionable strategy, David Allen developed what I call his Three Ds of dealing with new e-mail (Do, Defer, or Delegate), to which Sally McGhee's strategy adds a fourth: Delete. Put them together and you come up with the following list of techniques:

- ✔ **Do it:** If you can formulate a reply to an e-mail message within two minutes, go ahead and do it.

- ✔ **Defer it:** If you can't formulate a reply to a message within two minutes, defer it by moving it a folder where you won't forget it (a Deferred Mail subfolder or Action Mail subfolder, for example).

- ✔ **Delegate it:** If you're not the best person to reply to a message, send it on to the person who *is* by forwarding the message.

- ✔ **Delete it:** If you read a message (or its preview lines, if you view your e-mail messages using Messages with AutoPreview as your current Mail view) and find that it clearly falls into the junk category, move it into your Deleted Items folder by pressing the Delete key.

Personally, I don't think that determining whether an e-mail message is actionable (regardless whether that action takes two minutes or two hours) is the most strategic question. Instead, the basic question you need to answer is whether the message is important. In other words, ask yourself, "Is this e-mail message junk?"

If you answer yes to this question, you know right away what to do with the message: You move it into the Deleted Items folder and you're done with it. On the other hand, if you answer no to this basic question, that's when you have to ask yourself whether you need to respond to the message (either by simply acknowledging or by actually replying to it), and if you do, what kind of response is needed.

Therefore, so as not to be outdone by the experts, I've developed the Three Rs of dealing with new e-mail, which I offer as an alternative to the 4 Ds. These three techniques, as you see in the following list, are very different in nature from Allen's and McGhee's 4Ds because they only get you ready to work on so-called "actionable" e-mail, rather than actually calling for any action (in the Allen/McGhee sense) on your part:

- ✔ **Read it:** Determine from the subject and body of each new message whether it's junk.

- ✔ **Register it:** If the message is not a piece of junk mail, immediately assign it to the principal category that it seems to fit. (See Chapter 6 for details on categories and how to create and use them.) If it's a message you need to respond to, you also need to flag it for follow up.

- ✔ **Route it:** Move junk e-mail to the Deleted Items folder (and if you want to block the sender from being able to send future messages, choose Actions⇨Junk E-Mail⇨Add Sender to Blocked Senders List from the Outlook menu bar). Move the e-mail that requires a response into your Action Mail Inbox subfolder. Move mail that you want to keep for your own information or future reference to the appropriate Inbox subfolder that you set up for storing these kinds of messages until they're old enough to archive.

The assumption here is that batches of e-mail messages periodically flood your Outlook Inbox, and the most efficient way to deal with them is by batch processing them. You do this initial batch processing by going through the messages with the sole purpose of classifying each one and then moving it into the most appropriate Inbox subfolder (kind of the way your company's mail room or the U.S. Post Office does when it initially organizes snail mail by placing it into different pigeonholes or mail bags). At the end of this initial pass, all the messages that arrived together are moved out of your Inbox and safely tucked into their respective Inbox subfolders. and the only messages that concern you right away are the ones you routed to your Action Mail subfolder.

Categorizing new messages

In Chapter 6, I cover the care and feeding of Outlook categories that help you classify a module's various items for quick and easy grouping and retrieval. As part of the initial processing of new e-mail, I strongly suggest that you get in the habit of immediately assigning categories to all incoming messages that you determine are not junk mail.

Think of categorizing new e-mail messages as the very first step in the batch processing of them. If you find that a new message doesn't fall into the junk e-mail category, there must be other categories that you think pertain to it. By assigning the most obvious and important of those categories to the nonjunk mail message upon reading it, you get a head start on correctly routing it, the second step in batch processing.

Remember that you don't need to take the time to put junk e-mail messages into a junk category. Simply route the message straight to your Deleted Items folder by pressing Delete after reading its subject or text and determining that you need neither to respond to the message nor keep it around.

If you're using Outlook 2007, you can speed up the categorizing process by assigning shortcut keys to the categories that you assign to most of your nonjunk e-mail messages. This version of Outlook enables you to assign shortcut keys to eleven categories, using the keys Ctrl+F2 through Ctrl+F12. (See Chapter 6 for details on how to assign shortcuts to your top 11 e-mail message categories.) You can also assign a default, Quick Click category by clicking the empty rectangle in the Categories column displayed in the Information Viewer to the immediate right of the Date and Time column (thus turning the category rectangle red). To change the Quick Click category (initially the Red Category), choose Actions⇨Categorize⇨Set Quick Click from the Outlook menu bar and then click a new category in the drop-down list of the Set Quick Click dialog box before you click OK.

Flagging new messages for follow up

You need to flag all the new e-mail messages in your Inbox that you conclude require some sort of response on your part for follow-up (even if it's ultimately to forward the message to someone else in your organization who can better handle its content).

Adding the For Follow Up Search folder to the Outlook 2007 Navigation Pane

The great thing about flagging the new e-mail messages that require a response is that Outlook automatically adds any flagged message to a Search Folder named For Follow Up. This feature enables you to display all flagged messages in the Information Viewer by clicking the For Follow Up folder icon in the Navigation Pane (either in the Favorite Folders at the top or under Search Folders in the Mail Folders section below). It's a breeze to then select these messages and move them to your Action Mail folder for later processing.

Unfortunately, Outlook 2007 doesn't automatically add the For Follow Up folder to your Search Folders (although it does automatically add a Categorized Mail Search folder for you and displays the subject of all flagged items in its To-Do Bar).

However, these simple steps will add this custom Search folder to your Outlook 2007 Navigation Pane:

1. **Choose File➪New➪Search Folder or press Ctrl+Shift+P.**

   Outlook opens the New Search Folder dialog box, shown in Figure 8-1.

2. **Click Mail Flagged for Follow Up in the top Reading Mail section of the Select a Search Folder dialog box to select it and then click OK or press Enter.**

   Outlook closes the New Search Folder dialog box, and the For Follow Up folder is now added to the Search Folders section in the Navigation Pane.

Figure 8-1:
Creating
a custom
search
folder that
shows all
the flagged
e-mail
messages.

Adding the Flag column to the current view

If your current view in the Information Viewer of the Outlook 2003 Mail module doesn't include the display of the Flag column on the right, you can add the column to the Viewer by customizing the current view as follows:

1. **Choose View➪Arrange By➪Current View➪Customize Current View from the Outlook 2003 menu bar.**

   Outlook opens the Customize View dialog box for the current view (usually Messages or Messages with AutoPreview).

2. **Click the Other Settings button.**

   Outlook opens the Other Settings dialog box, similar to the one shown in Figure 8-2.

3. **Select the Show Quick Flag Column check box and then click OK or press Enter twice, first to close the Other Settings dialog box and then to close the Customize View dialog box.**

After Outlook 2003 closes the Customize View dialog box, the Quick Flag column appears on the right side of the Information Viewer in the Mail module.

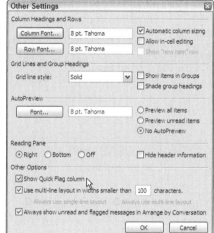

Figure 8-2: Customizing the current view to include the display of the Quick Flag column in the Outlook 2003 Information Viewer.

Changing the default Quick Click flag in Outlook 2003

Initially, Outlook 2003 uses the red colored flag as the default Quick Click flag automatically assigned when you click the empty flag icon in the Information Viewer (or set up a rule that automatically flags certain incoming messages). You can easily select another color for the default flag. You may want to reserve red for flagging the most urgent messages to which you must immediately reply and use a less cautionary color as the general marker for messages needing responses.

To change the default flag in Outlook 2003, choose Actions⇨Follow Up⇨Set Default Flag from the Outlook menu bar and then select one of the other color options (Blue Flag as Default, Yellow Flag as Default, Green Flag as Default, Orange Flag as Default, or Purple Flag as Default) from the continuation menu.

Changing the default Quick Click flag in Outlook 2007

In Outlook 2007, all the follow up flags are red (the only difference between them being the intensity of the red tint). In place of different colors, this newer version of Outlook adds different date labels to the reddish flags as a way of telling them apart. These flag labels not only identify the due date assigned to the e-mail message but also determine the group to which the message is

assigned in the Outlook To-Do Bar (in all Outlook modules), the Daily Tasks pane (in the Mail module), and the to-do list (in the Tasks modules).

Outlook 2007 gives you a choice of the following flags, each with its own start date and due date. The dates determine where the subject of the message appears on the Task List of the To-Do Bar in all Outlook modules, the Daily Task List in Calendar module, and the to-do list in the Tasks module and when the reminder appears — if you assign one:

- ✔ **Today:** This default flag assigns the current date as both the start date and due date. A Reminder appears one hour before the end time of the current workday.

- ✔ **Tomorrow:** Assigns the current date plus one day as both the start date and due date. A Reminder appears at the start time of the current date plus one workday.

- ✔ **This Week:** Assigns the current date plus two days for the start date and the last work day of current week as the due date. A Reminder appears at the start time of the current date plus two workdays.

- ✔ **Next Week:** Assigns the first workday of the following week as the start date and the last workday of the following week as the due date. A Reminder appears at the start time of the first workday of the following week.

- ✔ **No Date:** Uses neither a start date nor a due date. A Reminder appears one hour before the end time of the current workday.

- ✔ **Custom:** Enables you to assign a custom start date and due date to replace the provisional current date. A Reminder appears one hour before the end time of the current workday unless you've set a new due date — in which case, the reminder appears one hour before the end time on that date.

To select a new default Quick Click flag in Outlook 2007, choose Actions⇨Follow Up⇨Set Quick Click from the Outlook menu bar. The program then opens the Set Quick Click dialog box (shown in Figure 8-3), where you can choose Tomorrow, This Week, Next Week, No Date, or Complete (which replaces the flag icon with a check mark and marks the message as complete on all task lists) from the dialog box's drop-down list before clicking OK or pressing Enter to make your choice the new default flag.

Figure 8-3:
Selecting a
new default
Quick
Click flag
in Outlook
2007.

Keep in mind that flagging an e-mail message with any of the available flags automatically adds a reference to that message in your For Follow Up folder. The icon for this Search folder appears in the Favorite Folders section at the top of the Mail module's Navigation Pane as well as under Search Folders in the Mail Folders section (after you add the Search folder to the Navigation Pane, as explained earlier in this chapter in "Adding the For Follow Up Search folder to the Outlook 2007 Navigation Pane"). Also, note that clicking a flag you've already assigned in the Quick Click column of the Information View when this message is selected marks the message as complete (indicated by the check mark that replaces the flag icon). Marking a message as complete causes Outlook to immediately remove the reference to the message from the For Follow Up Search folder.

Routing new messages to the appropriate Mail folder

After you've gone through and completed the initial processing of all the messages in the new batch of e-mail in your Inbox, your Inbox should be in the following condition:

- ✔ All junk e-mail is moved from the Inbox to the Deleted Items folder.
- ✔ All e-mail that you have to respond to is flagged and appears listed in your For Follow Up Search folder.
- ✔ All e-mail that you want to store for future reference is classified by category.

Then, all you have to do at this point is move the flagged e-mail into your Action Mail Inbox subfolder and the other categorized e-mail messages to the Inbox subfolder set up for their respective categories:

1. **In the Inbox of the Mail Module, click the Arrange By drop-down button on your custom Productivity toolbar (see Chapter 6 for details) and then click the Flag option (in Outlook 2003) or the Flag: Start Date (in Outlook 2007) option.**

   Outlook displays all the e-mail messages you just flagged at the top of the Information Viewer.

2. **Click the first flagged message at the top of the Information Viewer and then hold down the Shift key as you click the last flagged message in the list.**

   Outlook selects all the messages in between — including the first one you clicked and last one you Shift-clicked.

3. **Press Ctrl+Shift+V.**

   Outlook opens the Move Items folder.

4. **Click the icon of the Inbox subfolder in which you store all the e-mail that you still need to respond to in some fashion (your Action Mail subfolder) in the Move the Selected Items to the Folder list box and then click OK or press Enter.**

   Outlook moves all the flagged messages from your Inbox into your Action Mail subfolder.

5. **Click the Arrange By drop-down button on your custom Productivity toolbar and then click the Categories option.**

   Outlook groups all the e-mail messages remaining in your Inbox by category (listed alphabetically by category name).

6. **Select all the messages in the first category by clicking the first message and Shift-clicking the last message, press Ctrl+Shift+V, and then click the name of subfolder where this category of messages is stored before you choose OK.**

7. **Repeat the process outlined in Step 6 for every category that contains e-mail messages in your Inbox until all the categorized e-mail messages are stored in their respective Inbox subfolders.**

   Once again, your Inbox is nice and empty (at least for the time being).

8. **Click the Arrange By drop-down button on your custom Productivity toolbar and then click the Date option (or whatever you normally prefer when viewing the new e-mail that comes into your Inbox).**

Prioritizing and dealing with messages that require a response

After doing the batch processing that empties your Inbox, if you still have some discretionary time for doing e-mail, you'll want to turn your attention to processing the e-mail messages you have moved into your Action Mail subfolder that still require some type of response on your part.

The response you make to an individual e-mail message can take the form of any of the following actions:

- ✔ **Reply to the Message:** Press Ctrl+R and then type your response at the top of the copy of the message before clicking the Send button.

- ✔ **Forward the Message:** Press Ctrl+F and then click the To button to select the recipient's e-mail address from your address book or type the e-mail address in the To text box. Type any message that you want to add above the message's header before clicking the Send button on the message editor's Standard toolbar.

✔ **Convert the Message into a Task:** To convert a message into a task on your Tasks module to-do list, drag the message from the Information Viewer to the Tasks navigation button at the bottom of the Mail module's Navigation Pane. Outlook then opens a Task dialog box (similar to the one shown in Figure 8-4) that displays the e-mail message in the bottom description area. You can then modify the Subject, Start Date and Due Date, Status, Priority, and % Complete fields as needed (see Chapter 12 for details) and specify a reminder, contacts, and categories as needed (again, see Chapter 12 for details) before you click the Save and Close button.

Figure 8-4:
Using the Task dialog box to convert an e-mail message into a task on your to-do list.

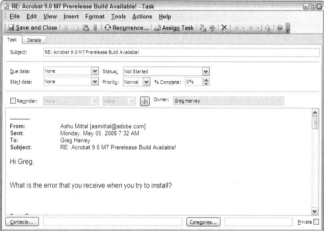

As soon as you reply to a message or forward it to another individual, don't forget to mark it as complete before moving on to the next message listed in your Action Mail subfolder. The easiest way to do this is by clicking its flag in the Information Viewer, thus converting the flag into a check mark. Note that when you order the messages using the Flag Arrange By option, all completed messages with check marks appear together (sorted by date at the end of the list), making it easy to move them out of the Action Mail subfolder and into their respective category subfolders for future reference.

In addition to converting a message into a task that then appears on your to-do list, you can also assign the message a new priority level (High or Low; Normal is the default) in your Action Mail subfolder. Assigning priority levels enables you to sort any e-mail messages that remain in a folder by their relative priority simply by selecting By Importance as the Arrange By option (choose View➪Arrange By➪Importance).

To assign a new priority to an e-mail message, follow these steps:

1. **Right-click the message in the Information Viewer and then click Options (Message Options in Outlook 2007) at the bottom of the contextual menu that appears.**

   Outlook opens the Message Options dialog box.

2. **Choose either High or Low from the Importance drop-down list at the top of this dialog**

3. **Click the Close button in the Message Options dialog box.**

   Outlook displays an alert dialog box asking you to confirm saving your changes.

4. **Click the Yes button in the alert dialog box.**

   After you assign a new priority, Outlook indicates that you've done so by placing a symbol in the Information Viewer. When you assign High importance to a message, Outlook indicates this status by adding a red exclamation point at the end of its Subject line in the Information Viewer, whereas items you've marked as being of low importance get a blue downward-pointing arrow added to them.

It's when you're determining the best response to the e-mail message gathered in your Action Mail subfolder that I think something akin to the Allen/McGhee two-minute rule kicks in. As you go through the e-mail messages in this subfolder, you probably want to take the time to reply only to those messages that you can answer very quickly — in, let's say, just five minutes total (two minutes may be pushing it). When you come upon a message in this subfolder that's going to take significantly more time to answer, convert that message into a task on your to-do list. That way, you can be sure that you won't forget about it and will take care of it as soon as you have adequate time to do so.

Creating message rules to automatically organize some of your e-mail

Message rules tell Outlook how to automatically handle certain messages you receive, either by flagging them or moving them into a particular Inbox subfolder. Message rules can really help automate the batch processing of new e-mail messages that you receive.

For example, if you periodically receive messages from a certain sender that you routinely store in a particular Inbox subfolder as valuable reference material, you can set up a message rule so that Outlook automatically moves the message into that subfolder. Likewise, if you receive messages from a particular sender (such as your boss or an important client) that you invariably have to respond to, you can have Outlook automatically flag any message that comes in from that sender and store that e-mail in your Action Mail subfolder.

To see how easy it is to create these kinds of rules, follow along with the steps for creating a rule that states that any e-mail message I receive from my Acquisitions Editor, K Feltman, is to be flagged with a red flag and moved into my Mail Action folder for processing:

1. **In the Mail module, choose Tools⇨Rules and Alerts from the Outlook menu bar.**

   Outlook opens the E-Mail Rules tab of the Rules and Alerts dialog box, similar to the one shown in Figure 8-5.

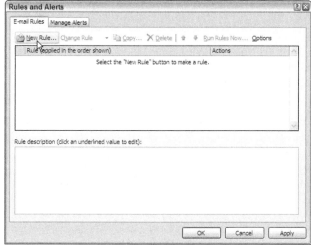

Rules and Alerts

E-mail Rules | Manage Alerts

New Rule... | Change Rule ▾ | Copy... | ✕ Delete | ⬆ ⬇ Run Rules Now... Options

Rule (applied in the order shown) | Actions

Select the "New Rule" button to make a rule.

Rule description (click an underlined value to edit):

OK | Cancel | Apply

Figure 8-5: Creating a new e-mail message rule in the Rules and Alerts dialog box.

2. **Click the New Rule button.**

   Outlook opens the initial Rules Wizard dialog box similar to the one shown in Figure 8-6. In Outlook 2003, the Start Creating a Rule from a Template option button selected (this setting is just assumed in Outlook 2007 and therefore its dialog box doesn't have this button) and the Move Messages from Someone to a Folder option highlighted in the Select a Template list box.

3. **Click the People or Distribution List link in the Step 2: Edit the Rule Description section at the bottom of the dialog box.**

   Outlook opens the Rule Address dialog box, similar to the one shown in Figure 8-7.

4. **In the dialog box's Rule Address list box, click the name of the contact whose e-mail message will trigger the new rule you're creating and then click the OK button.**

   Outlook closes the Rule Address dialog box and substitutes the name and e-mail address you select in the "Apply This Rule After the Message Arrives From" text in the Step 2: Edit the Rule Description list box.

Figure 8-6:
Editing
the rule's
description
in the Rules
and Alerts
dialog box.

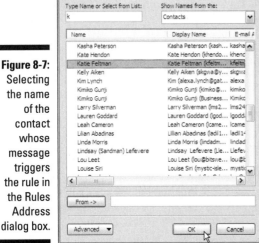

Figure 8-7:
Selecting
the name
of the
contact
whose
message
triggers
the rule in
the Rules
Address
dialog box.

5. **Click the underlined Specified link in the text "Move It to Specified Folder" in the Step 2: Edit the Rule Description list box.**

   Outlook opens the Rules and Alerts dialog box, shown in Figure 8-8.

Figure 8-8:
Selecting
the folder
into which
the mes-
sage is
moved in
the Rules
and Alerts
dialog box.

6. Click the icon of the folder into which the message is to be moved and then click OK or press Enter.

Outlook closes the Rule and Alerts dialog box and substitutes the name of the folder you select in the "Move It to Specified Folder" text in the Step 2: Edit the Rule Description list box.

7. Click the Next> button at the bottom of the Rules Wizard dialog box.

Outlook displays the second Rules Wizard dialog box, shown in Figure 8-9, where you can modify the conditions under which the new rule is activated.

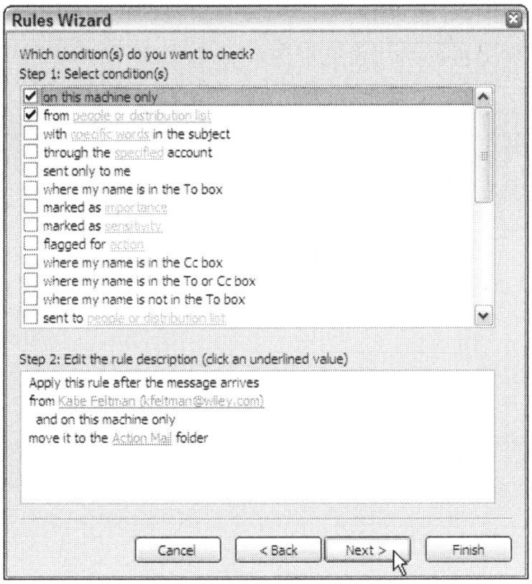

Figure 8-9:
Modifying
the
conditions
under which
the new rule
is activated
in the
second
Rules
Wizard
dialog box.

8. Modify any of the conditions by clicking their check boxes before you again click the Next> button at the bottom of the dialog box.

Outlook displays the third Rules Wizard dialog box, shown in Figure 8-10, where you can modify the actions that the new rule takes.

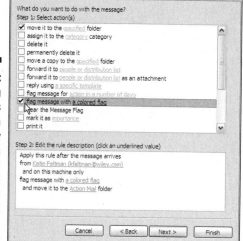

Figure 8-10:
Modifying
the actions
taken when
the new
rule is
activated
in the third
Rules
Wizard
dialog box.

9. **Click the Flag Message with a Colored Flag check box (in Outlook 2003) or the Flag Message For Follow Up at This Time check box (in Outlook 2007).**

Outlook adds the text "Flag Message with a Colored Flag" (Outlook 2003) or "Flag Message for Follow Up at This Time" (Outlook 2007) in the Step 2: Edit the Rule Description list box.

10. **Click the underlined Colored Flag link (Outlook 2003) or the Follow Up at This Time link (Outlook 2007) in the Step 2: Edit the Rule Description list box.**

Outlook opens the Select Flag Color dialog box (shown in Figure 8-11 as it appears in Outlook 2003).

Figure 8-11:
Setting the
flag color
for the
new rule
in Outlook
2003.

11. **Click OK or press Enter to accept the default Quick Click flag (red, unless you've changed it in Outlook 2003 and Follow Up for Today in Outlook 2007).**

Outlook replaces the text "Flag Message with a Colored Flag" with "Red" in Outlook 2003 and the text "Flag Message for Follow Up at This Time" in Outlook 2007 with "Follow Up Today" in the Step 2: Edit the Rule Description list box.

12. **Click the Finish button.**

Outlook closes the Rules Wizard dialog box, and your newly created rule now appears at the top of the list box on the E-Mail Rules tab of the Rules and Alerts dialog box.

13. **(Optional) Click the Run Rules Now button at the top of the E-Mail Rules tab if you want Outlook to apply the new rule to the e-mail messages that are currently in your Inbox.**

14. **Click OK or press Enter.**

Outlook closes the Rules and Alerts dialog box. After that, Outlook applies the new rule to all incoming e-mail messages in the order in which the rule appears in the list box on the E-Mail Rules tab of the Rules and Alerts dialog box.

Setting your e-mail options

In addition to using e-mail rules to help automate the management of the new batches of e-mail messages you receive, you can also sometimes reduce the amount of manual processing you have to do in your Inbox by the careful setting of Outlook's e-mail options.

In this regard, two kinds of e-mail options that you may want to take a look at are the following:

- ✔ **Junk E-Mail:** Enables you to set the level of junk-mail protection so that the more suspect e-mail messages go directly into your Junk E-mail folder; you can also specify which particular senders are to be considered safe and which ones are to be blocked.

- ✔ **E-Mail Options:** Enables you to set all sorts of message options, including how and where messages are stored and how Outlook alerts you to the arrival of new messages in your Inbox.

Junk e-mail options

To change any of Outlook's junk e-mail settings, open the Options dialog box (choose Tools⇨Options) and then click the Junk E-Mail button in the E-Mail section at the top of the Preference tab. Outlook opens the Junk E-Mail Options dialog box with the Options tab settings displayed (similar to the one shown for Outlook 2007 in Figure 8-12).

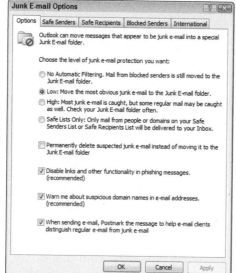

Figure 8-12:
Modifying
the junk
e-mail
settings in
the Outlook
2007 Junk
E-Mail
Options
dialog box.

The first group of settings on the Options tab enables you to change the general level of junk e-mail protection. By default, this level is set to Low, so if your Inbox is currently getting swamped with spam e-mail, you may well want to change this to High by clicking the High option button and see how this works. Because Outlook may well divert bona fide messages to your Junk E-Mail folder, you will want to check this folder on a regular basis after increasing the level to High to make sure that Outlook isn't moving too many messages that you need to respond to into this folder.

If you're really serious about weeding out spam from your Inbox, you can try using the Safe Lists Only setting. After you select this setting, Outlook delivers e-mail into your Inbox only from those people or Web domains you have added to the list boxes on the Safe Senders and Safe Recipients tabs of the Options dialog box. E-mail messages from all other sources are automatically diverted to your Junk E-Mail folder.

Don't select the Permanently Delete Suspected E-Mail Instead of Moving It to the Junk E-Mail Folder check box on the Options tab unless you're willing to thoroughly check your Deleted Items folder for bona fide messages that get sent there by mistake prior to emptying this folder.

E-mail message-handling options

If you want to change any of Outlook's general e-mail settings, open the Options dialog box (choose Tools➪Options) and then click the E-Mail Options button in the E-Mail section at the top of the Preference tab. Outlook opens the E-Mail Options dialog box (shown in Figure 8-13).

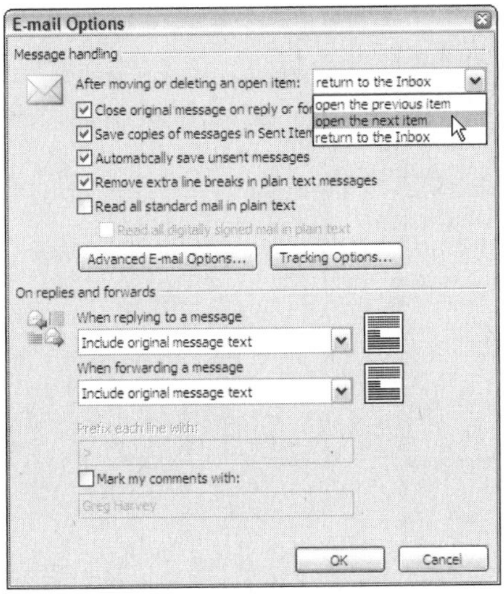

Figure 8-13: Modifying the general e-mail settings in the E-Mail Options dialog box.

Of the message-handling options displayed in the top section of the E-Mail Options dialog box, you may save a little time processing e-mail messages by changing the first two options:

- **After Moving or Deleting an Open Item:** By default, Outlook automatically returns you to the Inbox after you move or delete the message you currently have open in its own dialog box in Outlook. Select the Open Next Item option on this setting's drop-down list to have the program automatically open the next new e-mail message in your Inbox in this dialog box instead. That way, the next new message is automatically open for your inspection as soon as you finish the initial processing of its predecessor.

- **Close Original Message on Reply or Forward:** Select this check box to have Outlook automatically close the original e-mail message as soon as you click the Reply or Forward button to draft and send your reply or to forward it to someone else for processing.

In addition to changing these kinds of general message-handling settings in the E-Mail Options dialog box, you can also modify some of the more specialized e-mail options by clicking the Advanced E-Mail Options button. Clicking this button opens the Advanced E-Mail Options dialog box, shown in Figure 8-14.

The options in this particular dialog box cover three areas of message-handling: saving messages, receiving messages, and sending messages. When it comes to saving messages, you may want to select the In Folders Other Than the Inbox, Save Replies with Original Message check box to activate this option. That way, when you reply to messages in Inbox subfolders such as your Action Mail folder, Outlook saves your replies together with the original e-mail message.

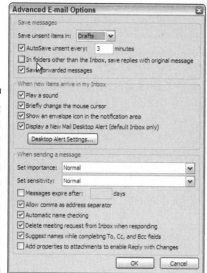

Figure 8-14:
Modifying
the
advanced
e-mail
settings
in the
Advanced
E-Mail
Options
dialog box.

When it comes to new messages coming into your Inbox, if you find that you're constantly being distracted by the audiovisual alerts that Outlook automatically gives you (such as playing a high-pitched sound and displaying a semi-transparent desktop alert on your computer's Status bar), by all means use the Advanced E-Mail Options dialog box to turn these alerts off. (The When New Items Arrive in My Inbox section houses all the controls for such alerts.) Most of the time you're much better off ignoring new batches of messages until you have time to deal with them.

Using AutoArchive to automatically clear out older messages

In the previous chapter, I cover the process for archiving your older e-mail messages to reduce the clutter of old e-mail that you'd stored up over time. Provided that your IT department permits it, after manually archiving your e-mail messages in this manner, you can then activate the AutoArchive feature and let Outlook take over doing this job for you.

To turn on the AutoArchive feature, follow these steps:

1. **Choose Tools➪Options from the Outlook menu bar.**

   Outlook opens the Options dialog box.

2. **Click the Other tab and then click the AutoArchive button.**

   Outlook displays the AutoArchive dialog box (see Figure 8-15).

3. **Select the Run AutoArchive Every check box to select this option and then set the archive interval, either by typing in the days between archive sessions in the option's text box or by selecting the value with its spinner buttons.**

4. **(Optional) If you want the program to prompt you each time before it starts archiving your messages, click the Prompt Before AutoArchive Runs check box to select it.**

   By default, when Outlook archives your e-mail, it cleans out all messages that are older than a year by moving them into an `archive.pst` file located inside your personal Outlook subfolder.

5. **(Optional) To change how messages are included in archiving, select a new value in the Clean Out Items Older Than text box and, if necessary, replace Months in the drop-down list box to its right with Weeks or Days.**

6. **Click OK or press Enter twice, first to close the AutoArchive dialog box and then to close the Options dialog box.**

Figure 8-15:
Modifying
the settings
for
automatically
archiving
older e-mail
in the
AutoArchive
dialog box.

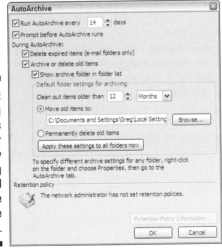

Backing Up Your Outlook Data Files

I'd be greatly remiss if I were to finish this chapter on developing good e-mail practices without adding a discussion of backing up your Outlook data files. After all, it won't do you much good to carefully maintain your various Inbox subfolders if you're only going to go and permanently lose all their messages in a computer hard drive crash.

Keep in mind that if you do suffer a serious computer crash that entails having to reinstall Outlook and restore backups of your active and archived e-mail, you'll also have to recreate your Inbox subfolders and go through the process of grouping the messages and then moving them into their appropriate folders. The good news, however, is that because you had the foresight to make regular backups of your Outlook data files, you will be able to recreate your original Outlook setup because the messages (and the contacts, tasks, notes, and so on) will still be available for your use. If you don't bother to back up your Outlook data files and you have such a computer disaster strike, you'll have nothing but the memory of this data, and you'll be starting literally from scratch!

Copying your .pst data files to a new drive or disk

If your company uses Outlook with Exchange Server, your messages are automatically stored on a server, and this server is probably automatically backed up on a regular basis by the network administration team. If, however, you don't use Outlook with Exchange Server, your active e-mail messages (along with addresses and other Outlook data) are stored in Outlook .pst files in your Personal Data folders, and your archived messages are stored in an archive.pst file in your Archived Data folders, both of which reside locally on your hard disk.

This means that, even when your computer is networked with others and the data on your company file server is routinely backed up, the local Outlook .pst data files stored on your hard drive are probably not. In such a case, you need to take the time to routinely back up your Outlook .pst data files by copying them to another hard drive (I have a USB 2.0 hard drive connected to my PC that I use for this kind of data file backup), backup tape, or optical disc such as a CD or DVD.

Backing up your Outlook .pst data files is a cinch when you know where to find them on your hard disk. (They are, I have to admit, buried pretty deeply on your hard disk, using a fairly convoluted file path.) Fortunately, Outlook helps in this regard, as you see in the following steps:

1. **Choose File⇨Data File Management from the Outlook menu bar.**

   Outlook 2003 opens the Outlook Data Files dialog box, similar to the one shown in Figure 8-16. Outlook 2007 opens the Account Settings dialog box with its Data Files tab selected. The list box in these dialog boxes shows the path for both your Archive Folders and Personal Folders.

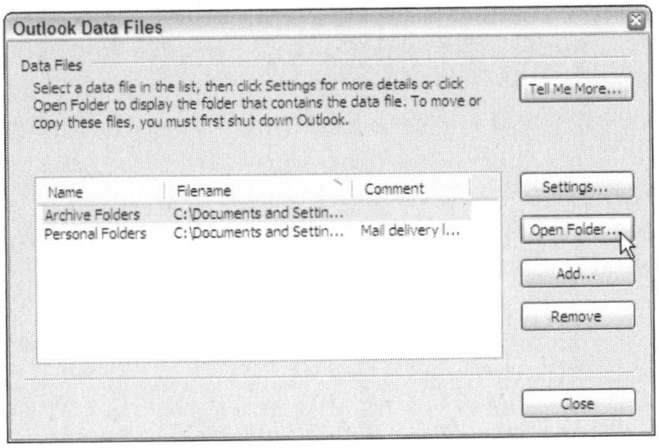

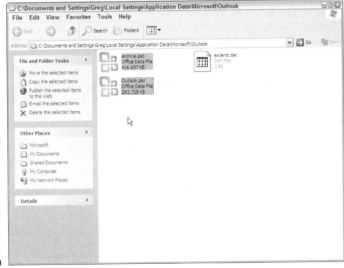

Figure 8-16:
Locating the
data files
containing
active and
archived
Outlook
items for
backing up.

2. **Click Archive Folders selection in the list box and then click the Open Folder button.**

   Outlook 2003 opens the Documents and Settings Outlook folder containing both your `archive.pst` and `Outlook.pst`, similar to the one shown in Figure 8-17. Outlook 2007 opens your Outlook folder containing these files.

Figure 8-17:
Selecting
the Outlook
.pst data
files for
copying to a
new drive.

3. **Control-click the file icons for both the `archive.pst` and `Outlook.pst` files and then copy them to the Windows Clipboard by pressing Ctrl+C.**

   After copying the Outlook `.pst` data files to the Windows Clipboard, you're ready to paste the copies of these files in a folder on the drive or disc you use to hold your backups in case of a computer drive crash.

4. **Use Windows to open a dialog box for the drive where you want to back up the `archive.pst` and `Outlook.pst` files and then paste them into one of its folders by pressing Ctrl+V.**

Restoring your backup .pst data files

If, heaven forbid, you should ever suffer a hard drive crash that makes it impossible for you to use the original Outlook data files, you can restore your backup copies of the `Outlook.pst` and `archive.pst` files to the new or repaired hard drive. All you have to do, after reinstalling Microsoft Outlook, is to copy these `.pst` data files into your rightful Documents and Settings Outlook folder.

To locate this folder, open the Outlook Data Files dialog box in Outlook 2003 or the Data Files tab of the Account Settings dialog box in Outlook 2007 by choosing File⇨Data File Management from the Outlook menu bar. Then, click the Personal Folders item before you click the Open Folder button to open a dialog box for this Outlook folder. Finally, use Windows to open the folder containing your backup `.pst` files and then drag its `archive.pst` and `Outlook.pst` file icons and drop them into the Documents and Settings Outlook dialog box.

After Windows finishes copying these backup `.pst` folders, when you next open Outlook your active e-mail will once again reappear in your Inbox folder (unfortunately, all the messages will be jumbled together and will not be all nicely organized into your various subfolders, meaning you'll have to retrace the housecleaning steps you followed in Chapter 7) and your archived e-mail shows up in your Archive Folders in the Mail module.

Part IV

Developing Your Outlook Productivity Practices

The 5th Wave   By Rich Tennant

"I like getting complaint letters by e-mail. It's easier to delete than to shred."

In this part . . .

The chapters in this fourth part contain the core Outlook personal productivity techniques. Here, you find individual chapters showcasing techniques for improving productivity using each of Outlook's many modules. Look to the information in this part for solid suggestions and practical methods for implementing personal productivity in every aspect of using Outlook as your personal information manager.

Chapter 9

Creating and Sending E-Mail Messages Like a Pro

. . . .

In This Chapter

▶ Guidelines for composing effective e-mail messages

▶ Deciding whether to use the Cc: line

▶ Attending to the care and feeding of e-mail attachments

▶ Creating your own personal signature and using digital signatures

▶ Tracking important e-mail and keeping copies of important responses

. . . .

*Y*ou've probably heard the old saying "it's far better to give than to receive" many times. When it comes to e-mail messages, I think you'll agree that this idea surely applies. For as the strategies for dealing with e-mail covered in the previous two chapters make plain, being inundated with e-mail messages day after day is one of the largest challenges to personal productivity that any knowledge worker faces.

Although being on the receiving end of way too much e-mail is consistently a number one personal productivity concern, you need to realize that an inability to efficiently and effectively compose and send out e-mail messages can also negatively impact your workflow as well. This is all the more true if your job relies heavily on e-mail as a primary means of communicating and keeping in touch with your clients and coworkers.

The focus of this chapter is on the ways you can be as effective in composing and sending out e-mail messages as you are in fielding the ones you receive. To that end, this chapter covers both the dos and don'ts for composing new e-mail messages, along with strategies for the most effective ways to track the messages you send out.

Composing Effective E-Mail Messages

Nothing wastes quite as much e-mail processing time as having to wade through a rambling e-mail message, which at the end leaves you as puzzled about its subject matter as you are about the response that the sender wants from you. Therefore, to avoid putting this same burden on a client or co-worker, you should endeavor to make sure that all your e-mails are concise and to the point.

This means that you need to think a bit about what you need to communicate and how best to say it. Before sitting down to draft a new message, you probably should consider the following things:

✔ What's the purpose of the e-mail? Is it to introduce yourself, give your recipient some important information, seek some sort of permission from him or her, set up some sort of one-time or ongoing communication, or some other function?

✔ Who's the intended recipient of the e-mail? Is it a coworker, team member, boss, client, or someone else? Given your relationship with the intended recipient, how will you strike the appropriate writing tone in your message?

✔ What kind of response, if any, do you want or expect? If you expect a reply, how will you make it clear what the alternatives are and the significance you place on receiving a response from your recipient?

✔ When you do need the response? If there's a deadline involved, especially a tight one, how will you communicate this fact and its importance?

If you take the time to think through these kinds of issues before you begin to write, chances are good that you'll end up with not only a more focused message but also one that gets a much better reception and quicker response.

Punching up the Subject line

The importance of the subject line in an e-mail message cannot be over-stated. The subject line is your recipient's first clue as to the nature of the message and its relative importance. In many e-mail programs (including Outlook, when Messages with AutoPreview is the not the current view), the subject line is the only piece of information other than the identity of the sender that is displayed in the list of new messages received.

This means that the subject lines of your e-mail messages need to effectively summarize the gist of the message in as few words as possible. Make sure when composing the subject line that you neither over- nor undersell the message, because if the subject line sounds too much like marketing hype, the recipient will likely treat the message as spam. Likewise, if the subject line is too nondescript, you run the risk of having the recipient pass it over in favor of the other hundred new messages competing for his or her attention.

Make every effort to create a subject line for your new message that immediately communicates the overall point of the message. And, if possible, make sure that the subject captures both the essence of the topics you're covering and your intention in covering them. For example, instead of the more generic subject line "Fall Team Meeting" to announce an upcoming, regularly scheduled team meeting, try something a little more informative, such as "Fall Team Meeting Invite & Line Up."

Making good use of e-mail abbreviations

The best use you can make of abbreviations in your business e-mail messages is to avoid them altogether, with the possible exception of the most commonly used and well-accepted business acronyms (GNP, MPG, and the like). As far as I'm concerned, all the *imo* ("in my opinion"), *eom* ("end of message"), *thx* ("thanks"), and *ttyl* ("talk to you later") types of e-mail abbreviations should be avoided at all costs, along with every single emoticon known to humankind [:-(].

Although such abbreviations may seem innocuous enough to you and appear to be real typing timesavers, they can all too easily send the wrong message to your readers (namely that you're either too lazy or don't care enough about them to take the time to spell out your words and phrases). Moreover, unless you're communicating with a co-worker or client with whom you regularly use abbreviations such as *btw* ("by the way") or *imho* ("in my humble opinion") in your messages, you can't be sure that your reader correctly understands them (*btw* can be taken as an abbreviation for "between," and as for *imho,* I won't even go there!).

Imho (oops!), abbreviations belong in text messages alone, if only because of the severe limitations placed on text entry by the inadequate design of far too many cell phone and PDA keyboards and the economic ramifications of exceeding the contractual restrictions placed on messaging by cell phone carriers themselves.

Composing concise and to-the-point messages

Even when avoiding the use of any and all e-mail abbreviations, you can, of course, still compose e-mail messages that are concise and to the point. Often the best way to do this is to present the ideas that you want to get across in the body of the message in a kind of outline form rather than in the paragraph form you'd use in the text of a regular card or letter.

In creating outline points, you generally try boil down your individual thoughts and ideas so that they're expressed in one or two lines of text, tops. This makes it particularly easy for your recipients to scan and take in the point you're making, especially online.

When considering the points to include in your message, be sure that they cover all the relevant information you feel your recipient needs to have. Also, be sure your points include all pertinent dates, times, and places and, if you need some sort of confirmation or feedback, be sure to include that point as well.

To Cc: or not to Cc: — that is the question

The first time a client asked me the meaning of the Cc: and Bcc: lines that appear in an e-mail message header, I gave him the correct answer — carbon copy and blind carbon copy — without knowing for sure whether my assumptions were correct.

Somehow, the idea that these terms straight out of the era of carbon-paper and typewriters would find their way over to electronic mail messages didn't seem right to me, although I was sure that the electronic equivalents of carbon copy and blind carbon copy worked in the exact same manner as their much earlier paper counterparts.

Just as with copies of a typed memo created with carbon paper, the original recipient of the message (that is, the person to whom the original message is addressed on the To: line) can see all the names (with e-mail address) listed on the Cc: line in an Outlook e-mail message (as can each carbon-copied recipient). And, as with typewriter carbon copies, the original recipient can see none of the names (and e-mail addresses) listed on the Bcc: line in an Outlook message (nor can the other blind-copied recipients).

When you want to send a completely blind message so that no one is listed as the original recipient on the To: line, enter the e-mail addresses for all your recipients on the Bcc: line of the new message.

Despite the similarities between paper and electronic carbon copies and blind carbon copies, there's a huge difference as well. For example, when you send a message with a bunch of recipients listed on the Cc: line of a message and one of them decides to reply to your message using the Reply All (rather than the simple Reply command), Outlook sends copies of the reply to not only you but also every one of the carbon-copied recipients (which can amount to a great many replies clogging up your company's e-mail system if you copied hundreds of coworkers). However, when you send the same message with all the non-original recipients listed on the Bcc: line instead, if one of them clicks the Reply All button to send you a reply, no one other than yourself as the sender and your original recipient on the To: line receives that reply.

Sending blind e-mail copies both protects the anonymity of your non-original recipients and ensures that they don't have to deal with replies from other copied recipients. This means that you want to use blind carbon copies on the Bcc: line rather than carbon copies on the Cc: line of the message whenever the privacy of your non-original recipients is any kind of an issue. Beyond that, using blind copies to prevent the possibility of involving your other (non-original) recipients in any replies you receive to a message from others shows a certain amount of respect for their time and their efforts to achieve and maintain their own work/life balance.

All about attachments

E-mail attachments have both upsides and downsides. The big upside of e-mail attachments is that they provide an easy means of sharing additional information you want your recipients to have without adding additional text to the body of the e-mail message itself. This confers the benefit of enabling you to keep the text of your e-mail message short, sweet, and to the point.

One large downside of e-mail attachments is that, depending on the type of information in the attachment files (graphics and video being among the worst), they can really bulk out your e-mail message. Depending on your recipients' Internet service provider and e-mail service, some of your messages with attachments may exceed the maximum size allowed for download, thus making it impossible for these folks to receive even your basic e-mail message.

To help keep the size of your Inbox under control, you may want to look into purchasing an Outlook add-in such as Attachment Save from Sperry Software, Inc. This software program automatically removes attachments from your incoming e-mail and saves them in whatever folder you specify on your hard drive. The message still retains the paperclip icon indicating that a file or files were attached to the e-mail message, which is convenient because the icon

can then act as a link to the attachment file saved elsewhere on your hard drive. For more information about this add-in product or to purchase it, go to `www.sperrysoftware.com/outlook/attachment-save.asp`.

Another significant downside to e-mail attachments is that because they've traditionally been carriers of all sorts of nasty computer viruses, many companies block the opening of certain types of files (especially executable files of all types — `.exe`, `.com`, and `.bat` files). As a result, your recipients may end up being unable to open the files that you take the time and spend the bandwidth to send. It's always best to check beforehand when dealing with a new client to see what e-mail attachment policies are in place before you start adding attachments.

When you know that sending attachments with an e-mail message is okay, you will want to use the following guidelines in doing so:

- ✔ **Attach the files before you compose the message:** To avoid embarrassing yourself by sending the e-mail message without the attachment file described in its text, always attach the file first and then compose the message text.

- ✔ **Briefly describe the attachment:** When describing the attachment, be sure to let your recipients know the file format (and, if it's not a well-known file type such as a Word `.doc` or Excel `.xls` file, what software program opens it).

- ✔ **Compress larger attachment files:** You need to compress any file you want to attach to an e-mail that's a megabyte or larger (as files with graphics and videos can sometimes be) even when you're sure that the file does not exceed your recipient's maximum.

Creating Your Own E-Mail Signature

One really simple method for saving time in composing new e-mail messages is to create your own e-mail signature that Outlook automatically inserts into any new message you create. These signature blocks can include a complimentary closing (such as "Sincerely" or "Yours Truly") and identify you as the message sender; they can also include standard contact information.

To get an idea of how easily you can create your own e-mail signature for new messages, follow along with the steps for creating my standard business e-mail signature in Outlook 2003:

1. **Choose Tools⇨Options from the Outlook menu bar.**

   Outlook opens the Options dialog box.

2. **Click the Mail Format tab and then click the Signatures button near the bottom of the dialog box.**

   Outlook opens the Create Signature dialog box similar to the one shown in Figure 9-1. Note that if you're using Outlook 2007, it opens a slightly different dialog box, this one called Signatures and Stationary dialog box (see Figure 9-3). This dialog box enables you to create your new signature right within its confines.

3. **Click the New button.**

   Outlook opens the Create New Signature dialog box in Outlook 2003 and the New Signature dialog box in Outlook 2007.

4. **Type the name for your new signature in the text box and then click the Next> button in the Create New Signature dialog box or the OK button in the New Signature dialog box.**

   Outlook opens the Edit Signature dialog box shown in Figure 9-2 in Outlook 2003 and returns you to the Signature and Stationary dialog box shown in Figure 9-3 in Outlook 2007, where you can enter and edit the stock text you want to appear in the message.

5. **Type the standard text that you want to appear in the new signature in the list box (this can include a standard salutation as well as a closing) and then use the various font and formatting buttons to format this text.**

   When creating a new signature, you can attach or insert your contact information in the form of a virtual business card if you want. (When creating a signature for Outlook 2007, you can also insert a picture stored in a separate graphic file by clicking the dialog box's Picture button or a link to a Web site by clicking its Insert Hyperlink button — again, see Figure 9-3.)

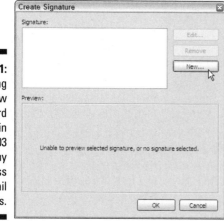

Figure 9-1:
Creating a new standard signature in Outlook 2003 for my business e-mail messages.

Figure 9-2:
Editing
the new
signature in
Outlook 2003
for my busi-
ness e-mail
messages.

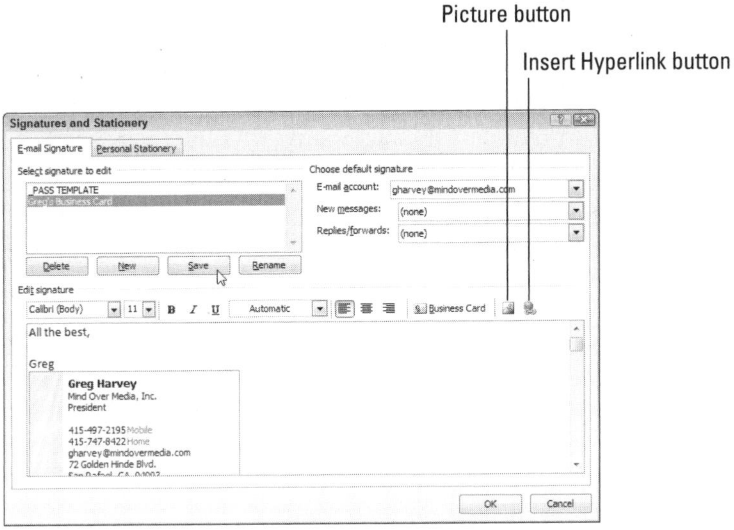

Picture button

Insert Hyperlink button

Figure 9-3:
Adding the
text and a
business
card for
my new
signature
in Outlook
2007.

6. **(Optional) To automatically attach a vCard to each new message as part of your signature in Outlook 2003, click the New VCard from Contact button. To automatically display the contact information on your vCard in each new message in Outlook 2007, click the Business Card button.**

In Outlook 2003, the Select Contacts to Export as VCards dialog box opens. In Outlook 2007, the Insert Business Card dialog box opens.

7. **If using Outlook 2003, click your name in the contact list to select it and then click the Add button before you click OK; if using Outlook 2007, just click the OK button.**

In Outlook 2003, the program adds your e-mail address to the Attach This Business Card (vCard) to this Signature combo box. In Outlook 2007, the program displays a facsimile of the business card with all its contact information in its Edit Signature list box.

8. **In Outlook 2003, click the Finish button to close the Edit Signature dialog box and then click OK to close the Create Signature dialog box. In Outlook 2007, click the Save button before you click the OK button.**

   Outlook returns you to the Mail Format tab of the Options dialog box.

9. **In Outlook 2003, choose the name of the signature you just created from the Signature for New Messages drop-down menu and then click the Apply button followed by the OK button. In Outlook 2007, simply click the OK button.**

   Outlook closes the Options dialog box.

After creating a new signature and selecting it as the one to use for new messages, Outlook automatically inserts its text (and graphics, if you assigned them) into each new message you create. Before you start using your new signature on a regular basis, however, you may want to send yourself a test message to see how the signature appears in a new e-mail. That way, you can ensure that the signature contains all the information you want your recipients to have and that all of its information is correct.

Note that you can also have Outlook automatically insert this signature into all messages you reply to and forward (or another signature that you've created) in Outlook 2003 by selecting it on the Signature for Replies and Forwards drop-down list on the Mail Format tab of the Options dialog box. In Outlook 2007, you need to click the Signatures button on the Mail Format tab of the Options dialog box and then select the signature from the Replies/Forward drop-down list in Signatures and Stationary dialog box.

Tracking Your Important E-Mail Messages

My last words of wisdom regarding e-mail productivity have to do with ways to successfully and automatically track some of the more important e-mail messages you send out. Many times with important messages, especially those requiring a response within a short timeframe, it's crucial to have verification that your recipients have not only successfully received the message but also have, in fact, opened and (presumably) read it.

Short of sending your recipients additional e-mails asking whether they got your original message and have looked at it, you can have Outlook automatically request that both a delivery and read receipt be sent to you.

Outlook enables you to automatically request delivery and read receipts either for all new messages that you send or just for the individual message you're composing. Because you don't need these kinds of receipts for messages that don't require any response or don't have information about important deadlines and because such requests can all too easily be misinterpreted and cause resentment through the implication that you don't trust your e-mail recipients to open and read your messages, I strongly suggest that you don't ever turn on the Read Receipt and Delivery Receipt settings in the Tracking Options dialog box. Instead, only turn these options on for the particular message you're composing in the Message Options dialog box, as explained in the upcoming section.

Requesting a delivery and read receipt for a single message

To track when the e-mail messages you send are received or read by your recipient, follow these steps:

1. **Open a new message (Ctrl+Shift+M) and then click the Options button on the Outlook 2003 toolbar or (in Outlook 2007) click the Options tab on the Ribbon in the Untitled Message window.**

   Outlook 2003 opens the Message Options dialog box, similar to the one shown in Figure 9-4.

2. **Click the Request a Delivery Receipt for This Message check box (simply called Request a Delivery Receipt in Outlook 2007) to select it when you want Outlook to send you verification of your recipient's receipt of the message.**

3. **Click the Request a Read Receipt for This Message check box (simply called Request a Read Receipt in Outlook 2007) to select it when you want Outlook to send you verification of your recipient's opening of the message.**

4. **In Outlook 2003, click the Close button to close the Message Options dialog box and return to the Untitled Message window, where you can compose and then send the new message. In Outlook 2007, you simply click the Message tab in the Untitled Message window and use its options to compose and send the message.**

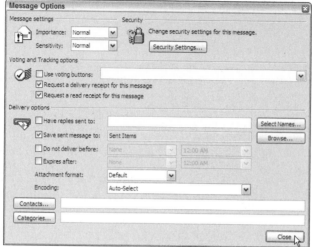

Figure 9-4:
Requesting
a delivery
and read
receipt for
a new mes-
sage you're
composing.

If you're composing an e-mail message that requires your recipients to give
you some sort of thumbs-up or thumbs-down response on a particular issue,
use the Voting Buttons option to make voting on the issue super simple. When
you select Voting Buttons, your recipients can quickly make their opinions
known on an issue by clicking the vote text that appears in the message's Info
bar and then clicking the appropriate response on its drop-down list. Outlook
will send you an e-mail with their responses (which recipients can edit or just
send back by clicking a simple button). To add voting buttons to a new message, click the Options button in Outlook 2003 or the Options tab in Outlook
2007. Then, click the Use Voting Buttons check box (Outlook 2003) or button
(Outlook 2007) and select the types of choices you want to present to your
recipients (Approve/Reject, Yes; No, or Yes; No; Maybe) on the drop-down list.

Modifying tracking options

By default, Outlook processes all delivery receipts that you attach to messages you send on their arrival so that you can verify the date and time your
recipient received the message. The program also automatically displays an
alert dialog box when you receive a message with a delivery request asking
for your confirmation to send that receipt to the message sender.

If you want, you can modify these and other Outlook tracking options by
opening the Tracking Options dialog box, similar to the one shown in Figure
9-5. To open this dialog box, click Tools⇨Options on the Outlook menu bar
and then click the E-Mail Options button on the Preferences tab to open the
E-Mail Options dialog box. Here, you click the Tracking Options button to
open the Track Options dialog box.

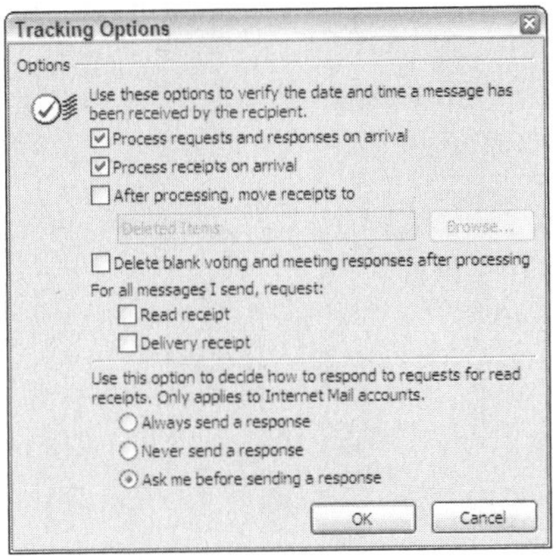

Figure 9-5:
Setting the
tracking
options for
the receipt
requests
you receive.

The additional tracking options that you might want to modify in the
Tracking Options dialog box include the following:

- **After Processing, Move Receipts To:** Select this check box to have
Outlook automatically move all read and delivery receipts sent to you
(see the For All Messages, I Send Request option below) to the Mail
folder listed in the text box immediately beneath it. By default, Outlook
moves these receipts to the Deleted Items folder unless you change the
name of the folder displayed in this text by either entering a new name
or using the associated Browse button to select it.

- **Delete Blank voting and Meeting Responses After Processing:** Select this
check box to have Outlook automatically move the voting and meeting
responses that you receive to the Deleted Items folder.

- **For All Messages, I Send Request:** Select the Read Receipt check box
to have Outlook generate a read receipt request for each message you
send, indicating when your message is read. Select the Delivery Receipt
check box to have the program generate a delivery receipt request that
indicates the date and time when you message is delivered.

- **Use This Option to Decide How to Respond to Request for Read Receipts:**
By default, Outlook selects the Ask Me Before Sending a Response option
button so you always have the choice whether or not to send a read receipt
back to the sender. Select the Always Send a Response option button to
have Outlook automatically send back a read receipt requested for any
message you receive. Select the Never Send a Response option to automatically prevent the program from ever sending a read receipt requested for
any message you receive.

Chapter 10

Using Calendar to Keep Yourself on Schedule

*T*he Calendar module in Outlook provides one of the most important means of attaining peak personal productivity and maintaining it in your pursuit of work/life balance. Because the Calendar module in both version 2003 and version 2007 adds basic task management to appointment and meeting scheduling, this module makes the perfect home base from which you can conduct all your Outlook business.

In this chapter, you discover the basic strategies and techniques for using the Calendar module to schedule all your appointments and meetings as well as keep on top of the tasks you need to accomplish on a given day. I hope that during this discovery process you not only become super comfortable using the Calendar's many wonderful features but also find the Calendar the most natural place from which to use Outlook as a full-fledged personal information manager.

Keeping Up with the Calendar Module

Although Outlook's Calendar module comes after the Mail module as far as using Outlook as your personal information manager, you can easily make it number one. This is because the Calendar module can provide you with a quick view not only of your daily, weekly, or monthly task list but also of the tasks currently on your to-do list.

Figure 10-1 shows the Calendar module as it typically appears in Outlook 2003. In the 2003 version, the program window is divided into the following three areas:

✔ **Navigation Pane:** This pane is divided into the following four sections:

Shortcuts: Here you'll find your My Calendars options, which enable you to hide and display the different Outlook calendars you keep.

Current View: The options here enable you to select a new view for the appointments and meetings scheduled on the current calendar, depending on how you've chosen the dates to be displayed.

Links: Click a link to open a shared calendar or customize the current Calendar view.

Navigation buttons: The buttons here enable you to select a new Outlook module.

✔ **Information Viewer:** This pane typically displays the appointments and meetings that are scheduled on your daily, weekly, or monthly calendar.

TaskPad: This pane is divided in the following two sections:

Date Navigator: Lets you select a new day, week, or month to display in the Information Viewer, depending on how you've chosen the dates to be displayed.

TaskPad: Displays the tasks currently on your to-do list.

Outlook 2007, as shown in Figure 10-2, has a slightly different look, with its replacement of the TaskPad with the To-Do Bar. In the 2007 version, the program window is divided into the same three areas, with these variations:

✔ **Navigation Pane:** This pane is divided into following three sections:

Groups: This section automatically includes the My Calendars familiar to you from Outlook 2003, but it also includes People's Calendars (where you can hide and display calendar snapshots other people send you by e-mail) as well as Other Calendars (where you can hide and display the Internet calendars to which you subscribe).

Links: Click the links here to display Internet help information on sharing calendars, find Internet calendars, send calendar snapshots by e-mail, publish a calendar to Office Online, and add a new group.

Navigation buttons: The buttons here enable you to select a new Outlook module.

Current View

Taskpad

Shortcuts

Links

Date Navigator

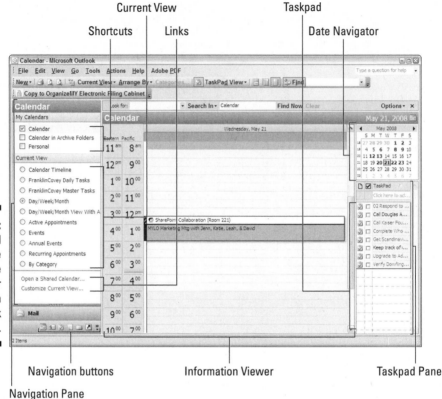

Figure 10-1:
Typical
appearance
of the
Calendar
module in
Outlook
2003.

Navigation buttons

Information Viewer

Taskpad Pane

Navigation Pane

✔ **Information Viewer:** This pane typically displays the appointments and meetings scheduled on your daily, weekly, or monthly calendar. It can also include the display of a Daily Task List subpane at the bottom, showing a list of the tasks that are overdue or have due dates corresponding to the dates displayed in the area immediately above it.

✔ **To-Do Bar:** This pane is divided into the following three sections:

Date Navigator: Use this section to select a new day, week, or month to display in the Information Viewer, depending on how you've chosen the dates to be displayed.

Appointments: In this section, the three most imminent appointments on your calendar are listed.

Task List: Here you'll find your to-do list tasks grouped by their due dates.

Shortcuts   Information Viewer   Appointments

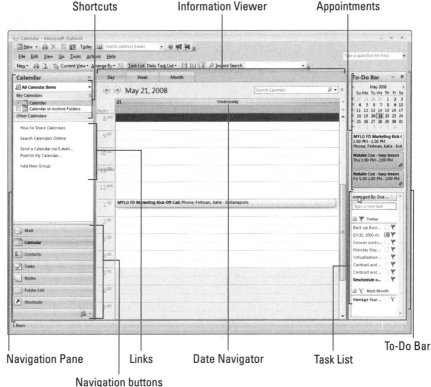

Figure 10-2:
Typical
appearance
of the
Calendar
module in
Outlook
2007.

Navigation Pane   Links   Date Navigator   Task List   To-Do Bar

Navigation buttons

Subscribing to and downloading Internet calendars

If you're now using Outlook 2007, you can easily download or subscribe to an Internet calendar (also known as an iCalendar, or iCal for short) to use in Outlook's Calendar module. You can even compare these Internet calendars side by side with any of the other regular Outlook calendars you maintain.

Keep in mind the difference between *downloading* and *subscribing* to an online calendar. When you download an Internet calendar, Outlook 2007 actually copies a Calendar Snapshot, in essence a static reproduction of the calendar with its current appointments and comments. When you subscribe to an Internet calendar, Outlook periodically refreshes the Calendar Snapshot it downloads, therefore keeping the iCalendar's information up-to-date. Note also that not all iCalendars that you download or subscribe to enable you to edit their contents. A few of these calendars are read-only, meaning that you can't add your own appointments and meetings to it.

When you start searching for them online, you'll find that there are all sorts of iCalendars available for use in Outlook. The most popular, of course, are those iCalendars that mark national holidays, the birthdays of famous people, or the anniversaries of significant historical events.

Downloading and subscribing to Internet calendars in Outlook 2007

The process for downloading or subscribing to an iCalendar from Outlook 2007 is a very straightforward one:

1. **Launch Outlook as you normally do and then, if necessary, open the Calendar module (press Ctrl+2).**

2. **Click the Search Calendars Online link in the Links section of the Navigation Pane.**

   Outlook launches your default Web browser, which displays the Outlook Internet Calendars Home page (similar to the one shown in Figure 10-3).

Figure 10-3:
Searching for iCalendars for Outlook 2007 on the Outlook Internet Calendars Home page.

3. **Click the iCALShare.com hyperlink under the Find Free Internet Calendars heading in the middle of the Web page.**

   Your Web browser opens the iCalShare – Share Your Calendars! Web page (similar to the one shown in Figure 10-4).

4. **Click the link for the category of the iCalendar you're interested in or enter keywords in the Search iCalShare text box and then click its Search button.**

   iCalShare displays a list (sometimes partial, if there's more than one page) of the iCalendars in the category you selected or that meet the search text you entered.

5. **(Optional) Click the Preview Calendar hyperlink to display a sample month (corresponding to the current month) of the calendar you're potentially interested in using.**

   Your Web browser displays a sample of the events noted on the selected calendar for the current month and year.

   When you've found the iCalendar you want to use in Outlook 2007, you can either download it or subscribe to it.

Figure 10-4: Selecting an iCalendar to preview and download to Outlook 2007 on the iCalShare Web page.

6. **If you previewed the iCalendar, click your Web browser's Back button to return to the page with the description of the iCalendar you're interested in. Then, to download a static Calendar Snapshot for Outlook, click the iCalendar's Download Calendar hyperlink. To subscribe to the calendar so that its content is periodically updated in Outlook, click the Subscribe hyperlink instead.**

   If you click the Download Calendar hyperlink, Outlook opens the File Download dialog box asking whether you want to open or save the calendar file. After you click Open, if you're running Internet Explorer under Windows Vista, an Internet Explorer Security alert dialog box opens, where you click the Allow button.

   If you click the Subscribe hyperlink and you're running Internet Explorer under Windows Vista, an Internet Explorer Security alert dialog box opens, where you click the Allow button. After you click Allow, a Microsoft Office Outlook dialog box appears on top of the Outlook window, asking whether you want to add this Internet calendar to Outlook and subscribe to updates. Click the dialog box's Yes button.

   No matter which hyperlink route you follow, Outlook adds the name of the iCalendar you just downloaded or subscribed to under the Other Calendars in the Navigation Pane. The program also displays this iCalendar side by side with the Outlook calendar that's currently being displayed in the Calendar module.

7. **Switch over to your Web browser showing the iCalShare Web page and then exit the browser (Alt+F4).**

   Windows returns you to the Calendar module in Outlook 2007.

8. **(Optional) To display just one calendar in Outlook's Information Viewer, select the check box in front of the name of the calendar you want to hide in the Navigation Pane. To display a tab for each calendar you have open in Outlook that you can then click to have that calendar displayed on top of the others, click the View⇨View in Overlay Mode on the Outlook menu bar instead.**

   Overlay mode makes switching between any of the calendars open in Outlook 2007 easy. Keep in mind, however, that whatever calendar display you select for the calendar on top (Day, Week, Month, and so on) is also used to display any other open calendar that you bring to the top in the Information Viewer.

Bringing your Google calendar into Outlook 2007

If you're a Google enthusiast who maintains an online Google calendar, you can download your Google calendar into Outlook 2007. All you have to do to import your Google calendar is follow these steps:

1. **Launch Outlook 2007 and then launch your Web browser and use it to log on to your Google calendar.**

The fastest way to bring up Google is by clicking the Google button on your Google toolbar, if you have it displayed in your Web browser.

2. **If necessary, select from the pane on the left side of the Web page the name of the Google calendar whose snapshot you want to import into Outlook.**

   Doing so ensures that the correct dates and appointments are displayed in the Web browser.

   Next, you need to display details about the Google calendar you're viewing.

3. **Back in left pane of your Google calendar Web page, choose Calendar Settings from the drop-down list to the immediate right of the name of your Google calendar.**

   Google replaces your calendar display with a list of details about your Google calendar.

4. **Scroll down and then click the ICAL button in the Private Address section of your Google Calendar details.**

   Google displays a Calendar Address dialog box containing a hyperlink to the private URL address for your Google calendar.

5. **Click the hyperlink address in the Calendar Address dialog box.**

   Your Web browser displays a File Download dialog box asking whether you want to open or save the calendar file.

6. **Click the Open button in this dialog box.**

   If you're using Internet Explorer on Windows Vista, the Internet Explorer Security dialog box appears.

7. **Click the Allow button.**

   Windows runs a program that adds a Calendar Snapshot of your online Google Calendar to your copy of Outlook 2007.

8. **Click the OK button in the Calendar Address and then exit your Web browser before you switch to Outlook 2007.**

   When you return to the Outlook 2007 Calendar module, the Calendar Snapshot of your Google calendar appears in its Information Viewer side by side your current Outlook calendar, and the name of your Google calendar is now displayed under Other Calendars in the Calendar Navigation Pane.

Sometimes you may have to synchronize the changes you make to your Google calendar online in your Web browser with the changes that you made to a snapshot of it in Outlook. (A Calendar Snapshot of your Google calendar is not read-only, so you are free to modify its contents.)

Unfortunately, Outlook doesn't yet provide some sort of synchronize command to automatically update different snapshots of the same calendar. This means that you have to manually reconcile modifications you've made online with your Web browser with those you've made to an earlier version in Outlook.

To do this, you need to follow the previous sequence of steps and download another (more recent) snapshot of your Google calendar that has all the changes you made online. This more recent Calendar Snapshot automatically has a number appended to its calendar name, such as Gregory Harvey (1), to differentiate it from an earlier download named just plain old Gregory Harvey (containing all the updates you made in Outlook that are not reflected in the online latest Google version). After that, you follow these simple steps to reconcile the differences between the earlier and more recent Google Calendar Snapshots so that you end up with just a single Google calendar in Outlook 2007:

1. **Select the check boxes in front of the names of the earlier and more recent Google calendars — Gregory Harvey and Gregory Harvey (1) in my example — in the Outlook Calendar Navigation Pane.**

   Leave all other check boxes deselected. That way, only the two versions of your Google calendars are displayed side by side in the Outlook Information Viewer.

2. **Click the Month button above the calendar display in the Information Viewer.**

   Now the entire current month for both versions of your Google calendars are displayed side by side in the Outlook Information Viewer.

3. **Drag any appointments you've added to the more recent Calendar Snapshot you just downloaded — Gregory Harvey (1) in my example — and then drop them on the same dates in the Google calendar you've been using in Outlook for some time — Gregory Harvey in my example.**

   Note that if you see that you've deleted some appointments from the more recent Google calendar snapshot that still show up on your original Google calendar in Outlook, you can delete them by clicking them and then pressing the Delete key.

4. **If you've made any online changes to months ahead of the current one, click the Forward button with the right arrow in Outlook and then use the same procedure outlined in Step 3 to reconcile these changes.**

   After you've finished reconciling all the months where you made changes online that were not reflected in the original downloaded version in Outlook, you're ready to jettison the recent Google calendar snapshot.

5. **Right-click the name of the more recent Google calendar you just downloaded in the Navigation Pane — Gregory Harvey (1) in my example — and then click the Delete option on its shortcut menu — Delete "Gregory Harvey (1)" in my example.**

   Outlook displays a Microsoft Office Outlook alert dialog box asking you to confirm the deletion.

6. **Click the Yes button in the alert dialog box.**

   Outlook deletes the more recent Google calendar snapshot, leaving only the originally downloaded version of your Google calendar that now reflects all the changes you made to it online. In my example, the Gregory Harvey (1) version disappears, leaving only the reconciled and updated Gregory Harvey Google calendar displayed in Outlook 2007.

Navigating your Outlook calendars with the greatest of ease

To achieve peak productivity using the Calendar module (especially if you make it your Outlook home base), you surely need to know how to work with and display different calendars as well as move easily between the components in the Calendar module. You also need to know how to quickly modify the date display in the Outlook Information Viewer when you select a Calendar View that displays dates graphically.

Adding new calendars and displaying them

Many Outlook users maintain at least two calendars: one to keep track of their business appointments and meetings and another to keep track of all their personal appointments and meetings. Some even try to maintain more than just a business and personal calendar, adding calendars that track special events or occasions such as the iCalendars discussed earlier.

Just because you *can* maintain multiple calendars in Outlook doesn't mean doing so is a particularly good idea, especially from the personal productivity point of view. Although keeping your personal appointments separate from business may make your workday appear less hectic, it can also mean — if you're still using Outlook 2003 — that you may miss a dental or doctor's appointment or double-book a business meeting with your child's soccer championship game. (Fortunately, if you're using Outlook 2007, this version automatically shows the appointments you may schedule on any one calendar on *all* the calendars you maintain, thus preventing just this kind of thing.)

Therefore, my advice (especially if you're still using Outlook 2003) is to keep a single Outlook calendar accessible either from home or office that tracks all your business and personal appointments and events. If doing this contradicts company policy (some managers don't want to see personal appointments showing up on company time) or if it's way too disheartening to see all those activities lined up one after the other in a single day, by all means maintain a separate business and personal calendar. However, in that case, you simply must know how to compare them side by side (as described in this section) to prevent any double-booking or missing out on important appointments or events that show up on one calendar but not the other.

Assuming that you're already using the default calendar (simply called Calendar) that Outlook automatically creates for you as your business calendar, here are the steps for creating a new, personal calendar and then displaying it side by side with your original business calendar:

1. **Launch Outlook as you normally do and then, if necessary, select the Calendar module (press Ctrl+2) before you press Ctrl+Shift+E.**

   Outlook opens the Create New Folder dialog box, similar to the one shown in Figure 10-5, with the Calendar folder already selected.

2. **Type the name you want to give your new personal calendar (such as Personal) in the Name text box and then click OK or press Enter.**

   Outlook adds the name of your new personal calendar to the list of calendars in the My Calendars section at the top of the Calendar Navigation Pane.

Figure 10-5: Creating a Personal calendar in the Create New Folder dialog box.

3. **In the Navigator Pane, select the check box in front of the name of the new personal calendar just added to the My Calendars section.**

   Outlook displays your new personal calendar side by side to the right of your default (business calendar) in the Information Viewer, as shown in Figure 10-6. Note that Outlook applies the same Day, Week, or Month date display to both calendars as was originally used to display the appointments and events on the sole business calendar in the Information Viewer.

I strongly suggest that after you create a personal calendar in Outlook 2003 to go with your original business calendar, you keep both of them displayed in this manner most of the time when using the Outlook Calendar module. Keeping both calendars displayed helps keep you from missing appointments that show up only on whatever calendar is hidden. It also helps you avoid creating conflicts when booking appointments and gives you an overview of what part of your day, week, and month is devoted to business rather than personal activities. This overview can actually end up helping in your ongoing endeavors to better balance your personal and professional lives.

If you're using Outlook 2007, you can overlay your business and personal calendars one on top of the other rather than have to always display their daily, weekly, or monthly contents (at a much smaller size) side by side. To overlay these calendars, click the View in Overlay Mode button (the one with the left-pointing arrow) on the tab of the right calendar or choose View➪View in Overlay Mode from the Outlook menu bar when the two calendars are already displayed side by side in the Information Viewer.

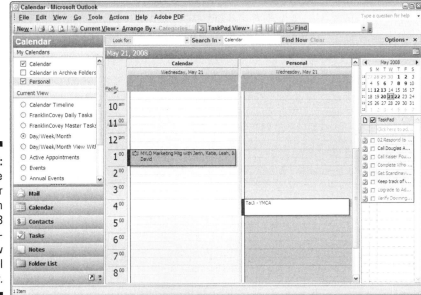

Figure 10-6: The Calendar module in Outlook 2003 after creating a new Personal calendar.

In Overlay mode, Outlook then displays both Calendar and Personal tabs that you can click to immediately display whichever calendar is currently hidden by bringing it to the top. If you later find that you need to compare a particular day or part of the day in each calendar, you can switch back to the side-by-side display by clicking the View in Side-by-Side button (with the right-pointing arrow) on the tab of either calendar or by choosing View⇨View in Side-by-Side Mode from the Outlook menu bar.

Using the Date Navigator to select different dates to display

Outlook automatically displays the Date Navigator (that miniature monthly calendar with current month and year displayed on its title bar) at the top of the TaskPad in Outlook 2003 or the To-Do Bar in Outlook 2007. Whenever you hide the TaskPad (choose View⇨TaskPad) or the To-Do Bar (choose View⇨To-Do Bar⇨Off or press Alt+F2), the program automatically displays the Date Navigator at the top of Navigation Pane (assuming that this pane is not also hidden).

As its name implies, you use the Date Navigator to select the different dates you want displayed in the Calendar module's Information Viewer when using a Calendar View that displays dates as days, weeks, or months.

Keep in mind that when you select a Calendar view in Outlook 2003 that doesn't display dates in the Information Viewer — the By Category view, for example, or Active Appointments — Outlook removes the Date Navigator from the window. (Outlook doesn't move the Date Navigator to the top of the Navigation Pane as it normally does when you close the TaskPad.) In Outlook 2007, the Date Navigator continues to appear at the top of the To-Do Bar as long as you don't close this pane by clicking its Close button.

To display a new date in the Information Viewer, you simply click it in the Date Navigator. To display multiple consecutive dates, drag through them in the Date Navigator.

If the date or dates you want to select aren't currently visible in the Date Navigator, you first need to select their month and year. You can do this by clicking the Forward or Back buttons that appear at the left and right edges of the Date Navigator title bar as needed.

If the month containing the date(s) you want to select is either three months before or after the month currently displayed in the Date Navigator, you can display it by clicking the current name of the month and year (such as May 2009) in the Date Navigator title bar. Doing so displays a pop-up menu with the names of the three previous months (April 2009, March 2009, and February 2009) listed above the current one on the menu and the names of the next three months (June 2009, July 2009, and August 2009) listed below. All you then have to do is click the name of the month and year you want displayed in the Date Navigator.

Note that as soon as you click a date in the Date Navigator, Outlook displays only that day, showing the times of all the appointments and events you've scheduled in the Information Viewer. So, for example, if Day/Week/Month with AutoPreview is the current Calendar view and Work Week the current date display and you click a date in the Date Navigator, Outlook immediately switches to the Day date display in the Information Viewer.

Typically, the Date Navigator displays the days and weeks for a single month — normally the current one — in the Outlook TaskPad (2003) or To-Do Bar (2007). If you can afford to give up screen real estate in the Information Viewer, you can expand the Date Navigator display to include two months (normally the current month and the one after). All you have to do is widen the TaskPad or To-Do Bar sufficiently to accommodate this two-month display by dragging the border between the Information Viewer and TaskPad/To-Do Bar to the left. This new arrangement not only makes it a snap to select dates in the current and upcoming month but also makes reading the list of tasks that appears in the pane on the right a great deal easier.

Switching the date display

In keeping with my Master Your Productivity Tools strategy, to be fully capable using the Outlook Calendar module, you need to know how to instantly switch from one date display to another in the Information Viewer. Table 10-1 gives you all the major shortcut keystrokes for quickly changing the date display in Outlook.

Table 10-1	Shortcut Keys for Changing the Calendar Display
Press This	*To Display*
Alt+1 through 9	The number of days equal to the number you type (Alt+1 displays the current day, Alt+2 displays the current and next day, Alt+3 displays the current day and next two days, and so on.)
Alt+0	The next 10 days, including the current day
Alt+– (hyphen)	The current seven-day week
Alt+= (equal sign)	The current month
Ctrl+Alt+1	The current day (Outlook 2007 only)
Ctrl+Alt+2	The current work week (Outlook 2007 only)
Ctrl+Alt+3	The current seven-day week (Outlook 2007 only)
Ctrl+Alt+4	The current month (Outlook 2007 only)

Note that when it comes to displaying the current month in the Information Viewer in Outlook 2007, you have a choice between pressing Alt+= (equal sign) and Ctrl+Alt+4.

If you want to display the current work week in Outlook 2007, you can do so by pressing Ctrl+Alt+2 or clicking the Week button at the top of the calendar display and then making sure that the Show Work Week option button is selected. If you want to do this same thing in Outlook 2003, you have to choose View⇨Work Week from the Outlook menu bar.

Customizing the Calendar options

You may find yourself a lot happier and more productive in the Calendar module if you change a few of its default settings. To make changes to the calendar defaults, you need to open the Calendar Options dialog box (similar to the one shown in Figure 10-7). To open this dialog box, simply choose Tools⇨Options from the Outlook menu bar and then click the Calendar Options button located in the Calendar section.

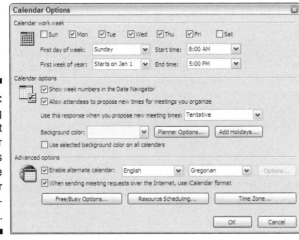

Figure 10-7: Modifying the default calendar settings in the Calendar Options dialog box.

As you can see in Figure 10-7, the calendar default settings are presented in three groups: Calendar Work Week, Calendar Options, and Advanced Options. You use the Calendar Work Week options to change the days that make up your work week or the day that begins a work week as well as to modify the start and end time of your workday. (If it were only as simple as 8 a.m. to 5 p.m.!)

You use the Calendar Options group to change a wide array of calendar options, including assigning a background color to your calendars (for the borders) and adding national holidays. (Outlook automatically adds the holidays celebrated in the United States of America to its calendars.)

You use the Advanced Options group to make such changes as enabling alternate calendars for different nationalities (such as Japanese or Chinese) and systems (such as the Hebrew lunar calendar) and changing the time zone used by your calendars or to add an additional time zone to them.

If you deal with people in an office in a different time zone with whom you routinely schedule appointments on your calendar, you may want to use the Advanced Option group's Time Zone button to add their time zone to your calendars. That way, when you schedule a telephone call or other online meeting, your calendar synchronizes the times by showing their alternate time zone to the immediate left of your local time zone in the Calendar Information Viewer when you select either the Day or Work Week display in Outlook 2003 or the Day, Work Week, or Week display in Outlook 2007.

For example, because I have so many meetings with people in the Eastern Time zone, I went ahead and added it as the alternate time zone to my calendar. Figure 10-8 shows you the results. Here, you see my calendar in Day display that now shows the Eastern time zone in a column to the immediate left of my local Pacific time. Note that I could easily modify this display so that the Pacific time appears in the column to the immediate left of the Eastern time zone simply by clicking the Swap Time Zones button in the Time Zone dialog box (opened by clicking the Time Zone button in the Calendar Options dialog box).

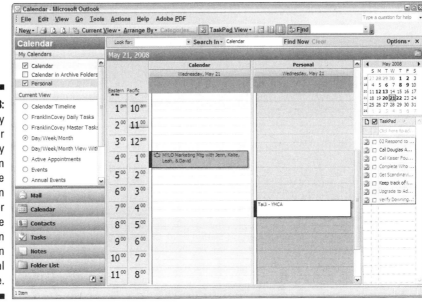

Figure 10-8: My Calendar in the Day display in the Information Viewer after adding the Eastern Time as an additional time zone.

Adopting a New Calendar View

As with the other Outlook modules, the Calendar program offers a number of different ways to view the appointment and event information you maintain in your calendars. By default, Outlook adopts a Day/Week/Month view for the Calendar module that depicts this information on a daily, weekly, or monthly calendar (as you'd typically enter it in a standard paper day planner). In addition, you have a choice between a variety of different predefined Calendar views, including a Day/Week/Monthly view with AutoPreview (that displays details for a selected appointment in a pane at the bottom of the Information Viewer) and an Active Appointments and All Appointments view that lists only upcoming appointments on your calendar or all the appointments (including past ones).

Keep in mind that you can also customize any of the predefined Calendar views as well as create new ones of your own design (following the same general procedure you would for customizing and creating new views for the Mail module, as outlined in Chapter 6). For example, you might want to create a new custom view — named something like Calendar Timeline view — which would use the Timeline type of view (one of the types of views that's not predefined) that presents your appointment and meetings on a daily, weekly, or monthly timeline (depending on the date display you select).

All About Scheduling Appointments and Events

The whole point of the Outlook calendar is to keep track of the time-bound obligations that you have. In Outlook, these kinds of obligations fall into one of three distinct types:

- ✔ **Appointment:** An activity normally involving you and one other participant that's scheduled at a particular time and often for a particular period of time but whose scheduling does not involve directly coordinating with the other participant's calendar and getting his or her agreement by e-mail.

- ✔ **Event:** An all-day occurrence that may or may not affect other workday activities you would otherwise try to accomplish that day. For example, the celebration of your spouse's birthday would not normally affect your workday in the same way as the celebration of a national holiday.

- ✔ **Meeting:** An activity normally involving you and multiple other participants that's scheduled at a particular time and often for a particular period of time, and whose scheduling very often involves coordinating with the other participants' calendars and getting their agreement by e-mail.

The practical repercussions of these distinctions are rather straightforward in Outlook. The procedure for adding a new appointment and an event to your calendar is identical except that when you specify an appointment, you also designate a particular start and end time, but when you schedule an event, you designate its duration as being all day.

When it comes to scheduling a new meeting, you send out e-mail invitations to all the participants that both inform them of the meeting's date and time as well as ask them confirm their ability and willingness to attend. If you're using Outlook with the Exchange Server, you can even check the other participants' Outlook calendars to determine those times when most are free so that you can figure out the best time for scheduling the meeting before you invite them to attend. Finally, if you're using Outlook with the Exchange Network, you can use Outlook to reserve available meeting resources (including physical meeting rooms and audio-visual equipment) and to set up an online Meeting Workspace, where you can store files containing all the supplementary material you want your participants to have beforehand, such as the meeting agenda and special informational handouts.

Scheduling one-time appointments and events

The process for putting a new appointment or event on your Outlook calendar is really quite simple:

1. **If the Calendar module is current, click the date of the new appointment in the Date Navigator and the hour of the appointment's start time in the Information Viewer before you press Ctrl+N. If the Calendar module is not current, press Ctrl+Shift+A instead.**

   If you're using Outlook 2003, the program opens the Untitled Appointment dialog box, similar to the one shown in Figure 10-9. If you're using Outlook 2007, the program opens a slightly different version of the Appointment dialog box, similar to the one shown in Figure 10-10.

2. **Type a short description of the appointment in the Subject text box.**

   Try to keep the appointment description as short as possible; otherwise, you won't have the foggiest idea of what appointment you have on a particular day when you switch your calendar display from Day to Week or Month.

3. **(Optional) Add the location of the appointment by clicking the Location text and then typing in a description of the locale or its actual address.**

   If you routinely schedule appointments in a particular spot, you may be able to enter the locale or address by choosing it from the drop-down list rather than having to type it into the text box all over again.

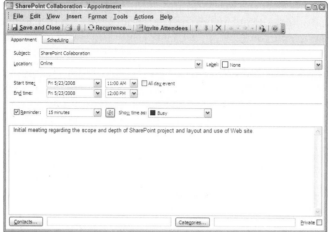

Figure 10-9:
Using the
Outlook 2003
Appoint-
ment
dialog box
to add
a new
appointment
to my
calendar.

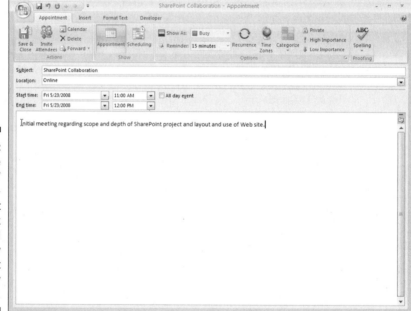

Figure 10-10:
Using the
Outlook 2007
Appoint-
ment
dialog box
to add
a new
appointment
to my
calendar.

4. **If necessary, modify the date and time of the appointment using the Start Time and End Time date and time combo boxes. If you're scheduling an event rather than an appointment, select the All Day Event check box instead.**

You can select the hour the appointment starts and ends in the Start combo boxes either by typing the 12-hour time (as in 3:30 p.m.) or 24-hour time (as in 15:30), or you can choose the hour (in half-hour increments) from the associated drop-down lists.

You can enter the start, or stop (or both) date for the appointment or event by typing the date number (6/6/09 or 6-6-09) in the appropriate date combo box or by clicking its drop-down button and then clicking the date on the drop-down Date Navigator.

Note that whenever you click the All Day Event check box, the combo boxes that record the starting and ending time are hidden, leaving only the date combo boxes visible in the Untitled Appointment dialog box.

 5. **(Optional) Click the list box in the bottom section of the Untitled Appointment dialog box and then type in a longer description of the appointment or note down any special information of which you need to be aware.**

Outlook automatically reminds you fifteen minutes before the start time of an appointment by displaying an alert dialog box and playing a default reminder sound. You can modify the reminder or remove it entirely.

 6. **(Optional) To reset the amount of time before the appointment that you're to be reminded, choose a different time from the Reminder drop-down list. To remove the reminder, select the Reminder check box in Outlook 2003 or choose None from the Reminder drop-down list in Outlook 2007. To reset the sound in Outlook 2003, click the Sound button or (in Outlook 2007) choose Sound from the Reminder drop-down list to open the Reminder Sound dialog box. There, you can select a new sound to play by entering its filename in the text box or mute any reminder sound by deselecting the Play the Sound check box before you click OK.**

Be default, Outlook automatically indicates the status of the time assigned to all new appointments as Busy and new events as Free on all copies of your calendar that you share with others (see the "Sharing Your Outlook 2007 Calendars" section that follows). Sometimes, you may need to change this default appointment or event status to something more appropriate, such as Out of the Office or Tentative.

 7. **(Optional) To change the status displayed for the new appointment or event on copies of the calendar you e-mail or share with others, click the Show Time As drop-down button (Outlook 2003) or the Show As drop-down button (Outlook 2007) and select the new status (Free, Tentative, Busy, or Out of Office) from its drop-down list.**

If the appointment or event falls into a category that you may later need to use to filter the engagements listed on your calendar, you may want to assign it to various categories.

8. **(Optional) To assign an existing category to the new appointment or event in Outlook 2003, click the Categories button at the bottom of the Untitled Appointment dialog box and then select the check boxes in the Categories dialog box that appears for all the categories you want to assign before you click OK. In Outlook 2007, click the Categorize button in the Ribbon and, in the new dialog box that appears, click the name and color of each appropriate category from its drop-down list.**

   Be default, Outlook shows any appointment, event, or meeting that you add to your calendar whenever you share that calendar with others. If you need to protect privacy by omitting a particular engagement from shared calendars, be sure to perform the following step.

9. **(Optional) To mark a new appointment or event as private to hide it on shared calendars in Outlook 2003, select the Private check box. In Outlook 2007, click the Private button in the Ribbon.**

   For some of the new appointments and events you put on your calendar, you may want to have instant access to the person's or company's contact information, just in case you need to look up the physical address or telephone number.

10. **(Optional) To insert the contact information for a person or company into the new appointment or event in Outlook 2003, click the Contacts button at the bottom of the Untitled Appointment dialog box and then click the name of the contact to add in the Select Contacts dialog box before you click OK. In Outlook 2007, click the Insert tab and then click the Attach Item button to open the Insert Item dialog box. There, click the Contacts folder in the Look In list box and click the name of the contact in the Items list box before you click OK.**

    Note that after inserting contact information in an appointment or event, you can display this information by opening the engagement in the Calendar Information Viewer and then clicking its contact link in Outlook 2003 in the Appointment dialog box or double-clicking the business card icon in the Event dialog box in Outlook 2007.

    Now you're ready to save your new appointment or event and add it to your calendar.

11. **Click the Save and Close button.**

    Outlook closes the Appointment or Event dialog box, and the engagement now appears on the calendar in the Calendar Information Viewer.

After you add an appointment or event to your calendar, a block covering the hours of the appointment and showing as much of the text of the subject that can appear in the current Day/Week/Month display appears in the Information Viewer (assuming that the Calendar module is in a view that uses a Day/Week/Month calendar display). In addition, the number corresponding to the date appears in boldface type in the Date Navigator.

Note that when you add an all-day event to your calendar, the text of the subject of that event appears at the top of the Information Viewer when it's in Day display mode.

Scheduling recurring appointments and events

Some of the appointments and events that you schedule on your calendar are not one-time affairs. For example, you may be adding an appointment that's just the first of a series of weekly or monthly engagements. In such a case, rather than spend your valuable time copying the first occurrence of the new appointment or event to the other pertinent days of the calendar in the Information Viewer, you can get Outlook to do all that for you simply by indicating that the appointment or event is a recurring one.

To indicate a recurring event, you follow the same steps I outline in the previous section for creating the first instance of the appointment or event and then, before you click the Save and Close button, you click the Recurrence button. Doing so opens the Appointment Recurrence dialog box, similar to the one shown in Figure 10-11.

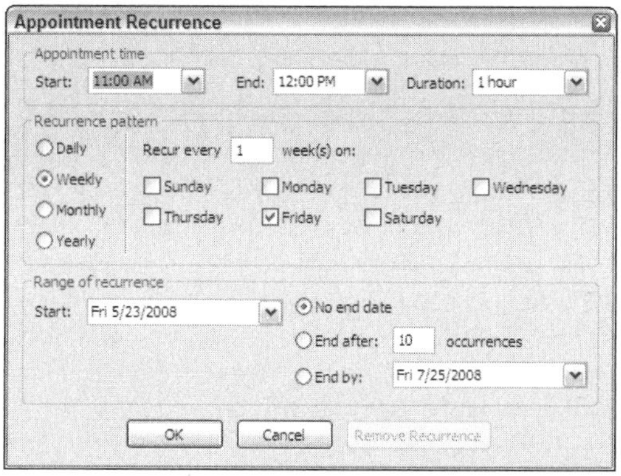

Figure 10-11: Using the Appointment Recurrence dialog box to indicate the recurrence pattern and end time for a recurring appointment.

When setting up a recurring appointment, you first need to click the appropriate Recurrence Pattern option button (Daily, Weekly, Monthly, or Yearly). Depending on which option button you choose, you have other option buttons and check box settings that you can change (such as whether a Weekly recurring appointment is every week, every second week, and so forth on the

same or a different weekday). Then, after you specify the Recurrence Pattern settings, you may still have to modify the end date or the number of occurrences in the Range of Recurrence settings before you click OK.

After you select OK and close the Appointment Recurrence dialog box, Outlook automatically adds as many appointments or events to the upcoming days, weeks, and months of your calendar as required by the settings you specified.

To later edit the settings of a recurring appointment, double-click the single occurrence on the calendar display in the Information Viewer that needs changing or any occurrence if they all require some modification. Outlook then opens an Open Recurring Item dialog box that enables you to choose between editing just the one occurrence or the entire series. To modify only the occurrence you selected, make sure that the Open This Occurrence option button is selected when you click OK. To edit the entire series, click the Open the Series option button before you click OK.

Note that the process for deleting a recurring appointment or event is very similar. When you press the Delete key after clicking a particular occurrence of a recurring appointment or event on the calendar display, Outlook opens the Confirm Delete dialog box, which enables you to choose between a Delete This Occurrence option button (to get rid of the single selected engagement) and a Delete The Series option button (to get rid of all appointments or events in the entire series).

Setting up a meeting and sending out meeting requests

The process for planning a new meeting and putting it on your Outlook calendar is very similar to that for adding a new appointment. The big difference comes at the time you set up the meeting's date, time, and location, when you have an opportunity to send out meeting requests that both inform all your potential meeting participants of the meeting's proposed date and time as well as seek their confirmation in attending.

The general steps for setting up a new meeting and sending out meeting requests to the potential participants are as follows:

1. **Launch Outlook as you normally do and then press Ctrl+Shift+Q.**

   Outlook 2003 opens an Untitled – Meeting dialog box with the Appointment tab selected, similar to the one shown in Figure 10-12. If you're using Outlook 2007, the program opens this dialog box with the Appointment button in the Show group selected on the Ribbon's Meeting tab.

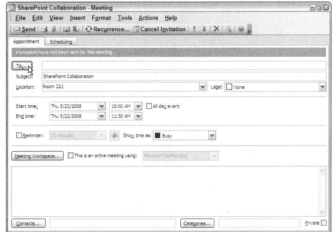

Figure 10-12:
Setting
up a new
meeting in
a Meeting
dialog box.

2. **Use the various fields to enter a descriptive meeting title along with the meeting's location, date, starting and ending times, and notes. If desired, specify what kind of meeting reminder to have Outlook display, just as you would do if you were specifying a new appointment for your calendar.**

   Now you're ready to send out meeting requests to all your potential meeting participants.

3. **Click the To button in the Untitled – Meeting dialog box.**

   Outlook opens a Select Attendees and Resources dialog box, similar to the one shown in Figure 10-13, where you specify the people you want to attend the meeting.

   Note that you can differentiate between those whose attendance is critical (by inserting their e-mail addresses in the Required text box) and those whose attendance is not mandatory (by inserting their e-mail addresses into the Optional text box). Step 4 shows you how.

4. **Ctrl+click each of the names of the mandatory attendees in the Name list box and then click the Required button to insert them into the Required text box. If you have any people you want to invite whose attendance is not mandatory, Ctrl+click their names in the list box and then click the Optional button to add them to the Optional text box before you click OK.**

   Outlook closes the Select Attendees and Resources dialog box, returning you to the Meeting dialog box, where the e-mail addresses of all the potential attendees you just selected appear in the To text box.

Figure 10-13:
Indicating
the required
and optional
attend-
ees and
resources
for the new
meeting in
the Select
Attendees
and
Resources
dialog box.

If you use Outlook with Microsoft Exchange server and your attendees
share their calendars on a free/busy server (see "Sharing Your Outlook
2007 Calendars," later in this chapter, for details), you can use the Untitled –
Meeting dialog box's Scheduling tab (in Outlook 2003) or the Scheduling
button (in Outlook 2007) to look for any conflicts and make any necessary
last-minute changes to the meeting date and time. Step 5 shows you how.

5. **(Optional) Click the Scheduling tab in Outlook 2003 or the Scheduling
   button in Outlook 2007.**

   The Scheduling tab (similar to the one shown in Figure 10-14) appears,
   indicating the busy times and times out of the office for each of the
   meeting attendees. Use this information to locate meeting conflicts
   and to make any necessary changes to the meeting date and starting
   and end times in the appropriate drop-down lists before you click the
   Appointment tab (2003) or button.

   Note that the Scheduling tab indicates the status of each of the attendees with the following icons:

   - *Magnifying glass* icon indicates the meeting organizer
   - *Upward-pointing arrow* icon indicates a required attendee
   - *Letter "I"* icon indicates an optional attendee

   The last thing you may need to do before e-mailing invitations to the
   attendees of your new meeting is to set up a Meeting Workspace, which
   is an online Web site (usually a Microsoft SharePoint site) where your
   participants find background information and materials they need for
   the meeting. Step 6 covers setting up a Meeting Workspace.

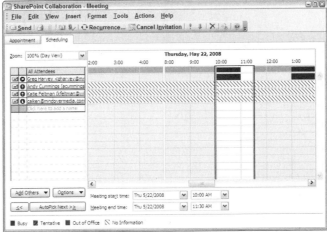

Figure 10-14:
Checking
the free and
busy times
of potential
meeting
attendees.

6. (Optional) To designate a Meeting Workspace that you've set up on your SharePoint Web site for the meeting, click the Meeting Workspace button to open the Meeting Workspace pane and then click its Create button.

7. (Optional) In the new pane that appears, choose an existing meeting location from the Select a Location drop-down menu.

   To select a new location, click the Other option on this drop-down menu and then enter the URL of the SharePoint Meeting Workspace in the Other Workspace Server dialog box before you click OK. You can then create a new workspace or select an existing one using the Select a Workspace drop-down menu before you click the OK button to close the Meeting Workspace pane.

Retaining meeting requests

As soon as you respond to an e-mail meeting request, Outlook automatically moves that e-mail message into the Deleted Items folder. If you prefer to retain the meeting requests you receive in your Inbox until you move them into the appropriate Inbox storage subfolders you've created, you can do so by following these steps:

1. Choose Tools➪Options to open the Options dialog box.

2. Click the E-Mail Options button in the Options dialog box.

3. Click the Advanced E-Mail Options button in the E-Mail Options dialog box.

4. Click the Delete Meeting Requests from Inbox when Responding check box to removes its check mark and then select OK three times to close all the open dialog boxes.

Now you're ready to invite your potential attendees to the meeting.

8. Click the Send button.

Outlook closes the Untitled – Meeting dialog box and e-mails meeting requests to each of your required and optional attendees.

Each of the potential attendees you added to the required and optional lists receives an e-mail message similar to the one shown in Figure 10-15. This message informs each attendee of the meeting date and time and contains a series of buttons in the Info Bar portion that gives him or her the option of responding in one of the following ways:

✔ **Accept:** Click this button to accept the meeting date and time without any change.

✔ **Tentative:** Click this button to tentatively accept the meeting date and time.

✔ **Decline:** Click this button to indicate that you can't attend the meeting at its scheduled date and time.

✔ **Propose New Time:** Click this button to open a Propose New Time dialog box, where you can select a new meeting date and time that you are able to attend and then propose it to the meeting organizer by clicking its Propose Time button.

Figure 10-15:
A typical
Meeting
Request
e-mail
asking you
to accept or
decline the
invitation or
to propose
a new
meeting
time.

When a potential attendee selects one of these options, Outlook sends you (as the meeting organizer) an e-mail with his or her response. Note that you can track the responses of the potential attendees you invited to the meeting. Simply double-click the meeting block on your calendar in the Information Viewer to reopen its Meeting dialog box, which now contains a Tracking tab (Outlook 2003) or a Tracking button (in the Show group in Outlook 2007). Click the Tracking tab or button to review the status of the response of each of the invited attendees.

Sharing Your Outlook 2007 Calendars

One of the best things about keeping your appointment schedule in an Outlook 2007 electronic calendar (as opposed to a paper day planner) is the ease with which you can share this information with other co-workers and clients who also need be informed of your daily, weekly, or even monthly activities.

The simplest way to share your Outlook 2007 calendar is to e-mail a copy of it. You can also publish it to the Internet and invite others to view it as a Web page.

E-mailing your calendar

To e-mail a copy of your calendar to a co-worker or client, follow these steps:

1. **Launch Outlook as you normally do and then make the Calendar module current, — if it's not already current — by pressing Ctrl+2.**

2. **Click the Send a Calendar via E-mail link in the Calendar Navigation Pane.**

   Outlook 2007 then opens a new message and displays the Send a Calendar via E-mail dialog box, similar to the one shown in Figure 10-16.

   By default, Outlook e-mails the default calendar named, appropriately enough, Calendar. You can, however, e-mail a copy of any other calendar you maintain in Outlook.

3. **(Optional) If you want to send a calendar other than the default Calendar, choose its name from the Calendar drop-down list.**

   By default, Outlook includes only the appointments and events that are scheduled for the current date on your calendar. You can, however, send any range of dates you wish, as Step 4 makes clear.

4. **(Optional) If you want more than just the current day's calendar information included in the e-mail, specify the dates you want included by choosing the appropriate option from the Date Range drop-down list: Tomorrow, Next 7 Days, Next 30 Days, or Whole Calendar. If you want to select another range of dates, click the Specify Dates option and then enter the beginning date in the Start combo box and the last date in the End combo box.**

    By default, Outlook e-mails only the availability information (Free, Busy, Tentative, and Out of the Office) for the hours on the dates specified by selecting the Availability Only option in the Detail section. You can, however, include the subjects of your calendar engagements with the availability information by selecting the Limited Details option or include full descriptions by selecting the Full Details option.

5. **(Optional) Choose the Limited Details option from the Details drop-down menu to display the subjects of your calendar engagements along with the availability information, or choose the Full Details option to display all the information about your calendar engagements, including availability.**

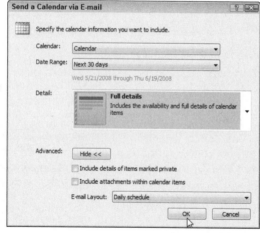

Figure 10-16:
Specifying
the calendar
and date
range to
send in a
new e-mail
message.

By default, Outlook shows engagements for all hours of the day on your calendar for the dates included. To limit the engagements to working hours only, perform Step 6.

6. **(Optional) To limit the engagements to working hours in the e-mailed calendar, select the Show Time Within My Working Hours Only check box. (If you need to check or reset your working hours, click the Set Working Hours link to open the Calendar Options dialog box, where you can modify the hours by editing the Start Time and/or End Time before you click OK.)**

   By default, Outlook e-mails your calendar using the Daily Schedule layout that includes the hours you're free as well as those when you're busy or out of the office. If you prefer to switch to the List of Events layout that displays a list without the free hours, follow Step 7.

7. **(Optional) Click the Show button in the Advanced section and then choose List of Events from the E-mail Layout drop-down list. If you've selected Limited Details rather than Availability Only as the Detail option (see Step 5), you can also click the Include Details of Items Marked Private to include all private engagements in the daily schedule or the list of events. If you have selected Full Details as the Detail option, you can also click the Include Attachments with Calendar Items to include any files that you may have attached to the appointment, event, or meeting to the new e-mail message.**

   Now you're ready to close the Send a Calendar via E-mail dialog box so that you can address and send the new message containing a copy of your calendar.

8. **Click the OK button.**

   Outlook closes the Select a Calendar via E-mail dialog box and adds the calendar information using the layout and level of detail you specified for the selected date range (see Figure 10-17) to the otherwise blank e-mail message.

9. **Fill out the e-mail header by selecting the e-mail address of the primary recipient(s) in the To text box and that of any secondary recipient(s) in the Cc text box. Make any modifications you deem necessary to the Subject text box and additions to the body of the message before you click the Send button.**

   Outlook e-mails the message to all your designated recipients containing the copy of your Outlook 2007 calendar.

Publishing your calendar to Microsoft Office Online

If you use Outlook 2007 with Microsoft Exchange Server, your free/busy schedule is automatically shared with the other users who have access to the server. If you want to share this type of calendar information with folks

who don't have access to the Exchange Server or don't use Outlook 2007 with Exchange Server, you can still share this info by publishing your calendar to Microsoft Office Online on the Internet (an Web-based, online extension of Microsoft Office software that offers you free workspaces where you can share items such as photos, documents, and calendars with others).

Publishing your calendar to Microsoft Office Online enables co-workers and clients who are not using Exchange Server to use your free/busy information to help them in scheduling meetings that you need to attend. This is because after you publish a calendar to Microsoft Office Online and grant people access to it, your free/busy information appears in their copies of Outlook. They can then use this information when they schedule a new meeting, thus potentially saving lots of time that would otherwise be spent in back-and-forth meeting requests trying to find a time when you're free to attend.

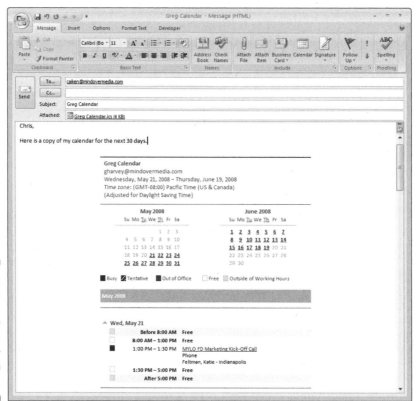

Figure 10-17:
New e-mail message with a copy of my calendar for the next 30 days.

The process of publishing your calendar to Microsoft Office Online is similar to sending your calendar to recipients via an e-mail message. (You even use a similar dialog box that enables you to specify the time span and type of detail to include.) The major difference is that you can allow anyone to search and view the calendar information (rather than keep it restricted to just those people you invite), and you can have Outlook periodically update the calendar information by automatically uploading new versions to the Microsoft Office Online Web site.

To publish your default Calendar to Microsoft Office Online, click the Publish My Calendar link in the Calendar Navigation Pane. (If you want to publish another calendar you maintain in Outlook, right-click the calendar in the Navigation Pane and then choose Publish to Internet⇨Publish to Office Online.) The first time you publish a calendar, you must log in to Microsoft Office Online using your Windows Live ID and password (which you get when you sign up for Microsoft Office Online by visiting http://office.microsoft.com).

Outlook then displays the Publish Calendar to Microsoft Office Online dialog box, similar to the one shown in Figure 10-18. Here, you use the various controls to specify the time span, level of detail, and permissions for your online calendar. Note that if you allow anyone to view and search for your published calendar, Outlook enables you to enter keywords that users can employ to find the calendar online in the Description list box.

Also, if you don't want Outlook to automatically upload updates to this calendar to Office Online and you want to include engagements marked private in the uploaded calendar, you need to click the Advanced button and then select the Single Upload: Update Will Not Be Uploaded option button and the Include Details of Items Marked Private check box before you click OK in Published Calendar Settings dialog box that appears.

Figure 10-18:
Publishing limited details from my calendar for the previous 30 days and next 60 days to Microsoft Office Online.

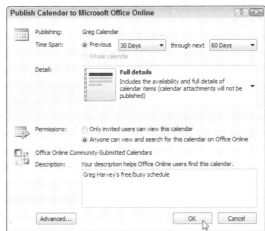

After you click OK in the Publish Calendar to Microsoft Office Online dialog box, Outlook publishes your calendar to a new Web page on Microsoft Online. If you restricted access to the published calendar to only those individuals you invite, you can then invite them to view your calendar by right-clicking the calendar you just published in the Navigation Pane and then choosing Publish to Internet⇨Share Published Calendar.

Outlook then opens a Share dialog box containing a new e-mail message with the subject line already filled in. All you have to do is select the e-mail recipient(s) in the To and Cc text boxes and then type any personalized text you want to add about your calendar in the body of the message before you click the Send button. Outlook mails this e-mail message to each of your recipients, and they can then click the message's Preview Calendar button (if they're using Outlook 2007) or paste the calendar's URL address into their Web browser's Address text box (Outlook 2003) to open your published calendar on its own Web page on the Microsoft Office Online Web site (see Figure 10-19).

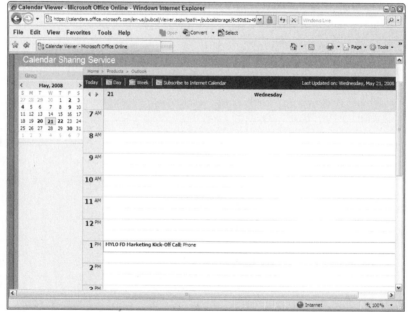

Figure 10-19:
Copy of my calendar published on its own Web page on the Microsoft Office Online site.

Chapter 11

Using Contacts to Stay in Touch

In This Chapter

▶ Efficient ways to add contacts to Outlook

▶ Organizing the contacts in your address book and creating new views for them

▶ Using your contacts to save time and be more productive

▶ Exporting your contacts for use with other applications

Although, the Contacts module comes third in the series of Outlook's major components, most folks treat this module as if it were number two on the list — right there behind Mail. Very few Outlook e-mail users are completely unfamiliar with its rudimentary features, and many use it to maintain their entire online address book.

In terms of personal productivity, the most important aspects of using the Contacts module include the ability to efficiently generate new records that store all the vital information you need about a new person or business, create new e-mail messages from existing contact records, and use views and categories to filter and sort your contacts list both for printing and exporting to other applications such as Microsoft Word for mail merge production. You can find all these aspects of using the Outlook Contacts module covered in this chapter.

Adding New Contacts Like a Pro

Outlook makes it a snap to add a new contact to your address book. If you're in the Contacts module, you simply press Ctrl+N to open an Untitled – Contact dialog box (similar to the one shown in Figure 11-1). If you're in any other Outlook module, you press Ctrl+Shift+C to open this same dialog box.

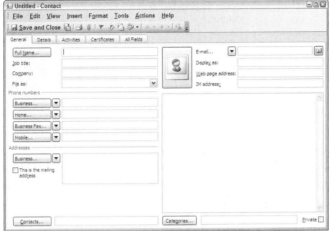

Figure 11-1:
Adding basic information for a new contact using the fields on the General tab of the Outlook 2003 Contact dialog box.

If you happen to be in the Mail module and have received a message from someone you need to add to the Contacts address book, you do this by right-clicking the name and e-mail address that appears at the top of the message in the Outlook Reading Pane and then choosing Add to Outlook Contacts from the shortcut menu. Outlook then opens a new Contact dialog box for the person — one that already has the Full Name, File As, E-Mail, and Display As fields filled in (using the selected name and e-mail address information).

If someone sends you an e-mail that contains his or her vCard (virtual business card — see Chapter 9 for more information), you can add a contact record for him or her with all the vCard information already filled in the appropriate fields. Simply double-click the name of the vCard attachment — it's the file with the .vcf extension — in the header area at top of the Outlook Reading Pane to call up the Open Mail Attachment dialog box. Click the dialog box's Open button to have the program open a new Contact dialog box with most of its fields filled in using the information on the vCard.

Note in Figure 11-1 that the Outlook 2003 Contact dialog box contains a series of tabs in addition to the default General tab. These additional tabs (which appear as buttons within the Show group on the Contact tab of the Outlook 2007 Ribbon) are Details, Activities, Certificates, and All Fields. Although most of the information you want to keep on your business and personal contacts is covered by the fields found on the General tab, for a few of your contacts you may want to use some of the fields found on the Details tab as well.

Figure 11-2 shows you the fields on the Details tab of the Outlook 2003 Contact dialog box. As you can see, the fields that appear on this tab include both business and personal details as well as online meeting information and an alternative, less-busy e-mail address to use.

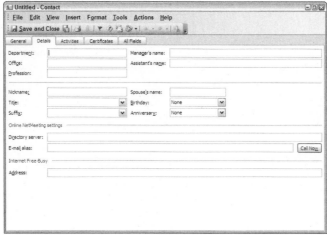

Figure 11-2:
Adding
more
information
about a new
contact
using
fields on
the Details
tab of the
Outlook 2003
Contacts
dialog box.

If you're adding a new record for a contact from the same company as someone who's already in your address book, you can save yourself from manually entering the company name, Web site address, basic business phone number, and business address by having Outlook 2007 use the existing record as the basis for a new one. To do this, first, open the existing record of the person in your address book with the same company information. Next, click the drop-down button on the Save & New button found in the Actions group on the Contact tab and then select New Contact From Same Company. Outlook then creates a new record for the company that you can personalize by entering the contact's name in the Full Name text box. As soon as you press Tab after entering the contact's name, Outlook replaces the company name with the person's name in the File As field, and you can then proceed to enter the person's e-mail address and edit his or her phone number before you save the record by clicking the Save & Close button.

Don't hesitate to assign categories to your new contacts right when you add them to your address book. A helpful division here would involve deciding whether a new contact belongs in the Business category or the Personal category. If you divide your contacts up right from the start, then whenever you select the By Category view in the Contacts module, Outlook automatically separates the business people from your friends and family. To add a new contact to the various categories that apply, open the record in the Contacts module by double-clicking it and then click the Categories button (in Outlook 2003) and select the check boxes for all the appropriate categories in the Available Categories list box before you click OK. In Outlook 2007, click Categorize button in the Options group of the Contact tab and then click the color of each category that applies.

Organizing Your Contacts

When you first begin working with Outlook's Contacts module, the program displays all the records for all contacts you add to your address book in alphabetical order using a card layout. (Address cards in Outlook 2003 are shown in Figure 11-3, and business cards in Outlook 2007 are shown in Figure 11-4.)

As with the other Outlook modules, you can easily switch the Contacts module from this default view into one of the other predefined views. In Outlook 2003, you do this either by clicking the option button in front of the name of the view in the Current View section of the Navigation Pane (Detailed Address Cards, Phone List, By Category, By Company, By Location, or By Follow-up Flag) or by choosing View⇨Arrange By⇨Current View from the menu bar and then clicking the name of the predefined view you want to use.

In Outlook 2007, you can switch views by clicking the option button in front of the view name in the Current View section of the Contacts Navigation Pane (Address Cards, Detailed Address Cards, Phone List, By Category, By Company, By Location, or Outlook Data Files). You can also switch views by choosing View⇨Current View from the menu bar and then clicking the name of the predefined view to apply.

Figure 11-3: Viewing the contacts in my Outlook 2003 address book in the default Address Cards view.

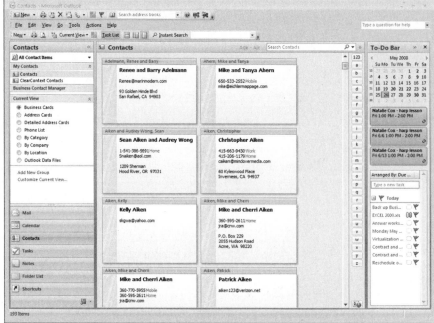

Figure 11-4:
Viewing the contacts in my Outlook 2007 address book in the default Business Cards view.

Eliminating duplicates in the contact records

Sometimes, despite your best efforts, you end up with duplicate records in your Outlook Contacts address book. Outlook does its best to prevent this by trying to alert when you're about to create a new record with the same name as an existing one, but sometimes those duplicates still sneak in there. (This has happened to me once when I merged records from an old address book kept on an old computer with a new address book I had just started on a new computer, and I forgot to prohibit duplicates during the importing.)

One of the quickest ways to locate duplicate records so that you can eliminate one of the copies is to make Phone List the current view in the Contacts module and then sort the contact records in the table alphabetically on either the Full Name or File As field.

Figure 11-5 illustrates how you might do this. For this figure, I first switched the view in my Contacts module to Phone List by clicking the Phone List option button in the Navigation Pane. Then, I clicked the Full Name column header one time to sort the table by first and then last name in reverse

alphabetical order (Z to A). I then noticed right away that somehow my address book has duplicate entries for Richard Redmond, one of which I can get rid of right away by clicking and then pressing the Delete.

Figure 11-5:
Finding
duplicate
contacts by
switching to
the Phone
List view
and then
sorting the
records in
descending
order
(Z to A)
by the Full
Name.

Then, after scrolling through the entire sorted Phone List and making sure that there are no other duplicates that I need to remove, I can return the list to regular alphabetical order (A to Z) by clicking the Full Name column header a second time before returning the Contacts module to its default Address Cards view by clicking the Address Cards option button.

Customizing the Contacts module's views

You can customize any of the Contacts module's predefined views or create new custom views for Contacts just as you can for any other Outlook module. To customize an existing view, make it current in the Contacts module before choosing View⇨Arrange By⇨Current View⇨Customize Current View from the Outlook 2003 menu bar (or View⇨Current View⇨Customize Current View from the Outlook 2007 menu bar). If you want to create an entirely new view for the Contacts module, you follow the same command path in Outlook 2003 and 2007 except that you click the Define Views option rather than Customize Current View on the final submenu.

If you're like me and you want to keep a phone list printout of your contacts that you *know* will print out on a minimum number of pages, you can create a custom view that displays just the fields you want printed in the order you want to see them. Since I consistently use the basic Business and Personal Contact categories in order to separate professional from personal contacts, I created two custom views for this job: Business Phone List and Personal Phone List.

The custom Business Phone List view uses a Table view type to display a list of records using only the following Contacts fields in this order: Icon, Flag Status, Full Name, Company, Business Phone, Business Fax, Mobile Phone, and Web Page. In addition, the business phone list is sorted alphabetically in A to Z order by the Full Name field and filtered with the Business category so that only business contacts appear in it (see Figure 11-6).

Figure 11-6:
The
Customize
View dialog
box for my
custom
Business
Phone list.

Customize View: Business Phone List		☒
Description		
Fields...	Icon, Flag Status, Full Name, Company, Business Phone, Bu...	
Group By...	None	
Sort...	Full Name (ascending)	
Filter...	Contacts: More Choices	
Other Settings...	Fonts and other Table View settings	
Automatic Formatting...	User defined fonts on each message	
Format Columns...	Specify the display formats for each field	
Reset Current View	OK Cancel	

To sort the custom Business Phone list in this manner, you click the Sort button in the Customize View dialog box and then, in the Sort dialog box that appears, select Full Name from the Sort Items By drop-down list as well as the Ascending option button. To filter this custom list, you click the Filter button in the Customize View dialog box and then, in the Filter dialog box that appears, click the More Choices tab where you select Business in the Categories drop-down list (assuming that you've set up a Business category and assigned it to particular business contacts in your address list).

The Personal Phone List custom view likewise is built upon the Table view type, but its records contain only the following Contact fields in this order: Icon, Flag Status, Full Name, Home Phone, Mobile Phone, Business Phone, IM Address, and Web Page. In addition, this phone list is sorted in the same way by the same Full Name field. However, in this view, the list of contact records is filtered with the Personal category rather than Business so that just my personal contacts are included. To filter this list in this manner, click the

Filter button in its Customize View dialog box and then, in the Filter dialog box that appears (see Figure 11-7), click the More Choices tab where you select Personal in the Categories drop-down list.

Then, when it comes time to print out a new phone list either for my professional and personal contacts, all I have to do is follow these few steps:

1. **In the Contacts module (Ctrl+3), click the Business Phone List or Personal Phone List option button (that are added automatically as soon as these custom views are created as described earlier) in the Navigation Pane.**

   Outlook makes the custom view you click the current one in the Contacts module.

2. **Choose File⇨Print Preview from the menu bar (or you can press Ctrl+F2 if you use Outlook 2003).**

   Outlook opens the Print Preview window (similar to the one shown in Figure 11-8), which shows the contact information that will print on the first page of the report. This window also shows you the total number of pages on the left side of the status bar.

3. **Press the Page Down key to check out the contents of each page of the report.**

   To print all the fields (columns) used in the Business Phone List across a single page of the report, you need to change the page setup so that Outlook prints the report using the Landscape orientation.

4. **Click the Page Setup button on the toolbar at the top of the Print Preview window.**

   Outlook opens the Page Setup: Table Style dialog box.

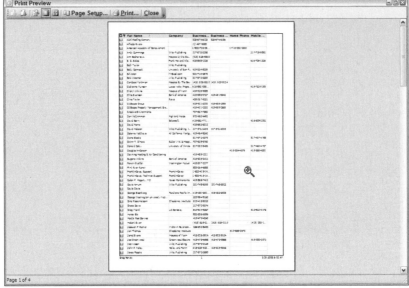

Figure 11-8:
Using Print
Preview to
check the
paging of
a phone
list report
before
printing it.

5. **Click the Paper tab and then click the Landscape option button before clicking OK.**

   The Print Preview window now shows the currently displayed report page in landscape mode with all the fields (columns) on a single page. In addition, the number of total pages displayed on the status bar decreases significantly.

6. **Click the Print button on the toolbar at the top of the Print Preview window.**

   Outlook closes the Print Preview window and then opens the Print dialog box.

7. **Adjust any print settings that need tweaking (printer, print range along with the number of pages and copies) and then click OK.**

   Outlook closes the Print dialog box and sends your report to the selected printer.

Adding contacts to a distribution list

Another thing you should know about organizing your contacts for maximum productivity is how to create and use a distribution list. A distribution list contains all the contacts that you routinely e-mail as a group. By creating a

distribution list with the names of all the people in the group, you save a lot of time when you either need to send an e-mail to everyone in the group or set up a meeting with them.

To create a new distribution list, follow these steps:

1. **Launch Outlook as you normally do and then press Ctrl+Shift+L.**

   Outlook opens the Untitled – Distribution List dialog box, similar to the one shown in Figure 11-9.

2. **Type in the name of the new distribution list in the Name text box.**

3. **Click the Select Members button.**

   Outlook opens the Select Members dialog box.

4. **Ctrl+click the names of the people in your address book that are part of the new distribution list and then click the Members button before you click OK.**

   All the names you selected in the Select Members dialog box now appear listed in the Distribution List dialog box.

5. **Click the Save and Close button.**

   Outlook closes the Distribution List dialog box and adds the new distribution list to your list of Contacts. (It appears under the name you assigned it and is identified with an icon of two heads in profile.)

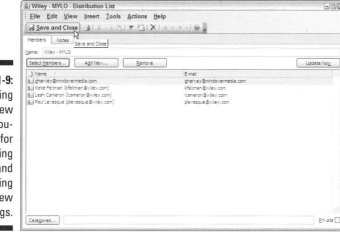

Figure 11-9: Creating a new distribution list for e-mailing and scheduling new meetings.

After you create a distribution list, you can use it to send a message or meeting requests (see Chapter 10) to all of its members. All you do is right-click the name of the distribution list in the Contacts Information Viewer and then, in Outlook 2003, choose either New Message to Contact or New Meeting Request to Contact from the shortcut menu and in Outlook 2007, choose Create from the shortcut menu and New Message to Contact or New Meeting Request to Contact from the continuation menu.

Outlook then opens either an Untitled Message or Untitled – Meeting dialog box with the name of the distribution list automatically entered in its To text box. You can then fill in the rest of the e-mail message or meeting request fields as required before you click the Send button to send the message or meeting requests to all the people listed as part of the distribution list.

If you don't need to send the e-mail message or meeting request to all the members in the distribution list, click the plus sign in front of the distribution list name in the Untitled Message or Untitled – Meeting dialog box (and OK in the Expand List alert dialog box) to expand the list so that the e-mail addresses of all the members appears in the To box. You can then delete the addresses of those members who don't need to have a copy of the message or meeting request before you click the Send button.

Putting Your Contacts to Good Use

You can put the contacts you keep in your address book to plenty of good uses. Here's a list of the more important contact-related things you can do to save time and make you as productive as possible in Outlook:

- **E-mailing:** One of the quickest and easiest ways to send a new e-mail message is by opening the record of the contact you want to e-mail (by typing some or all of the contact's name in the Find a Contact text box on the Standard toolbar and then pressing Enter). Then, click the New Message to Contact button on the Standard toolbar in the Contact dialog box in Outlook 2003 or the E-Mail button in Outlook 2007 to open a new e-mail message already addressed to that contact in the To text box.

- **Calling:** If your computer is set up to do automatic dialing, you can telephone a contact by pressing Ctrl+Shift+D (from any Outlook module) and then selecting the Contact in the New Call dialog box.

- **Web site browsing:** If you entered the URL address of your contact's Web site into the Web Page Address text box of the contact record, you can browse the Web site simply by clicking the contact in the Information Viewer of the Contacts module and then pressing Ctrl+Shift+X. (You don't have to open the contact's card.)

✔ **Mapping:** If you have to visit a new contact and need to see a map of his or her location, open his or her contact card in Outlook and then click the Display Map of Address button in Outlook 2003 or the Map button in Outlook 2007 (both use a road sign icon). Outlook then opens your Web browser and connects to the Live Search Maps page with your contact's address already displayed in the text box at the top of the page. All you have to do at that point to display a map of the address is to click the Search Maps button to the immediate right of the address text box.

✔ **Tracking activities:** To review the e-mail history or upcoming tasks or appointments with a particular contact, open his or her contact card and then click the Activities tab (Outlook 2003) or the Activities button (Outlook 2007). To restrict the list of activities to a particular arena such as e-mail messages, journal entries, notes, or upcoming tasks and appointments, choose the item to display from the Show combo box's drop-down list.

✔ **Flagging for follow-up:** You can easily flag a contact to remind yourself to do some sort of follow-up with him or her. Simply right-click the contact name and then choose Follow Up from the contextual menu that appears. In Outlook 2003, the program opens a Flag for Follow Up dialog box that enables you to select the type of flag (Follow Up, Call, Arrange Meeting, Send E-mail, or Send Letter) along with the due date and time before you click OK. In Outlook 2007, a continuation menu appears, on which you click the type of date flag to attach to the contact (Today, Tomorrow, This Week, Next Week, No Date, Custom, or Add Reminder).

Note that you can also assign the default flag to a selected contact in Outlook 2007 by pressing the Insert key and that, in Outlook 2007, after you flag a contact, his or her name appears in the Task List both in the To-Do Bar and Task module. (In Outlook 2003, the program merely adds a flag icon to the contact name in the Contacts module.)

✔ **Scheduling meetings:** You can save time when scheduling a new meeting and sending out meeting requests by first selecting all the participants in the Contacts module. Ctrl+click each contact name (this is often easiest when using the Phone List view) to select them and then drag the selected contacts and drop them on the Calendar Navigation button. Outlook then opens an Untitled – Meeting dialog box with the e-mail addresses of all the contacts you selected already entered into the To text box. (See Chapter 10 for more information on scheduling a meeting and sending out meeting requests.)

✔ **Assigning tasks:** You can assign a new task to a contact in your address book simply by clicking his or her name (Ctrl+click to select multiple contacts) in the Information Viewer of the Contacts module and then dragging and dropping it on the Tasks Navigation button. Outlook then opens a new Untitled – Task dialog box with the contact's e-mail address already listed in the To text box. (See Chapter 12 for details on assigning tasks.)

Exporting Contacts to Other Programs

Sometimes, you may want to use the contacts you keep in your Outlook
address book in other applications programs. For example, you might export
the contact list over to a Microsoft Excel workbook file so you can use Excel's
features to sort and filter its records (assuming that you're familiar with
Excel or have my *Excel 2003 For Dummies* or *Excel 2007 For Dummies* [both
published by Wiley] on hand — sorry, just couldn't resist the plug). You
can then use Excel as the data file in a mail-merge procedure conducted in
Microsoft Word.

To export the contacts in your address book to another file format for use
with another application program, follow these steps:

1. **Choose File⇨Import and Export from the Outlook menu bar.**

   Outlook opens the first dialog box of the Import and Export Wizard.

2. **Choose Export to a File from the Choose an Action to Perform list box
   and then click Next.**

   Outlook opens the Export to a File dialog box containing the Create a
   File of Type list box with all the file format choices you have when wanting to export a file. Click Microsoft Excel or Microsoft Access to export
   your contact data to a worksheet or data table that Excel or Access can
   open and work with. Click one of the other comma- or tab-separated file
   formats when exporting contacts for use with a DOS- or Windows-based
   application program that can read these file formats.

3. **Click the name of the type of file you want to create in the Create a
   File of Type list box and then click the Next button.**

   Outlook opens the first version of the Export to a File dialog box, this
   one containing the Select Folder to Export From list box. This list box
   contains a standard folder tree with a complete hierarchy of the Outlook
   folders and subfolders that mirrors the folder tree that appears in the
   Navigation Pane when the Folder List button is selected. This is where
   you select the folder whose data you want to export by clicking its
   folder icon where it appears in the hierarchy.

4. **Click the Contacts file icon in the folder hierarchy displayed in the
   Select Folder to Export From list box of the Export to a File dialog box
   and then click the Next button.**

   Outlook now opens a version of the Export to a File dialog box that contains
   just the Save Export File As text box. This text box is where you indicate the
   folder path and filename for the new data file before proceeding with the
   export.

5. **Click the Browse button to open the Browse dialog box: Use the Save In drop-down list to select a new folder and then enter a new filename (or modify the existing filename if one is automatically supplied for your type of data file) in the File Name text box.**

6. **Click OK to close the Browse dialog box.**

7. **Click the Next button in the Export to a File dialog box.**

   Outlook opens the Export to a File dialog box with a Following Actions Will Be Performed list box containing the command to export the contacts in your Contacts folder. Before clicking its Finish button to export your contacts, you can use the Map Custom Fields button in the following step to ensure that only data from the fields you want in the new file are used.

8. **(Optional) Click the Map Custom Fields button to open the Map Custom Fields dialog box. Click the Clear Map button to remove all entries from the To list box on the right and then drag all the fields in the From list box on the left and drop them into the To list box in the order in which they are to appear in the new export file. When you're finished, click OK to close the dialog box.**

   Now, you're ready to export your contact list to the new file.

9. **Click the Finish button in the Export to a File dialog box.**

   Outlook displays an Import and Export Progress dialog box, showing the program's progress in exporting your contact records to the new file. After this dialog box closes, you can then open the new file using an appropriate program.

Exporting your Outlook contacts list to another file format is no substitute for periodically backing up all your Outlook data as outlined in Chapter 8. If your computer experiences a catastrophic crash that affects the ability to read the data on your hard drive, chances are good that your exported contact list files won't be readable either. Of course, if you do keep a copy of the exported file stored on a different disk or backup media and you do ever need to restore your contact list in Outlook, you can do so by importing the file into the program.

Chapter 12

Using Tasks to Successfully Stay on Top of Your Obligations

In This Chapter

▶ Understanding when to put something onto your task list

▶ Tracking tasks in the Outlook 2003 TaskPad or the Outlook 2007 To-Do Bar

▶ Using the Tasks module to manage your workload and personal responsibilities

▶ Adding one-time and recurring tasks to your to-do list

▶ Keeping completed tasks from cluttering up your task list

▶ Assigning tasks to others to complete

*M*any experts in the field consider effective task management second only to organization in determining your success in achieving peak personal productivity. And while I don't have an opinion about whether task management is first or second in terms of importance, I'm clear that without effective task management, you have little hope of achieving the peak personal productivity and work/life balance you seek.

Therefore, this chapter covers best productivity strategies and practices for doing task management in Outlook. You manage your workload and personal responsibilities in Outlook through a judicious use of the Tasks module and the TaskPad in Outlook 2003 and To-Do Bar in Outlook 2007.

The Tasks module is the place where you keep and manage your complete to-do list. The task list that appears in the TaskPad in the Outlook 2003 Calendar module and the To-Do Bar in every Outlook 2007 module is designed to give you a quick look at pending tasks with upcoming due dates. Both the TaskPad and To-Do Bar show all overdue tasks in red and tasks with forthcoming due dates in black. The Outlook 2007 To-Do Bar even goes so far as to automatically group the tasks by due day into Today, This Week, Next Week, and Next Month groups.

To introduce you to this very important topic, I've broken the subject of task management with Outlook down into three simple components: the definition of a task, task management via the TaskPad or To-Do Bar, and task management via the Tasks module.

What Makes a Task So Special?

Before going on to find out about how Outlook helps you manage your tasks, you need to be clear about what sets a task apart from other Outlook items, especially appointments and events on your calendar. Simply put, a *task* represents some discrete action that you plan to get done that may entail a single step or a whole series of steps.

A task is similar to an appointment or event that you place on your Outlook calendar in that it's something you plan to get done by a particular date (and, sometimes, by a particular time).Therefore, you normally give a task both a planned start date and due date.

However, a task can differ significantly from an appointment or event on your calendar, especially when the task is sufficiently complex to warrant the charting of its progress during the period between the start and due date. For example, the task of preparing a final PowerPoint sales presentation for the monthly marketing meeting is an example of a complex task, one that may require several weeks of preparation and work.

Deciding whether a simple task belongs on your calendar or your task list

Deciding when to enter a simple task, such as telephoning a business colleague tomorrow at 11:00 a.m., as an appointment on your calendar rather than as a task on your tasks list is a personal one. Because Outlook enables you to assign both a date and time as well as a reminder to a task on your tasks list just as you can to an appointment on your calendar, it's really not so important where you put it (as long as you enter it somewhere in Outlook).

However, if you're the type of Outlook user who looks more to your daily calendar for direction than any other Outlook module, you may want to enter these types of simple time-bound tasks as appointments on your calendar. If the daily calendar is your go-to place for keeping a handle on things, then add such simple tasks as an appointment on your daily calendar because you're sure to get an immediate sense of the task's timing the moment you spot it, something that you don't get from seeing it displayed on the daily task list in the Outlook 2003 TaskPad or Outlook 2007 To-Do Bar.

During the period between your start date and due date, you may mark your overall progress on a complex task such as creating the sales slide presentation through a series of several milestones (for example, gathering sales information for the presentation, creating the initial presentation in PowerPoint, editing and formatting the design presentation, and checking the final presentation). Reaching the next milestone in the series then represents achieving a new level of progress in your goal of completing the task. (In an Outlook task, such levels are measured as percentages of completion, with 0% meaning that you've yet to begin the task and 100% meaning that you've completed the task.)

In my opinion, the question of whether or not to record the milestones for a complex task as individual tasks on your Outlook task list depends largely on how you how work best. If you find that you need periodic Outlook reminders to help you stay on course and reach your milestones, then by all means, enter each milestone as an individual task. On the other hand, if you find it sufficient to have just the overall due date staring you in the face, then instead of taking the time to record a bunch of simple tasks, stick with recording just the single, master task. In that case, however, just be sure to list your milestones as notes in the list box of this master task and to open the task in the Tasks module and update the % Complete setting whenever you reach a milestone.

Task Management with the Outlook 2003 TaskPad

The TaskPad automatically appears whenever you're in the Calendar module (Ctrl+2) of Outlook 2003. The Outlook TaskPad gives you a quick way both to enter new tasks and to track them.

Figure 12-1 shows the Calendar module in Outlook 2003. The TaskPad appears in the pane on the far-right side of the window, immediately beneath the Date Navigator.

The Outlook 2003 TaskPad itself is divided into three columns: Icon, Complete, and Subject. You click the task Icon in front of a listed task to select that task. You click its Complete check box to mark the task as completed (whereupon Outlook displays the entire task in strikeout text). And the Subject field displays as much of the task description as fits within the current width of the TaskPad (which you can increase by dragging the border between it and the Calendar Information Viewer to the left).

Complete   Subject

Icon   New Task

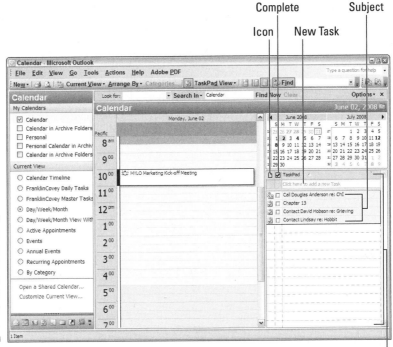

Figure 12-1:
The
TaskPad
in the
Outlook 2003
Calendar
module.

TaskPad

Keep in mind that, by default, the Outlook 2003 TaskPad displays all uncompleted tasks sorted by their due dates in ascending order (present to future). This means that you see overdue tasks first, followed by tasks with no due date. Then you see the tasks that have the current date as their due date (which just happened to be the due date automatically assigned to all new tasks you add in the TaskPad) followed by those with future due dates. To list the tasks in the TaskPad by due date in descending order (future to present), click the TaskPad subject header at the top of the third column. Outlook re-sorts the list in descending due date order, as indicated by the triangle now pointing downward instead of upward.

Adding a new task in the TaskPad

To add a new task on the TaskPad, you simply click in the Subject column in the top row immediately above the very first listed task. Basically, this means clicking anywhere in the area that contains the light gray text, "Click Here to Add to New Task."

As soon as you click in this area, the light gray text disappears, replaced by a flashing cursor. Outlook also adds a Complete check in front of the now empty text box. You then type a short description of the task in this text box and press Enter when you finish.

To help ensure that your task descriptions are brief and always to the point, make them into commands that begin with an active verb followed by a simple object, such as Call Dr. Bennett, Schedule appt with A. Smith, E-mail John, and Complete Q2 sales report.

After you press Enter, Outlook adds the new task to the TaskPad list. You can then later refine and update the details of the task, including specifying the start date and due date, adding notes, associating the task with a contact in your address book, assigning categories to the task, and logging your progress by opening the task's dialog box. To do this, you double-click either the task in the TaskPad in the Calendar module or the Information Viewer of the Tasks module or right-click the task in these locations and then choose Open from its shortcut menu.

Selecting a different TaskPad view

Outlook's View menu contains two command items related to the display of the TaskPad:

- ✔ **TaskPad:** Select this command to hide or redisplay the TaskPad. When the TaskPad is hidden, Outlook displays the Date Navigator at the top of the Navigation Pane.

- ✔ **TaskPad View:** Select this command to display a continuation menu with options for changing which tasks are displayed in the task list. The view options on this submenu include All Tasks, Today's Tasks (the default), Active Tasks for Selected Days, Tasks for the Next Seven Days, Overdue Tasks, Tasks Completed on Selected Days, and Include Tasks with No Due Date.

When you select the Active Tasks for Selected Days view, Outlook displays all incomplete tasks with due dates on or before the date selected in the Date Navigator. This means that the TaskPad shows you daily tasks when only the current date is selected in the Date Navigator, but it displays tasks with upcoming due dates when you select future days in the Date Navigator (by dragging through them). This particular TaskPad view, therefore, offers a highly effective means of controlling the contents of this task list as well as a quick-and-easy way to glance over future obligations without having to sort the list again in order to be able to select other options on the View menu.

Task Management with the Outlook 2007 To-Do Bar

Outlook 2007's To-Do Bar represents a significantly enhanced version of the TaskPad in Outlook 2003. As such, the To-Do Bar now appears in Outlook 2007 in every single module. This even includes the Tasks module, where the To-Do Bar's a bit of overkill and can usually be dispensed with no adverse effects (simply by pressing Alt+F2).

Figure 12-2 shows the To-Do Bar as it appears in Outlook 2007 when the Calendar module is current and the next three days are displayed in the Information Viewer of Calendar (after selecting them in the Date Navigator).

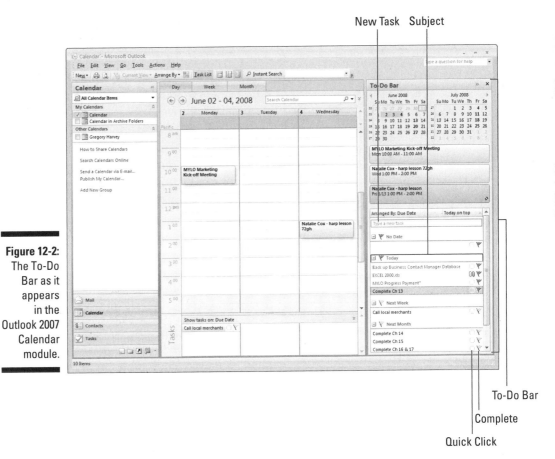

Figure 12-2:
The To-Do Bar as it appears in the Outlook 2007 Calendar module.

As you can see in this figure, Outlook 2007 automatically arranges the tasks (called to-do items) displayed in the tasks list at the bottom of the To-Do Bar into groups such as No Date, Today (which includes overdue tasks), This Week, Next Week, and Next Month, with the groups arranged by due date in ascending order (present to future). You can collapse any of these groups so that only the group heading is displayed by clicking its Collapse button (indicated by the minus sign) and then expand a contracted group to once again display all of its tasks by clicking the group's Expand button (indicated by the plus sign).

You should note that the to-do items in tasks list in the To-Do Bar are divided into three fields or columns: Subject, Quick Click, and Complete. The Subject field displays a short description of the task. The Quick Click field enables you to assign whatever category you've designated as the Quick Click category to a task simply by clicking (and then coloring) its empty rectangle. The Complete field shows the follow-up flag associated with the task's due date and enables you to mark a particular task on the list as completed simply by clicking its flag icon.

To add a new to-do item to the task list in the To-Do Bar, click the text box containing the light gray text, "Type a New Task." As soon as you click in this area, the light gray text disappears and is replaced by a flashing cursor in the now empty text box. You then type a short description of the task in this text box and then press Enter when finished.

After you press Enter, Outlook adds the new to-do item to the task list in the To-Do Bar as part of the Today group by automatically assigning the current date as both the start date and due date. You can then later modify and update the details of the task, including changing the start date and/or due date, adding notes, and recording your progress on the task by opening the task's dialog box. To do this, either double-click the task in the task list in the To-Do Bar or Tasks module or right-click the task and then choose Open from the top of the shortcut menu that appears.

Getting Productive with the Outlook Tasks Module

The Outlook Tasks module (Ctrl+4) is the place to go when you need a complete look at all your tasks, both those that you've already completed and those you've yet to complete. By default, the Tasks module displays all these tasks in your to-do list in a simple table layout, which is called, appropriately enough, Simple List. (If you aren't in Simple List view, choose View⟿

Current View⇨Simple List.) This layout contains fields (columns) for Icon, Complete, Subject, Due Date, and, in the case of Outlook 2007, Flag.

The great thing about the Tasks module is that, in addition to the Simple List view, the program offers a number of other useful ready-made views you can apply to the tasks in your to-do list. Just choose View⇨Current View and then pick a view. For example, you can switch to the Detail List view to add Priority, Attachments, Status, % Complete, and Categories fields to the Icon, Subject, and Due Date fields seen in the Simple List view.

And, when you need to see only the tasks on your to-do list that are currently overdue, you can do this simply by switching to the Overdue Tasks view. When you need to see just the tasks with due dates in the upcoming week, switch to the Next Seven Days list. And when you need to remind yourself just how far you've come in achieving peak productivity by getting on top of your obligations, you can switch to the Completed Tasks to see all the tasks that you've successfully completed!

Switch to the Task Timeline view to see your tasks represented graphically as bars extended over time (with the beginning of the bar representing the planned start date and the end of the bar the due date) against a scale of hours, weeks, or days (depending upon whether you select the Day, Week, or Month display on the View menu). This view is perfect for immediately spotting overlapping tasks that may represent conflicts in terms of your time and energy and ability to meet to their due dates.

Removing completed tasks from your task list

One of my pet peeves with the Outlook Tasks module is that its default Simple List view continues to show all tasks that I complete, albeit in strike-out text, along with the ones that are still pending. And although it makes me feel good, on the one hand, to see all the to-do items displayed in the Tasks module that I've gotten done, it does tend to distract me from the ones that still need doing.

Keep in mind that you can always temporarily filter the completed tasks out of the task list in the Tasks module by making Active Tasks the current Tasks module view (by clicking the Active Tasks option button in the Navigation Pane). That way, you're no longer thrown off course by the completed tasks and can concentrate solely on the tasks that are still pending.

If you'd rather not have to look at the completed tasks in the default Simple List view or other common views such as Detailed View, Next Seven Days, and By Category, you can easily round them up periodically using the Completed Tasks view and then move them to another folder for safekeeping. Here's how:

1. **Create a new, custom Completed Tasks folder. (Ctrl+Shift+E opens the Create a New Folder dialog box, which you can use to create this custom folder.)**

   The Completed Tasks folder can even be a subfolder of the Outlook Tasks folder, if you want.

2. **Select the Completed Tasks view in the Tasks module to filter out all active tasks and display only the completed ones.**

3. **Select all these tasks (Ctrl+A) before you right-click the highlighted block of tasks and then choose Move to Folder from its shortcut menu.**

4. **Make sure that your Completed Tasks custom folder is selected and then click OK in the Move Items dialog box.**

   Outlook moves all of the completed tasks into the Completed Tasks folder, leaving the current view of your Task module empty.

Then, to remove the filter and once again display your active tasks in the Tasks module, choose View⇨Current View and select another predefined view, such as Simple List, Detailed List, Next Seven Days, and so forth.

Adding a new task from any module

Outlook makes it really easy to add a new task. You can open an Untitled – Task dialog box (with the Task tab selected, similar to the one shown in Figure 12-3) from any Outlook module by pressing Ctrl+Shift+K. You can also quickly enter a new task as a to-do item in the task list portion of the Outlook 2003 TaskPad in the Calendar module or as a to-do item in the tasks list portion of the Outlook 2007 To-Do Bar in any module, as described in the "Task Management with the Outlook 2003 TaskPad" and "Task Management with the Outlook 2007 To-Do Bar" sections, earlier in the chapter.

When you enter a new task as a to-do item in the Click Here to Add a New Task text box in the TaskPad or in the Type a New Task text box in the To-Do Bar, you can enter only a short description of the task in the Subject field. (If you want to modify the start date and due date or enter other details or notes, you have to open its Task dialog box by double-clicking the task or right-clicking it and then choosing Open from its shortcut menu.)

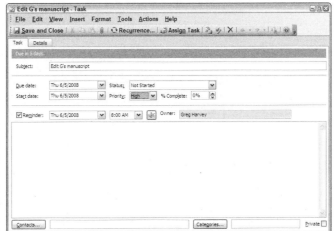

When, however, you enter a new task in the Untitled – Task dialog box, you can not only enter a longer description for the Subject field in its text box but fill in or modify any of the following fields:

- ✔ **Due Date:** Outlook doesn't automatically assign a due date to a new task entered into the Untitled – Task dialog box. To specify the due date for the new task, click the Due Date's drop-down button and then click the date in the drop-down Date Navigator. Note that if you try to specify a due date that comes before the start date you've assigned the task, Outlook displays an alert dialog box informing you of this fact, and when you click OK to close the alert dialog box, the program doesn't update the Due Date field.

- ✔ **Start Date:** Outlook doesn't automatically assign a start date to a new task entered into the Untitled – Task dialog box. To specify the start date for the new task, click the Start Date's drop-down button and then click the date in the version of the Date Navigator that drops down. Note that if you specify a start date without specifying a due date, Outlook assigns the same date to both the Due Date and Start Date fields. And if you specify a start date that comes after the due date you've assigned, Outlook automatically adjusts the date in the Due Date field so that it's the same as the one entered in the Start Date field.

- ✔ **Status:** Outlook assigns Not Started as the default status for a new task. To assign a different status to the task, click the Status drop-down button and then select the new status (In Progress, Completed, Waiting on Someone Else, or Deferred).

✔ **Priority:** Outlook assigns Normal as the default priority for a new task. To assign a different priority to the new task, select either Low or High from the Priority drop-down list.

✔ **% Complete:** When you create a new task, by default, Outlook considers it zero-percent complete. To indicate a different percentage rate of complete, type a number into the % Complete text box or use the upward-pointing spinner button to select a new percentage (25%, 50%, 75%, or 100%).

✔ **Reminder:** Outlook doesn't automatically alert you when a task is about to come due. To have Outlook display an alert dialog box reminding you of an impending task, click the Reminder check box and then select the date and time you want this alert displayed in its associated drop-down list boxes. To prevent a sound from being played when the reminder alert dialog box is displayed or to change the sound that's played, click the Reminder Sound button (the one with speaker icon) and then click the Play This Sound check box to mute the reminder or Browse to select a new alert sound using an existing sound file in a folder on your computer before you click OK.

✔ **Owner:** If you're the one to whom the Outlook program is licensed, then, by default, you're listed as the owner of each new task. To specify another user as the owner of the task (for whom any reminders should toll or to whom any task request responses should be sent), select your name in the Owner text box and then replace it by typing in the name of the new owner.

In addition to editing these fields on the Task tab, you can also enter notes into the list box that appears immediately below the row with the Reminder and Owner fields. And, in Outlook 2003, you can associate the task with particular contacts in your address book, assign categories to it, or mark it as private by using the Contacts or Categories button and Private check box that appear on the final row of the dialog box.

In Outlook 2007, you can add categories to a new task by clicking the Categorize button or make it private by clicking the Private button, both in the Options group. To add a contact to the list box of a new task, click the Insert tab and then click the Attach Item button to open the Insert Item dialog box. Then click the Contacts folder in the Look In list box and then click the name of the contact to add in the Items list box below before you click OK.

While the fields on the Task tab enable you to record basic information about the new task, the fields on the Details tab enable you to document your work on the task. Display these fields by clicking the Details tab in Outlook 2003 or the Details button in the Show group of the Task tab in Outlook 2007.

You can then use any of the following fields to document your work and progress on the new task:

- ✔ **Date Completed:** Select the date that you actually complete the task — especially when this date differs from the due date — by clicking the Date Completed drop-down button and then clicking the date on the Date Navigator that drops down.

- ✔ **Total Work:** Enter the total number of hours, days, or weeks you expect to work on the project. Type the units (hours, days, or weeks) after the value (as in 45 hours).

- ✔ **Actual Work:** Enter the number of hours, days, or weeks you worked on the project up to now using the same units (hours, days, or weeks) as you specified in the Total Work field.

- ✔ **Mileage:** Enter any driving mileage associated with completing the task — especially if this mileage is reimbursable or tax-deductible — in this text box.

- ✔ **Billing Information:** Enter any billing information, such as the hourly rate, the address of the company to bill, and the name of the person to whom you'll send the bill.

- ✔ **Companies (Company in Outlook 2007):** Enter the names and/or contact information of relevant companies (clients, suppliers, and so forth).

- ✔ **Update List:** When you assign a task to others (see "Assigning a task," later in this chapter), this text box displays your name and the names of any other people who received the task request.

- ✔ **Create Unassigned Copy:** Click this button to send a copy of the task to someone other than the person or people you've assigned it to (thus, this button remains unavailable as long as the Update List field is empty, indicating that no task request has been sent asking someone else to take it on).

After you click the Save and Close button in the Task dialog box (which is no longer the Untitled – Task dialog the moment you enter a task description in the Subject field text box), Outlook adds the task as an item to the task list on the TaskPad or To-Do Bar as well as to the to-do list in the Tasks module (depending upon the due date you specify).

Whenever you need to update a task or edit its settings, just open its Task dialog box again by double-clicking its to-do item in the TaskPad or To-Do Bar or Task Module or by right-clicking it and then choosing Open from its shortcut menu.

You can quickly create a new task from any other Outlook item (including an e-mail message, appointment, contact, or note) simply by selecting its module and then dragging the item to the Navigation pane and dropping it on the Tasks navigation button. Outlook then opens a new task dialog box containing the information in the Outlook item where you can fill in all the pertinent information as outlined in this section before clicking the Save and Close button to add it to your to-do items on your tasks list.

Specifying recurring tasks

Some of the tasks that you add to your to-do list in Outlook are repetitive in nature, reoccurring at set intervals (like turning in your mileage or sales receipts before the end of the month). When you record a task that you know is going to repeat at specific intervals, you can specify it as a recurring task. That way, you don't have to manually copy the task and adjust its due date for each subsequent occurrence.

To indicate that a task is recurring, open its Task dialog box and then click the Recurrence button located on the Standard toolbar in Outlook 2003 or in the Options group on the Task tab of the Ribbon in Outlook 2007. Outlook then opens a Task Recurrence dialog box similar to the one shown in Figure 12-4.

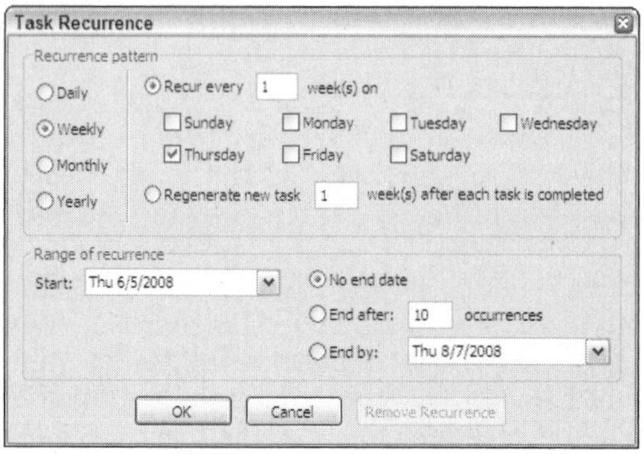

Figure 12-4: Specifying when and how often a task reoccurs in the Task Recurrence dialog box.

> **Task Recurrence**
>
> **Recurrence pattern**
> ○ Daily   ⊙ Recur every [1] week(s) on
> ⊙ Weekly   ☐ Sunday   ☐ Monday   ☐ Tuesday   ☐ Wednesday
> ○ Monthly   ☑ Thursday ☐ Friday   ☐ Saturday
> ○ Yearly   ○ Regenerate new task [1] week(s) after each task is completed
>
> **Range of recurrence**
> Start: [Thu 6/5/2008 ▾]   ⊙ No end date
>   ○ End after: [10] occurrences
>   ○ End by: [Thu 8/7/2008 ▾]
>
> [OK] [Cancel] [Remove Recurrence]

Here, you indicate the recurrence pattern by selecting the interval in the Recurrence Pattern section at the top (Daily, Weekly, Monthly, or Yearly). If the task naturally reoccurs at so many weeks after the current task is completed, click the Regenerate New Task option button and then enter the number of weeks in its associated text box. After specifying the recurrence pattern, you indicate the start and stop date (if any) for the recurring task in the Range of Recurrence area of the Task Recurrence dialog box.

As soon as you close the Task Recurrence dialog box (by clicking OK) and the Task dialog box (by clicking Save and Close), a new icon appears for the task in the Icon column in the TaskPad, To-Do Bar, and Tasks module, indicating that it's a recurring task. And the moment you mark this occurrence of the task as complete (either by clicking the Complete column in the TaskPad or To-Do Bar or right-clicking the task in the Tasks module and choosing Mark Complete from its shortcut menu), Outlook automatically adds another occurrence of the task to your to-do list (with a new due date that's a day, week, month, or year ahead, depending upon your Recurrence Pattern selection) until you reach the stop date or the last occurrence you've specified in the Range of Recurrence settings.

Assigning tasks to others

When you add a new task to your to-do list in Outlook, the task belongs to you alone, unless and until you decide to farm it out by assigning the task to someone else.

The process for assigning a task to another person is very similar to that for sending meeting requests to potential meeting participants. (See Chapter 10 for more on sending meeting requests.) After you click the Assign Task button in the menu bar of the task's Task dialog box, Outlook modifies the Task dialog box by adding a To text box and a message at the top indicating that the task reassignment message has not yet been sent (see Figure 12-5).

After you select the e-mail address of the person to whom you want to reassign the task (by clicking the To button and then clicking the name in the Select Task Recipient dialog box) and then click the Send button, Outlook e-mails a task request to him or her.

When you return to the task list in the TaskPad, To-Do Bar, or Tasks Module, the icon for the to-do item you just assigned to someone else is changed. To indicate that the task is in the process of being reassigned, Outlook adds a Hand icon below the normal icon denoting a task — the clipboard with check mark icon across it. When you reopen the Task dialog box, the person to whom you sent the task request is now listed as the owner of the task, and a message indicating that you're currently waiting for a response from this person appears at the top of the Task tab.

Meanwhile, the task request e-mail message that your task recipient receives in his or her Outlook Inbox displays the subject of the task in the e-mail Subject line in the Mail Navigation viewer. When the recipient selects the message, the number of days until the due date, the due date, status, priority, and percent complete information appear in the Info Bar at the top of the Reading Pane, right below the Accept and Decline buttons.

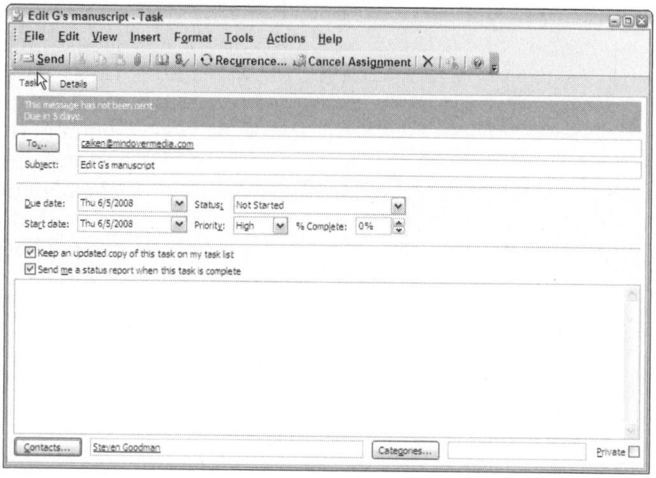

Figure 12-5:
Assigning
an existing
task to a
co-worker
on the team.

When the task recipient accepts the task assignment by clicking Accept and then clicking OK in the Accepting Task dialog box, you automatically receive an e-mail in your Inbox, indicating that the task has been accepted. The task recipient can then update you on the progress he or she makes on the task simply by clicking the Send Status Report button after updating the % Complete field in the Task dialog box. When he or she completes the task and marks it as complete, you also automatically receive an e-mail in your Inbox, indicating the task is now complete. In addition, Outlook automatically marks the task as complete in the task list in the TaskPad or To-Do Bar, as well as in the Task module.

Should your task recipient refuse to accept the task you've tried to assign to him or her by clicking the Decline button at the top of the task request's Info Bar, Outlook sends you an e-mail indicating that your task recipient has declined the task. In such a case, when you reopen the task's Task dialog box, you're still listed as the owner (although the to-do item continues to carry the icon of the hand-under-the-clipboard, indicating that you tried to reassign the task).

To remove this icon indicating that the task is in the process of being reassigned and restore the task as a normal to-do item on your Outlook task lists, open the Task dialog box and then choose Action⇨Return to Task List from the dialog box's menu bar. You can then either complete the task yourself or repeat the task assignment procedure, this time hopefully sending it to a co-worker who will accept the task and complete it for you.

Chapter 13

Using Notes to Capture Your Ideas

In This Chapter

▶ Using Outlook Notes to record your bright ideas and keep them in your face

▶ Adding and organizing your Outlook notes

▶ Sharing your Outlook notes with co-workers

▶ Effectively integrating Outlook Notes with OneNote 2007

A s you're probably well aware, the invention of Post-it or "sticky" notes by 3M's Art Fry (and absolutely not the zany characters, Romy and Michele in the 1997 hit comedy movie, *Romy and Michele's High School Reunion*) forever changed the way people take and use short, individual notes. This is because Post-it notes not only enable you to quickly capture random thoughts and to-do items, but you then get to stick the notes in obvious places where you can't easily ignore them. (All around the computer monitor is one of my favorite places.)

As you soon discover, Outlook Notes are definitely modeled off of Post-it notes. Their icons resemble a pad of notes with the lower-left corner of the first note turned up, and they're even a canary yellow color (although you can change them to blue, green, pink, or white). Moreover, you can drag Outlook notes out of the Notes module and stick them anywhere you want on your Windows desktop. And with some skillful window placement, this makes it possible to have certain Outlook notes up while you're working on documents in other applications, such as a report in Word or financial statement in Excel. It also makes it possible to declutter the periphery of your computer screen.

This chapter shows you how to use Outlook notes to quickly capture your bright ideas (and find them again) as well as how to use them as visual reminders that stay in your face when you're using your computer but not working in Outlook. This chapter also introduces you to ways that you can effectively use the notes you keep in Microsoft's standalone note-taking program, OneNote 2007, in Outlook.

Making Outlook Notes a Routine Part of Your Productivity Practices

Outlook notes are definitely being underutilized by today's Outlook users. (Most don't even know they're there.) This is really too bad because Outlook notes can really help you achieve what many leading experts tout as one of productivity's most important aspects; namely, the ability to document all your random thoughts that just seem to pop into your head, often at the most unlikely times. These thoughts can run the gamut from pedantic lists of things you have to do, want to do, and might never do all the way to inspiring quotes, deep questions, astounding insights, and personal aspirations.

The theory here is that by getting all these types of things down on paper (all right, digitally stored in bits and bytes), you never have to go through the painful experience of remembering that you had a really great idea while at the same time not being able to remember exactly what it was. By documenting all your spontaneous ideas as Outlook notes, the worse that can happen is that you'll have to take a tiny bit of time searching for the note that contains them.

I urge you to make good friends with the keyboard shortcut Ctrl+Shift+N, enabling you to create a new note from any Outlook module, and I hope that you then *use* this shortcut relentlessly to note every seemingly significant idea that pops into your head. Further, I suggest that you do this kind of routine note-taking without regard to whether the idea you're documenting would be better placed on your to-do list as a task item or on your calendar as an appointment or event. (I show you how to convert your Outlook notes into other Outlook items in "Using notes to create other Outlook items," later in this chapter.) Simply put, you should make every effort to get your idea fully documented by getting it completely recorded and saved. (Fortunately, Outlook notes are automatically saved without requiring you to click any button or press any other keyboard shortcut.)

Creating and Organizing Notes

When you press Ctrl+Shift+N in any Outlook module, the program opens a new note, similar to the one shown in Figure 13-1. As you can see in this figure, an Outlook note bears a strong resemblance to a physical Post-it note, except for the fact that the Outlook note is divided into the following three areas:

- **Title bar:** This bar along the top of the note doesn't actually show the title of the note. (The text you enter on the first line in the body of the note serves as the note title.) It does, however, contain a Menu button that you click to open a menu of options, a blue Moving handle you drag to reposition the note on top of an application or Windows desktop, and a Close button you click to close the note. (Outlook automatically saves the note when you close it.)

- **Note body:** This is the area in the middle that contains the text of the note.

- **Status bar:** This bar along the bottom contains the Date stamp, which displays the note's creation date and time, and a Sizing handle you can drag to modify the height and width of the note.

Menu Button   Close button

Moving handle   Title bar

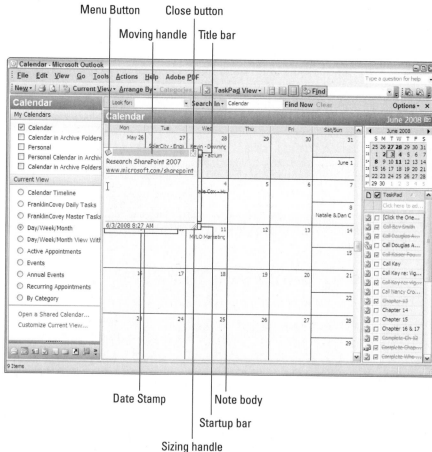

Figure 13-1:
Creating a
new note
from the
Outlook
Calendar
module
using the
Ctrl+Shift+N
keyboard
shortcut.

Date Stamp   Note body

Startup bar

Sizing handle

When you open a new note, Outlook automatically places the cursor/insertion point at the beginning of the first line in the note body. You can then start typing the text of the note, or you can paste any text in place (Ctrl+V) if you've previously copied the text to the Windows Clipboard (as you would if you wanted to store text in another document or Web page in Outlook note form).

If you type a Web address or e-mail address in the note body in a format that Outlook understands such as www.dummies.com or mailto:greg@harveyproductivity.com, the program automatically adds a live hyperlink to that Web or e-mail address. This means that when you click the Web address link in the note, Outlook actually launches your Web browser and takes you to the Web page associated with that address. Similarly, when you click an e-mail address link, Outlook opens a new e-mail message with that e-mail address in its To field.

One thing clearly lacking in Outlook notes is the presence of scroll bars. This means that as you add more lines of text than fit in the current size of the note, Outlook moves existing lines of text up and out of sight to accommodate the new lines without also adding a vertical scroll bar to bring them back into view. This means that you either have to use the Sizing handle to increase the size of the note to display all the note text or press the ↑ and ↓ arrow keys to scroll through the text to display hidden lines.

Customizing and printing your notes

Outlook's Menu button in the upper-left corner of an open note (refer to Figure 13-1) makes it easy to customize your note. The menu attached to this button contains a list of commands, many of which you're sure to be familiar with:

- ✓ **Color:** (Outlook 2003 only) Enables you to assign a new note color (Blue, Green, Pink, or White) that you can then use to group notes by selecting By Color as the current view in the Notes module.

- ✓ **Categories:** (called Categorize in Outlook 2007) Enables you to assign categories to a note that you can use to group notes by selecting By Category as the current view in the Notes module. In Outlook 2007, assigning a category to a note also changes the note's color to the color used by the category.

- ✓ **Contacts:** Enables you to associate the note with particular contacts in your address book. To associate a contact with a note, simply click the note's Menu button and then click the Contacts item to open the Contacts for Note dialog box. Here you can click the Contacts button to open the Selects Contacts dialog box, where you click the name of the contact and then click OK.

After associating a contact with a note, you can then call the contact, send him or her an e-mail, schedule a meeting, or open the contact's record from within the note. To perform one of these activities using a contact's information, you can double-click the contact's name in the Contacts for Note dialog box to open a dialog box with the contact's record and the use the appropriate buttons (E-Mail, Meeting, Call, and so on).

✓ **Print:** Enables you to print the contents of the note.

If you want to change the relative size of the notes you create and/or change their default font or font color, here's what you do:

1. **Click the Note Options button in the Notes section of the Options dialog box (Tools⟶Options).**

   Outlook then opens the Note Options dialog box shown in Figure 13-2.

2. **Click the Font button to open the Font dialog box where you can select a new font (or new font style, font size, or font color, if you want) for the appearance of the note text. Then click OK.**

3. **Click the Size drop-down button to select either the Small or Large size to change the relative size of the open note.**

4. **If you want to change the default note color from Yellow to another color, select a new color (Blue, Green, Pink, or White) from the Color drop-down menu.**

5. **Click OK to close the Note Options dialog box.**

Figure 13-2:
Changing
the default
font and size
assigned for
new notes
in the Notes
Options
dialog box.

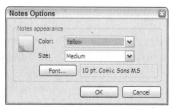

Using notes to create other Outlook items

Earlier in the chapter, I make a case for getting in the habit of entering notes indiscriminately without regard to whether they'd be better off entered as some other Outlook item, including a new e-mail message in your Mail module, appointment or event in your Calendar module, to-do item in your Tasks module, or journal entry in your Journal module.

My rationale for suggesting this strategy is simple: Outlook makes it so easy to later move your notes to the appropriate module that you're better off worrying about nothing more than capturing the potential e-mail, contact, appointment, task, or journal entry information in note form.

For example, say you suddenly remember that you need to call your doctor to discuss some recent lab test results. So, you press Ctrl+Shift+N, type "Call Dr. Smith to discuss lab results," and then click the Close button. Now, you have an electronic sticky note in Outlook that you can drag onto your Windows desktop to remind you to make that call. However, this particular note really belongs on your Outlook to-do list rather than just being a visual reminder in virtual Post-it note form.

Therefore, to convert this note into a bona fide to-do item on your tasks list, simply open the Notes module (Ctrl+5) in Outlook and then drag and drop the note's icon onto the Tasks button in the Navigation Pane. Outlook responds by opening a Call Dr. Smith to Discuss Lab Results – Task dialog box with the date stamp and text of the note displayed in its list box. Then, all you have to do is assign the new task a due date and time and assign Dr. Smith as a contact (assuming that you don't know his phone number by heart) before you click the Save and Close button.

Alternatively, you could use this note to create a new appointment on your calendar rather than a to-do item on your tasks list. To do this, drag the Dr. Smith note icon onto the Calendar button in the Navigation Pane of the Notes module instead. This causes Outlook to open a Call Dr. Smith to Discuss Lab Results – Appointment dialog box where you can specify the date and time of the call before you click Save and Close to put it on your daily calendar.

If you take down contact information in a note and want to use it as basis for creating a formal contact record for the person, drag its note icon onto the Contacts button in the Navigation Pane. Outlook opens a new Untitled – Contact dialog box with the person's contact information from the note entered into its list box. You then have to copy and paste pertinent pieces of contact information into their respective fields (Full Name, E-Mail, and so on) before you click Save and Close.

Creating notes from other Outlook items

Not only can you use your Outlook notes as the basis for creating other Outlook items — including e-mail messages, contacts, tasks, appointments, and journal entries — but you can also create notes from any of these Outlook items. All you have to do is open the appropriate Outlook module and then drag and drop the item you want to appear in the new note onto the Notes button in the Navigation Pane.

After you drop the Outlook item on the Notes Navigation button, Outlook opens a new note on top of the Outlook program window containing the contents of that item. This item's text is inserted below a blank line and separated from it by a partial dotted line. You can then enter the subject of the note into this blank line and edit the item's text as needed.

The primary reason for converting other Outlook items into notes is to use these notes as visual reminders on your Windows desktop. This means that you normally don't want to close the new note after creating it. The idea here is to drag the note outside of the confines of the Outlook program window and drop it somewhere else on your Windows desktop where it will never be out of sight and therefore out of mind.

Figure 13-3 illustrates this situation. This figure shows my Windows Vista desktop after dragging a new note that I created from an appointment on my calendar onto the desktop. Here, it will serve as a visual reminder when I minimize the Outlook program window in order to work in some other application.

Figure 13-3: Windows desktop with a new note used as a visual reminder created from an appointment on my calendar.

Searching Outlook notes

One of the big advantages of keeping your notes electronically in Outlook is that you can use the program's search ability to quickly find the ones to which you need to refer. The steps for searching notes are really straightforward and very easy to follow:

1. **If you're not already in the Notes module in Outlook, press Ctrl+5.**

   Outlook makes the Notes module current.

2. **If your notes aren't displayed as a list in the Notes Information Viewer, click the Notes List option button in the Navigation Pane.**

   Outlook displays a list of your notes sorted alphabetically by Subject (see Figure 13-4).

3. **Click the Look For text box in Outlook 2003 or the Search Notes text box in Outlook 2007 at the top of the Notes Information Viewer; then type in the text you want to search for in your notes in this text box. In Outlook 2003, you also click the Find Now button.**

   Outlook filters the list of notes so that only those notes containing the search text are displayed. You can then open any of the notes by double-clicking it in the list, and you can once again display all the notes in the list by clicking the Clear button in Outlook 2003 or the Clear Search button (the one with the *X* in it to the immediate right of the Search Notes text box) in Outlook 2007. Doing this clears the filter so that all your notes are once again listed in the Information Viewer.

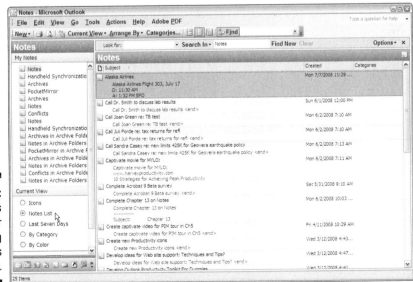

Figure 13-4: The Notes module after selecting the Notes List view.

Sharing your Outlook notes

Outlook makes it a snap to share your notes with other co-workers and clients via e-mail. All you have to do is right-click the note in the Notes module (Ctrl+5) and then choose Forward from its shortcut menu. Outlook then opens a new e-mail message that uses the subject of the note (the first line of text) as the Subject of the e-mail message and automatically appends the note to the message as an attachment.

Then, all you have to do is specify the e-mail recipients in the To, Cc, and/or Bcc fields, type any additional explanatory text in the body of the message, and click the Send button to share the note. When your recipients receive this e-mail, they can then open the note by double-clicking the attachment icon in header of the message and then drag it onto on their Windows desktop.

Successfully Using OneNote 2007 with Outlook

OneNote 2007 is the current version of Microsoft Office's standalone note-taking software program. This program offers sophisticated abilities not only for taking notes, but also for organizing them. It is particularly useful for students and workers in professions in any profession that relies heavily on note taking.

As part of Microsoft Office (although always sold separately from the rest of the Office bundles), OneNote is designed to work well with other Office applications, especially Outlook. For example, you can insert Outlook meeting details into OneNote where you can elaborate on them. (This is especially useful if you then use OneNote 2007 to take your meeting notes.) So, too, you can add tasks, appointments, and new contacts in Outlook from information you enter in OneNote 2007.

Inserting Outlook meeting details into OneNote

OneNote enables you to insert details of an appointment or meeting that you've placed on your Outlook calendar directly into its notes, including details such as the date, time, location, attendees, and subject. This feature enables you to use the essential meeting information stored in Outlook as the header for the meeting notes that you then take in OneNote.

To see how nicely this works, follow along with the steps for taking the details for a meeting scheduled on an Outlook calendar into a new page of notes in OneNote:

1. **With OneNote open, click the Notebook button to open the notebook where you want to keep the meeting notes and then click the tab of a blank page at the top of the notebook to make it active or click the New Page button if no blank pages are available.**

   OneNote opens a new page in the current notebook.

2. **Choose Insert⇨Outlook Meeting Details from the OneNote menu bar.**

   OneNote opens the Insert Outlook Meeting Details dialog box, similar to the one shown in Figure 13-5.

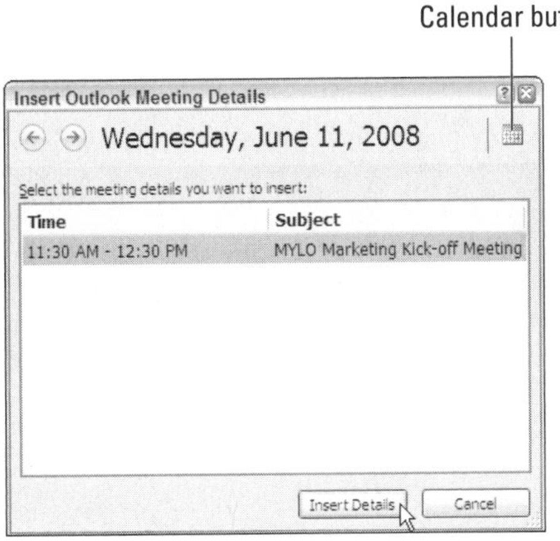

Calendar button

Figure 13-5: Selecting the Outlook meeting whose details you want to copy into a new page of an existing notebook in OneNote 2007.

Insert Outlook Meeting Details

(←) (→) Wednesday, June 11, 2008

Select the meeting details you want to insert:

Time	Subject
11:30 AM - 12:30 PM	MYLO Marketing Kick-off Meeting

Insert Details   Cancel

3. **Click the Calendar button to display the drop-down Date Navigator and then use it to select the date of the meeting you've scheduled on your Outlook calendar.**

   The Select The Meeting Details You Want to Insert list box in the Insert Outlook Meeting Details dialog box displays all of the appointments and meetings you've scheduled in Outlook on the date you select.

4. **Click the meeting whose details are to be copied into OneNote in the Select The Meeting Details You Want to Insert list box and then click the Insert Details button.**

5. **Depending upon the level of your security settings, OneNote may then display an alert dialog box warning you that another program is asking you to allow this access. If this is the case, click the Allow Access check box in this alert dialog box and then click Yes.**

OneNote then inserts the meeting details into the new page of the currently open notebook, inserting the Subject field into the page's header box and the rest of details about date, time, attendees, and so on appearing in a separate text box below, as shown in Figure 13-6.

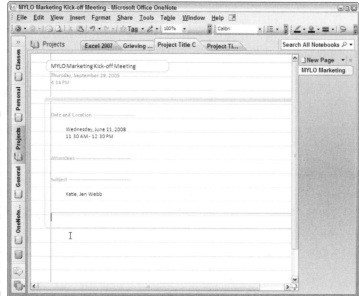

Figure 13-6: Outlook meeting details after inserting them into a new page of an existing notebook in OneNote 2007.

Creating Outlook tasks, appointments, and contacts from OneNote

OneNote also enables you to convert information you store in the pages of its notebooks to bona fide Outlook items. These items include tasks, appointments, and contacts. Presumably, the idea here is that you're taking notes on your computer in OneNote during a meeting, presentation, or seminar, and as part of this note-taking you record information that you also want to appear in Outlook as a to-do item on your tasks list, an appointment on your calendar, or a contact record in your address book.

Creating a new Outlook task from a note in OneNote

To convert a note in a OneNote notebook into an Outlook task that appears as a to-do item in your Outlook task list, select the note's text box and then choose Insert➪Outlook Task from the OneNote menu bar and click the flag associated with the task's due date that appears on the continuation menu: Today, Tomorrow, This Week, Next Week, No Date, or Custom. (Note that

when you select the Custom item on this continuation menu, OneNote opens the Outlook Task dialog box where you can assign the due date and time and start date and time along with the priority, status, and percentage complete.)

After you do this, the flag icon associated with the due date appears in front of the note in its text box in your open notebook in OneNote. In addition, this task appears as a to-do item in your tasks list in Outlook Tasks module (under the generic subject heading, Click the OneNote Link in Task Body for Details).

In the notebook in OneNote, you can then right-click the flag icon that appears in front of the note's text to change the task's due date, mark the task as complete, delete it from OneNote and Outlook, or to open the task's Outlook Task dialog box in OneNote. In Outlook, you can open the Task dialog box for this new to-do item by double-clicking the to-do item in the task list in the Tasks module, and in the dialog box you can modify the settings and details.

Creating a new Outlook appointment from a note in OneNote

To convert a note that you've recorded in a OneNote notebook into an appointment that appears on your Outlook calendar, select the note's text box in OneNote and then press Alt+Shift+A. (You can also choose Tools⇨ Create Outlook Item⇨Create Outlook Appointment from the OneNote menu bar.)

OneNote then opens a new Outlook Appointment dialog box that appears on top of the OneNote program window with the text of the selected note copied into the list box that appears on its Appointment tab. You can then fill in the information for the missing fields, including the subject, location, start and end dates and times, as well as assign contacts and categories to the appointment before you click the Save and Close button to save this appointment on your Outlook calendar and close the Appointment dialog box.

Creating a new Outlook contact record from a note in OneNote

The process for converting a name, address, telephone number, and Web site address in OneNote into a new contact in your Outlook address book is almost identical to that for creating a new Outlook appointment. However, after selecting the text box of the note in OneNote that contains your contact information, you press Ctrl+Shift+C (or choose Tools⇨Create Outlook Item⇨Create Outlook Contact from the OneNote menu bar).

OneNote then opens a new Contact dialog box that appears on top of the OneNote window. This Outlook dialog box contains the contact information from the note in the OneNote notebook copied to its list box. You can then copy and paste the pieces of this contact information to the appropriate contact fields, such as Full Name, E-Mail, Web Page Address, and so forth before you click the Save and Close button to save this contact record in your Outlook address book and close the Contact dialog box.

Chapter 14

Using the Journal to Keep an Eye on Your Activities

In This Chapter

▶ Understanding how using the Journal can help you increase your productivity

▶ Turning on (and customizing) automatic journaling in Outlook

▶ Manually recording an activity with the Journal

*L*ast, and very often least for most Outlook users, comes the Journal module. This module rates so low on the Outlook totem pole that it doesn't even get a navigation button on the Navigation Pane unless you go to the trouble of placing the Journal button there yourself. (Curiously enough, the Journal module *does* have its own keyboard shortcut — Ctrl+8.)

One reason that the Outlook Journal may be so underrated is that, at first glance, it doesn't seem as active and full-featured as the other modules, at least not in the same way that the Mail processes your e-mail messages, the Calendar keeps your appointments, and Tasks maintains your to-do list. Compared with these worker-bee modules, the Journal module appears downright anemic and rather passive.

Another part of the problem, I think, is that referring to this module as a journal is somewhat misleading. Typically, you associate a journal with a diary — a place where you write down your daily activities, thoughts, and feelings. And the Outlook Journal, as a rule, acts more like a mechanical log that automatically records an array of different daily activities that you want documented.

This log can not only automatically document when you sent and received e-mail messages to and from a particular contact but also your meeting and task requests and responses, thus helping you keep track of important correspondence you receive and events that have transpired. In addition, the Journal can help you keep track of your interactions and activities by recording the amount of time you worked with a contact as well as the date and time you worked with files in other Office applications, including Word, Excel, Access, and PowerPoint. And perhaps most important of all, this

document tracking feature enables you to quickly locate the documents that you've worked on, an invaluable feature when you discover you need to reopen a file.

Understanding How the Journal Can Help You Be More Productive

Although the run-of-the-mill Outlook user may not find the Journal's time- and activity-tracking capabilities particularly useful, I trust that that's not the case for someone like you who's approaching Outlook as a means by which you can increase your personal productivity. In your case, the Outlook Journal provides an easy way to chronicle a lot of the time you spend working on particular projects and with particular clients and co-workers.

Having the Journal's log to refer to can really help you become more aware of where you spend your time. In turn, this awareness can help you find new ways to better manage the time you spend with the people and projects that you have to work with. Moreover, if you regularly work with other Office applications such as Word or Excel, you can use the Journal not only to chronicle the time you spend editing their documents, but also to help you quickly locate their files later on when they once again need printing or editing. This is because the Journal keeps a record of the directory path to every document you create and modify with a tracked Office application — which means you'll never have to worry again if it has completely slipped your mind where on your system you've saved a particular document or file you'd recently been working on.

Making the Most of the Journal Module

The first time you open the Outlook Journal (Ctrl+8), Outlook 2003 displays an alert dialog box asking whether you want to turn on the Journal, while at the same time seeming to downplay some of its capabilities by means of the following notice:

> The Journal can automatically track Office documents, and also e-mail associated with a contact. However, the Activities tab on the contact item is the best way to track e-mail and does not require the Journal. Do you want to turn the Journal On?

In Outlook 2007, you receive a similar message. According to this version of the introductory message, the Activities page in a Contact record simply provides another way (not necessarily the "best" way) to track e-mail messages from this contact without requiring the use of the Journal.

Using automatic journaling

If you dare to go ahead and click the Yes button to turn on the Journal after reading this faint praise of its capabilities (at least as far as e-mail goes), Outlook opens the Journal Options dialog box, similar to the one shown in Figure 14-1.

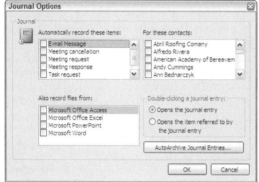

Figure 14-1:
Selecting the items and contacts you want the Journal to automatically track in the Journal Options dialog box.

In the Automatically Record These Items list box, click the check boxes for all the Outlook items you want the Journal to automatically record. Next, click the names of the contacts in your Outlook address book for whom you want them recorded in the For These Contacts list box.

To also record file usage with documents you create and modify in other Microsoft applications, select all of the check boxes for the programs you want tracked (Microsoft Office Access, Microsoft Office Excel, Microsoft PowerPoint, and Microsoft Word) in the Also Record Files From list box.

And, if you want Outlook to open the item referred to in an entry when you double-click it in the Journal (rather than simply open a dialog box for the Journal entry), select the Opens the Item Referred to by the Journal Entry option button in the Double-Clicking a Journal Entry section of the dialog box before you click OK.

If you ever decide that you no longer need to track Outlook items for a particular contact or certain Office application files, you can remove them from the Journal. Simply open the Journal Options dialog box by choosing Tools⇨Options from the menu bar and then clicking the Journal Options button. When you have the dialog box open, deselect the check boxes for those Outlook items, contacts, and file types you no longer want to record and then click OK.

Is tracking e-mail messages on the Activities tab/page of a contact record really superior to the Journal?

You may be curious as to whether or not tracking your e-mail messages with a particular contact is better done on the Activities tab/page of the contact's record rather than in the Journal itself (as Outlook 2003's introductory message would have you believe). The fact is that the Activities tab/page of the contact record provides you with a terrific way of listing all your e-mail correspondence with a particular contact in your address book (along with other Outlook items you share, including contacts, notes, and all the items you track for the contact in the Journal). The Activities tab/page shows you a list of just the messages (sent and received) involving the contact whose record is open. The Journal, on the other hand, shows a timeline with the record of the e-mails messages for all the contacts you selected in the Journal Options dialog box. To me, this simply means that the Activities tab/page gives a more condensed view of your electronic correspondence with a particular contact, and this, in turn, can sometimes be easier to deal with than the more extensive view you get in the Journal.

After you select the Outlook items and Office applications that you want Outlook to track automatically in the Journal, Outlook begins adding them to this module using the default By Type view shown in Figure 14-2.

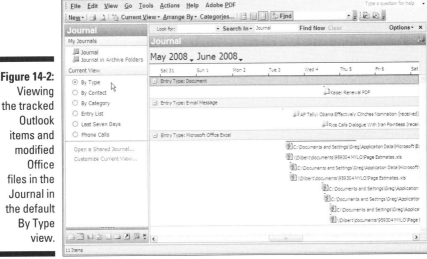

Figure 14-2: Viewing the tracked Outlook items and modified Office files in the Journal in the default By Type view.

As you can see in this figure, this default Journal view groups together the various Outlook items and Office applications that the Journal automatically tracks and records and then places them on a timeline using a daily scale. When an item or file has a duration that spans more than one date, the Journal shows this by drawing a bar on the timeline, the start of which indicates the start time and the end of which indicates the end time.

Changing the Journal view

As with any other Outlook module, you can switch from the default view to any of the predefined views (By Contact, By Category, Entry List, Last Seven Days, Phone Calls, or Outlook Data Files) by clicking its option button in the Current View section of the Journal Navigation Pane.

 Switch to the Entry List view when you want a tabular view of your Journal entries that you can re-sort and edit easily. When you make Entry List the current view, Outlook displays the entries in groups by type and sorts them by start date in descending order (most recent to least recent). To sort the entries in this list on another field or in ascending order in the Start field (least recent to most recent), all you have to do is click the field name. To edit or print entries in the list, select them, then right-click the selection and then choose the appropriate option from its shortcut menu (Open, Print, or Delete).

Of course, you can also customize any of the predefined Journal views as well as create new ones of your own. To customize the current view, choose View⇨Arrange By⇨Current View⇨Customize Current View (in Outlook 2003) or View⇨Current View⇨Customize Current View (in Outlook 2007). If you want to create a new view for the Journal module, choose the Define Views option rather than Customize Current View from the Current View submenu.

Manually creating Journal entries

Although most of your Journal entries will undoubtedly be created automatically by setting their items and application options in the Journal Options dialog box, you can manually add Journal entries as well. You would want to do this, for example, when you spend time on a telephone call that isn't generated through Outlook or on a document that's not saved in an Office file format automatically tracked by the Journal but which you still want recorded as a Journal entry.

To add a manual Journal entry, follow these simple steps:

1. **Press Ctrl+Shift+J from any Outlook module.**

   Outlook then opens an Untitled – Journal Entry dialog box, similar to the one shown in Figure 14-3.

2. **Enter a description for the new entry in the Subject field.**

   By default, Outlook assigns all new manual Journal entries to the Phone Call category. If your manual entry falls into another classification, you need to follow Step 3 to select a different Entry type.

3. **If you're not recording a phone call, select the appropriate classification for your entry in the Entry Type drop-down list.**

4. **(Optional) Fill out as much supporting information about the journal entry as you can.**

   This information can include any or all of the following:

   - *Company:* If you want to associate the Journal entry with a company, enter its name in the Company text box.

   - *Start Date:* If needed, click the drop-down buttons on the two Start Date combo boxes to assign a new date and time to the Journal entry's start date. By default, Outlook assigns the current date and time as the Start Time for the new Journal entry.

   - *Notes:* Enter any notes that you want to record about the entry in the dialog box's text box. Just as with other Outlook items, you can add notes describing the entry in more detail.

   - *Associate a contact:* When using Outlook 2003, you associate the entry with a particular contact in your address book or assign it categories by clicking the Contacts button or Categories button, respectively. In Outlook 2007, you associate contacts by clicking the Attach Item button on the Insert tab and assign categories by clicking the Categories button on the Options tab.

   - *Private:* To mark the entry as private, click the Private check box (Outlook 2003) or Private button (Outlook 2007).

   - *Start Timer:* To have Outlook calculate the amount of minutes you spend on an entry, click the Start Timer button.

   - *Duration:* To designate the amount of time you intend to work with the entry or to have the entry last, click the Duration combo box and enter the number of minutes, hours, days, or weeks you intend to spend (followed by one of these units) or select the amount of time on its drop-down list.

5. **Click the Save and Close button.**

   After you click this button, Outlook adds your new entry to the current Journal view.

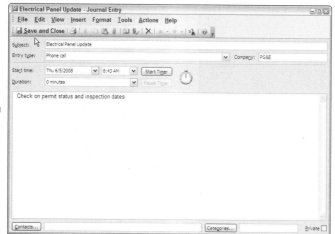

Figure 14-3:
Creating a
new manual
entry in a
Journal
Entry dialog
box.

Use the automatic timer in the Journal Entry dialog box to have Outlook calculate the total amount of time you spend working with or on a Journal entry (phone call, meeting, document, and so forth) whenever it's important to track this kind of information. Simply open the entry in the Journal module of Outlook right before you're ready to start timing the entry and then click the Start Timer button to begin. You can minimize the Journal Entry on the Windows task bar while Outlook times the event, but you can't close the Journal Entry dialog box (because doing so automatically pauses the timer). When you've finished working on or with the entry and you want Outlook to calculate the elapsed time, select its Journal Entry dialog box to maximize it again on your desktop and then click the Pause Timer button before you click the Save and Close button.

Keep in mind that you can speed up the process of creating a new Journal entry for a particular contact in your Outlook address book by right-clicking the contact's name in the Contacts module and then, in Outlook 2003, choosing New Journal Entry for Contact from the shortcut menu. In Outlook 2007, you do this by pointing to Create on the shortcut menu and then clicking New Journal Entry for Contact on its continuation menu. Outlook then opens a new Journal Entry dialog box with the contact's name already entered in its title bar and in the Subject field.

Chapter 15

Outlook on the Go

. . . .

. . . .

A large part of maintaining the peak personal productivity you've achieved is being able to be productive even when you're on the go. More and more, it's not enough simply to have access to your Outlook e-mail messages, calendars, and task list when you're in your office. You also need to be able to deal with these items when you're on the move, whether it's close to home on your daily commute to and from the office or far away on business trips to other cities and countries.

With the large-scale introduction of wireless technology in the form of Wi-Fi and Bluetooth, it's now possible to take your Outlook data with you wherever you go, not only on your laptop computer, but also on your Smartphone (a mobile phone equipped with at least Internet and text messaging capabilities, such as the BlackBerry Curve or Palm Treo) or PDA (personal digital assistant such as an HP iPAQ or Palm T/X).

In response to this new reality on the ground — and on the seas and in the air — this chapter covers accessing your Outlook data from your mobile devices and keeping it synchronized, as well as ways you can access your e-mail messages and calendar on the Internet during those times when you can't access these items using the traditional Outlook program.

Getting Outlook Data onto Your Mobile Devices

The good news is that once you get your mobile device (be it a Smartphone or a PDA) configured to accept Outlook data items, synchronizing those items between your mobile device and laptop or desktop computer is no

harder than establishing a connection between them. To configure your mobile device for Outlook, you first need to install the utility programs for managing data supplied with the mobile device on the computer that runs Outlook. These programs generally enable you to load various applications on your mobile device as well as back up its data and, most importantly, synchronize data between your computer and the mobile device.

After installing this data management software, you next need to connect the mobile device to the laptop or desktop computer. Connections between a mobile device like a Smartphone or PDA and a computer are normally accomplished via a USB connector between the two devices or, alternatively, wirelessly via Bluetooth technology (although some mobile devices can also connect to a computer via a serial cable connection).

Then, to get Outlook data such as the contacts in your address book, appointments and events on your calendar, and to-do items on your task list onto your mobile device and keep these items updated, you need to find and launch the utility program installed on your computer that synchs your mobile device.

For my BlackBerry Pearl Smartphone, this particular utility is called Synchronize and is part of the BlackBerry Desktop Manager that I use to control all aspects of synchronization with the cell phone. Figure 15-1 shows you the options that appear on the Synchronize tab of this utility's Synchronize dialog box; these options enable me to specify automatic synchronization whenever the Smartphone is connected to my computer. Figure 15-2 shows you the Configuration dialog box that enables me to specify which Outlook data items to keep synchronized on my cell phone.

Figure 15-1:
Selecting how and when desktop Outlook data is synchronized on my BlackBerry Pearl Smartphone.

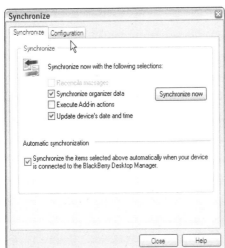

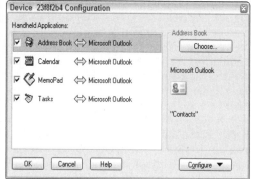

Figure 15-2:
Specifying
which
Outlook
items are to
be synchro-
nized on my
BlackBerry
Pearl Smart-
phone.

As you can see in Figure 15-2, not only can I use the configuration options in this dialog box to specify that I want to keep the Outlook address book, calendar, notes, and tasks current on my BlackBerry, but in so doing, I also specify which Outlook folders to use. This means, for example, that I can keep a calendar different from my default Outlook calendar synched on my BlackBerry should I feel the need to. (See Chapter 10 for information on keeping more than one calendar in Outlook.)

Keep in mind that synchronization between your computer and mobile device is a two-way street. So, for example, if I change the Status from Busy to Tentative on an appointment on my BlackBerry calendar or the Status from In Progress to Completed on a to-do item on my BlackBerry task list, then the very next time I synchronize the data, the Synchronize software will modify the appointment in my Outlook calendar and the to-do item on my Outlook task list to reflect these changes.

Sending Text Messages from Outlook to a Mobile Phone

If you have a teenager at home, then I certainly don't have to tell you that text messaging is all the rage with the younger generation. Of course, you don't have to be sixteen years old to appreciate the ability to send messages to a cell phone, especially if that phone isn't equipped to send and receive regular e-mail. Being able to send text messages from Outlook on your computer in the office to cell phones "somewhere out there" can save you a tremendous amount of time in keeping in touch with co-workers and clients who are either traveling or working in the field.

Outlook 2007 makes it simple to send a text message to any cell phone that supports text messaging. All you need to do is install Outlook Mobile Services (OMS for short) on the computer running Outlook 2007. And to accomplish this installation, you need to select an SMS (Short Messaging Service) provider who covers the cellular network (T-Mobile, Verizon Wireless, AT&T Wireless, and so on). To find such an SMS provider, set up an account with them and download the OMS software, visit `http://messaging.office.microsoft.com` on the Internet.

After you set up an account and install the SMS software, you can then send a text message to any cell phone directly from Outlook 2007 by choosing File⇨New⇨Text Message from any Outlook module's menu bar. (The OMS software adds this new option to the bottom of the New submenu.)

Outlook 2007 then opens a new Untitled – Text Message window, similar to the one shown in Figure 15-3. As you can see in this figure, this window is divided into two sections: a Preview pane on the left and the pane where you type in the text of your message on the right.

To compose a new message in this window, enter the recipient's cell phone number in the To text box or select it from your address book by clicking the To button and then clicking the name and cell phone number in Select Names: Contacts (Mobile) dialog box before you click OK.

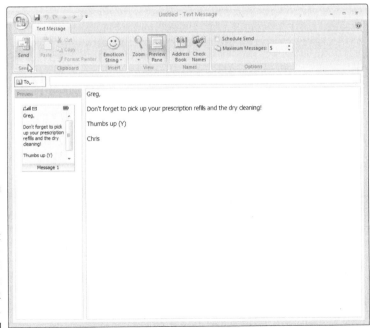

Figure 15-3:
Sending a new text message to my cell phone from Outlook 2007.

Then, click the cursor in the pane on the right and type in the text of your message. (You can see how its lines wrap in the Preview pane on the left.) After you finish typing the message text, you're ready to send your text message by clicking the Send button.

 Keep in mind that, if you're still using Outlook 2003 and you want to be able to send text messages from this version of Outlook, you can do so by finding an SMS provider who covers your cellular network and then downloading and installing a separate SMS (Short Messaging Service) plug-for Outlook. One such provider who offers an Outlook plug-in and support for a wide array of different cellular networks (both here in the United States and abroad) is SMSCountry at www.smscountry.com.

Using Outlook with Instant Messaging

Instant messaging (IM, for short) makes it possible for you and another co-worker or client to exchange text messages, video, and audio over the Internet in real time (unlike the back-and-forth of e-mailing and, too often, that of telephone tag). Instant messaging facilitates impromptu communication of all sorts, all the way from quick question-and-answer sessions to keeping in touch with colleagues, friends, and family and catching up on the latest chitchat.

Lots of different IM software programs are available for Internet real-time communication. One of the most popular IM programs (and possibly the most compatible with Outlook) is Microsoft's Windows Live Messenger (see Figure 15-4). This IM software enables you to exchange real-time text messages as well as video (assuming that both contacts have webcams on their computers).

When using use an instant messenger program such as Windows Live Messenger, you can tell whether or not people in your Outlook address book are online and available for messaging by adding their IM addresses in their contact records and by turning on the Display Messenger Status in Outlook feature. To do this, follow these steps:

1. **Launch Outlook as you normally do and then choose Tools⇨Options from the Outlook menu bar.**

   Outlook opens the Preferences tab of the Options dialog box.

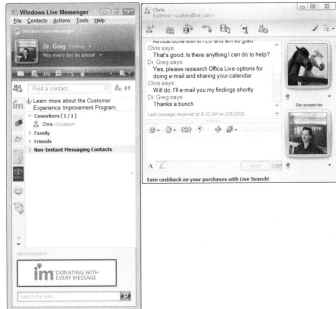

Figure 15-4:
Using
Windows
Live
Messenger
to con-
duct an
impromptu
discussion
with a
co-worker.

2. **Click the Other tab in the Options dialog box and then in Outlook 2003, select the Enable the Person Names Smart Tag check box in the Person Names section at the bottom of this tab. In Outlook 2007, you select the Display Online Status Next to a Person Name check box, instead.**

   As soon as you select the Enable the Person Names Smart Tag check box in Outlook 2003 or the Display Online Status Next to a Person Name check box in Outlook 2007, the Display Messenger Status in the From Field check box becomes active.

3. **Select the Display Messenger Status in the From Field check box and then click OK.**

   After turning on the Display Messenger Status in Outlook, you still have to add the IM address for each contact with whom you do instant messaging.

4. **In the Find button's text box on the Standard toolbar (or on your custom Productivity toolbar if you created one), type the name of the contact whose IM address you want to add and then press Enter.**

   Outlook opens the Contact dialog box for the contact name you entered.

5. **Click the IM Address field and type in the contact's instant message address and then click the Save and Close button.**

After adding the IM address for each contact with whom you want to be able to conduct instant messaging, Outlook then displays the current status of any contact when he or she sends you a regular e-mail message. All you have to do is open the e-mail message in the Mail module and then position the mouse pointer over the person's name in the From field at the top message (see Figure 15-5). Outlook then displays a colored circle indicating the person's current online status (green for online and available, red for offline, and tan for online and busy).

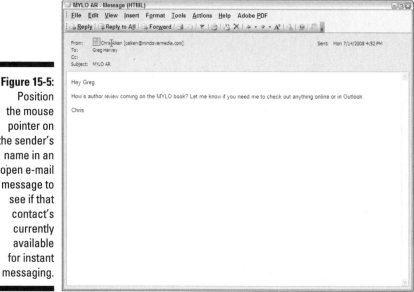

Figure 15-5:
Position the mouse pointer on the sender's name in an open e-mail message to see if that contact's currently available for instant messaging.

If the person's status indicates that he or she is now online and available for messaging, you can then reply by sending an instant message instead of sending a standard e-mail reply. All you have to do is position the mouse pointer on the green indicator ball next to the person's name in the From field until a drop-down button appears. Then, click the drop-down button and choose Reply with Instant Message from the menu that appears.

Part V
The Part of Tens

The 5th Wave   By Rich Tennant

"...so if you have a message for someone, you write it on a piece of paper and put it on their refrigerator with these magnets. It's just until we get our e-mail fixed."

In this part . . .

The two chapters in this fifth and final part, the Part of Tens, reflect the dual nature of this book: Chapter 16 gives you my top ten personal productivity strategies designed to help you visualize how you might go about achieving your goal of greater work/life balance. Chapter 17 gives you my top ten Outlook productivity techniques designed to help make this goal a reality.

Chapter 16

Top Ten Personal Productivity Strategies

Achieving work/life balance through increased personal productivity isn't simply a matter of developing new work habits. You also need to develop new approaches to your work and innovative tactics for dealing with the inevitable changes and uncertainties you're bound to meet along the way.

In this chapter, I cover my top ten tactics for developing and maintaining peak personal productivity. They necessarily begin with a frank assessment of where you're currently at and where you ultimately hope to be. They conclude with suggestions on the attitudes you'll want to develop and maintain in order to realize these aspirations.

Know Yourself When It Comes to Productivity

You can't expect to make much progress on achieving increased productivity if you don't know where you're at currently. Therefore, I suggest that you

begin this entire "personal productivity" endeavor with an assessment of where you're starting from. As part of this assessment, you need to acknowledge the areas where you could stand some definite improvement as well as those where you're naturally strong (be it the area of organization, prioritizing, planning, or time management). Doing this will indicate the areas you need to concentrate on, while at the same time preventing you from reinventing the wheel, so to speak.

As part of this productivity self-assessment, I also suggest you take a look at where you expect yourself to be after developing some new skills and habits in the areas that need improvement. I find it tremendously important to have a clear and concrete image of what work/life balance means to you and what it looks like in your life. This image can then serve both as a motivator and a model that enables you to judge your success.

View Personal Productivity as Part of Self-Fulfillment

Remember that peak personal productivity is not a goal in itself. Rather, it's merely the means of achieving the real goal of balancing your professional and personal life. Further, keep in mind that the underlying purpose of this work/life balance is to be as happy and fulfilled in all aspects of your life as you can possibly be.

I think maintaining this perspective on personal productivity is important in keeping you going and keeping your eye on the prize. Too many gurus in the productivity field aren't clear enough about this. Because they're so personally jazzed about the subject, they tend to give off the misimpression that achieving peak productivity should be a sufficient reward in and of itself. I not only don't think that this is the case, but I also caution you against making personal productivity more than it is: a worthy means to a lofty end.

Master Your Productivity Tools

I use the term "productivity tools" in the loosest sense. Your day planner, personal computer, cell phone, and Outlook software are only the most obvious tools that you need to master in order to achieve peak personal productivity.

Your intelligence, motivation, and attitudes are also key productivity tools that you need to master. Therefore, I urge you not only to give a makeover to your computer files and your Outlook program interface, but also to your attitudes toward work and play. Also, I urge you to adopt an open attitude that enables you to welcome every opportunity you get to develop new abilities and skills that help actualize you both personally and professionally.

Get Yourself Organized

Remember that solid organization provides the foundation upon which you build your personal productivity. As such, it's important to get your workspace organized at the outset of the process of becoming more productive. Just be aware of the definite trade-off between the time it takes to maintain peak levels of organization and the time it takes to actually get your work done.

Also, keep in mind that being organized doesn't just describe the state of your files, but also the state of your mind. This means that you need to be on top of your mental/emotional game when it comes to work in order to have any chance of achieving your productivity goals. This, in turn, means that you need to take care of both your body and your mind by paying attention to nutrition, exercise, and recreation. (All work and no play is definitely not the way to go.)

Prioritize Your Tasks

The real key to achieving peak personal productivity is being able to realistically assess the relative importance of all your obligations. By evaluating their relative merit, more often than not you end up determining the order by which you need to take them on and find the means by which you can get them done. This means that in the ongoing fight to maintain your personal productivity, establishing the priority of the things that still need doing is often more than half the battle.

Plan for the Future

When you think about your day planner, you undoubtedly think "calendar." And when you think "calendar," you probably think "scheduling." And so you should, for effective time management is often little more than effective scheduling.

Just keep in mind that effective scheduling isn't just a matter of juggling and filling the open timeslots on your Outlook calendar. It's also being able to find ways to make good use of the slots you don't fill, the time that isn't planned and accounted for. Also, planning isn't just a matter of dealing with your immediate obligations. It's also a matter of being able to anticipate those commitments that aren't yet on the horizon but which you're bound to meet up with in the near future.

Focus on What You Can Do

The power of positive thinking just can't be overstated. When it comes to personal productivity, you have to be able to keep your focus on what you can do now and get done in the near future and not what you can't accomplish.

Whenever you're unable to maintain this kind of "can do" focus, you run the risk of being stopped dead in your tracks and then wasting time getting absolutely nothing done (the very antithesis of personal productivity). For, even when you can't get everything done and your best-laid plans go awry, you need to be able to keep on doing whatever you can to have any chance of later regaining the upper hand and getting back on track.

Stay Open to Change

Staying open to change isn't just a platitude. It's an essential component of successfully dealing with the vicissitudes of modern life. In fact, it may be the people who are the most adept at dealing with change, both in the workplace and their personal lives, who end up being the most successful in terms of personal productivity.

It surely takes a certain amount of mental jujitsu to deal effectively with having to switch your gears and change your plans. The best way to cope with ongoing change and reduce the stress associated with it is to learn how to stay relaxed and mentally open in the face of it so you're ready to go off in a new direction whenever you're situation requires you to do so.

Deal Tactically with Information Overload

By anticipating information overload, you have half a chance of not being completely overwhelmed by it. As I'm very fond of pointing out, however,

information overload is, all too often, the result of ineffective or nonexistent data filtering (which is why, in my computer training classes, I stress knowing how to filter out of your data all but the information you need to work with).

When it comes to personal productivity, the big problem with information overload is that it can render you ineffective, either by leading you down a lot of blind alleys or by stopping you in your tracks. Either way, you need to guard against it whenever possible in order to maintain peak productivity.

Develop a Healthy Sense of Interdependence

To paraphrase John Donne, "No person is an island." For, at the end of the day, personal productivity isn't simply a matter of being the best at your own game, but also a matter of being at your best playing with others.

This is the case because so many knowledge-based and service-related professions make communicating and working well with others an essential part of the job. This makes honing your interpersonal skills part and parcel of achieving true peak personal productivity. It also means that you must face the twin challenges of effectively staying in touch with others as well as successfully relying upon them at various times to meet certain obligations.

Chapter 17

Top Ten Outlook Productivity Techniques

In This Chapter

▶ Making the most of every single Outlook module

▶ Keeping your Inbox organized

▶ Keeping your Inbox near empty

▶ Sending effective e-mail messages

▶ Making Outlook Today or the Calendar the center of your productivity system

▶ Sharing your calendars with everyone who needs to know

▶ Efficiently charting all your upcoming tasks

▶ Noting all your random ideas

▶ Using automatic journaling to evaluate your time management

▶ Taking Outlook with you on the road

*T*o help you in your quest to make Outlook a key component in your achieving peak personal productivity, in this chapter, I've brought together my top ten techniques for using Outlook as a full personal information manager.

As you go through these ten techniques, keep in mind that not all of them may apply to your particular work situation and the challenges you face. However, whenever you do come upon a technique that seems to fit, I urge you to implement it in your use of Outlook, using the detailed information referenced to in the text.

Utilize Every Single Bit of Outlook

The only way you can hope to have Outlook truly help you in your goal of achieving peak personal productivity is by making full use of the program's

capabilities. This means being able to put Outlook to its best use in communicating with your co-workers and clients, organizing your ideas and supporting materials, prioritizing your tasks, planning your schedule, and evaluating your prowess in the area of time management.

One way to initiate this process is by expanding your Outlook horizons beyond e-mail in the Mail module. You can do this by getting an overview of the capabilities of Outlook's various modules and by learning the shortcut keys as outlined in Chapter 5 and then, perhaps, by making Outlook Today or the Calendar module the new center of your Outlook productivity system, as outlined in Chapter 6.

Organize Your Inbox

Like the paper inbox you may keep on your desk, the Inbox folder in the Outlook Mail module is meant to be a *temporary* holding bin for the stuff that comes in (e-mail messages, in this case).

Too often, however, Outlook users treat the Inbox like it was a semipermanent storage container and then soon end up always dreading having to open it to read new messages. You simply must take the suggestions outlined in Chapter 7 to heart and clean out that overflowing Inbox if you're to have any hope of removing your Inbox-phobia. And the best way I know to do this is by organizing your e-mail, archiving what you can and then putting the rest of the messages into the appropriate subfolders for later processing and easy retrieval.

Keep That Inbox Near Empty

Doing radical housecleaning in your Inbox periodically to empty it out is just not an effective way to deal with your ongoing e-mail problem. You'll be much happier and more productive by keeping your Inbox in a manageable state near empty.

As Chapter 8 suggests, this means being able to deal with incoming batches of e-mail messages through a combination of automatic processing via e-mail rules and manual processing by means of categorizing the messages and then moving them into their appropriate processing and holding Inbox subfolders.

Send Really Effective E-Mail Messages

Most of the time when contemplating your e-mail productivity, you think exclusively of dealing with the e-mail messages you receive, with no real thought regarding the effective composition and strategic sending of new messages.

In Chapter 9, however, I maintain that improving the e-mail messages you send out can also result in improving your personal productivity. This happens because by making communication with co-workers and clients notably more effective, you often dramatically decrease the amount of time and energy lost in your recipients seeking further clarification and your involvement in continued e-mail message reply-and-send.

Make Outlook Today or the Calendar the Center of Your Productivity World

One surefire technique for transforming Outlook into much more than a mere e-mail program is to either make Outlook Today (Personal Folders) in the Mail module or the Calendar module the center of the program as a personal information manager.

To implement this change, simply follow the general instructions I give in Chapter 5 for selecting a new Outlook startup folder and use them to make either the Personal Folders (for Outlook Today) or the Calendar folder the new program default. That way, each time you launch Outlook, you're immediately confronted with either the overview of your calendar and tasks presented in Outlook Today view or with the daily, weekly, or monthly appointments on your Calendar.

Share Your Calendar As Needed

Successfully charting and maintaining your upcoming appointments, events, and meetings on your calendar is only one part of the story. To really give a boost to your productivity with the people with whom you need to collaborate, start sharing your calendar (as described in Chapter 10) with all those who need to know your whereabouts and would benefit from having access to your immediate schedule.

In sharing this vital scheduling information with those who need it, you'll not only find it a great deal easier to hit upon those times when you can meet and work together, but you'll also find that it helps build and solidify a sense of teamwork and cooperation.

Do Terrific Task Management

As soon as you understand how to effectively maintain your to-do list in Outlook (as I describe in Chapter 12) and actually get into the habit of doing it, I'm pretty sure the use of the other Outlook modules in your pursuit of peak productivity will fall right into place.

I say this because I find the ability to maintain a thorough to-do list central to other aspects of personal productivity, including organizing your ideas and successfully managing and scheduling your time. For this reason, you may want to make mastering task management your first priority (right after organizing and cleaning out your e-mail Inbox, of course).

Take Note of Every Idea

Productivity is akin to creativity, and in order to maintain any semblance of creativity, you can't be laden down with niggling details. And, as I point out in Chapter 13, one of the most effective ways to clear out space in your head is by getting all those small details and stray ideas stored on your computer in the form of Outlook notes.

With Outlook notes, note taking can be very painless and quite ad hoc (assuming, of course, that you have the Outlook program running whenever your computer is turned on and Windows is booted). When jotting down ideas as Outlook notes, concentrate only on capturing the idea with little or no regard for its classification or organization. Later on, you can easily arrange your notes and, if necessary, turn them into to-do items on your task list or appointments on your calendar.

Use Automatic Journaling to Evaluate Your Productivity

As I describe in Chapter 14, the Outlook Journal enables you to automatically track your interactions with certain contacts in your address book as well as log your edits with other Office programs such as Word and Excel.

As such, in some work situations, this type of automatic journaling can provide you with a fairly accurate timeline on your major work interactions. You can then use the timeline to evaluate the current state of your time management and, if necessary, to find ways to improve upon it.

Take Outlook with You Wherever You Go

Applying all these nifty Outlook productivity skills and habits is of little consequence when you have to leave it all behind on your work computer when you're not in the office. Therefore, if telecommuting or work-related travel form a significant part of your job, you'll definitely want to take Outlook with you when you're on the go or not working at your office computer.

And the most convenient way to do this, as Chapter 15 points out, is by synchronizing key Outlook data items you maintain in the program on your desktop computer with your mobile device, such as a Smartphone or personal digital assistant (PDA). That way, you can access any of your Outlook contacts, calendars, to-do lists, and, in most cases, notes any time you need to while you're away from the office without having to worry the least bit that you've left someone or something vital behind.

Appendix A

Personal Productivity Resources

● ●

*T*he subject of how increasing personal productivity can work to enhance work/life balance is, to say the least, a big one, and this book on becoming more productive with Microsoft Outlook only begins to scratch its surface. To help you delve a little more deeply into this important topic, I list some of my favorite print and online personal productivity resources in this appendix.

Print Resources

The books in the following list can help you deepen your understanding of many productivity principles and ideas, not to mention Outlook features that I've only been able to briefly touch upon in this book:

✔ *Outlook 2007 Business Contact Manager For Dummies* by Karen Fredricks and Lon Orenstein (Wiley Publishing). This is the book to have if you're using Outlook 2007 and you want more information about its basic features.

✔ *Outlook 2007 All-in-One Desk Reference For Dummies* by Jennifer Fulton and Karen S. Fredricks (Wiley Publishing). If you're using Outlook 2007 and you want to have a more complete understanding of the full range of its features, then this is definitely the book to have.

✔ *The 7 Habits of Highly Effective People* by Stephen R. Covey (Free Press). This is Stephen Covey's classic text on the seven basic behaviors that, in his estimation, all people need to cultivate in order to be truly successful.

✔ *Getting Things Done: The Art of Stress-Free Productivity* by David Allen (Penguin Books). This is David Allen's classic text on what it takes for you to cultivate what he calls the "art of stress-free productivity."

✔ ***Ready For Anything: 52 Productivity Principles For Work and Life*** by David Allen (Viking). In this book, David Allen reiterates the principles of personal productivity he first introduces in his book *Getting Things Done,* here presenting them in 52 short and to-the-point chapters.

✔ ***Take Back Your Life: Using Microsoft Office Outlook 2007 to Get Organized and Stay Organized*** by Sally McGhee and John Wittry (Microsoft Press). This is the updated edition for Outlook 2007 of Sally McGhee's original title on using Microsoft Outlook to organize your life and become more productive. In it, she shows you how to use Outlook 2007 to create what she calls her Integrated Management Productivity system that you can use to stay on top of your workload.

✔ ***Total Workday Control Using Microsoft Outlook,*** 2nd Edition, by Michael Linenberger (New Academy Publishers). This is the updated version of Michael Linenberger's original book (entitled *Seize the Workday*) on developing what he calls the best task and e-mail practices using Microsoft Outlook.

✔ ***Leave the Office Earlier*** by Laura Stack (Broadway Books). This book covers the ten key factors that personal productivity expert and motivational speaker, Laura Stack, considers to be essential in order to improve productivity, reduce stress, and help you achieve work/life balance.

✔ ***Organizing For Success*** by Kenneth Zeigler (McGraw-Hill). This book is a compilation of the habits, strategies, and practices that time management consultant, Ken Zeigler, feels are essential to taking control of your workday and being both professionally and personally successful.

✔ ***Order From Chaos: A 6-Step Plan for Organizing Yourself, Your Office, and Your Life*** by Liz Davenport (Three Rivers Press). This book gives you organization consultant Liz Davenport's step-by-step plan for becoming more organized and using the newfound freedom it brings to be more productive and successful in all aspects of life.

✔ ***The Time Trap: The Classic Book on Time Managment,*** 3rd Edition by Alec Mackenzie (AMACOM, American Management Association). This book is the latest edition of time management consultant Alec Mackenzie's classic work on how to effectively avoid all the time traps that tend to stand in the way of true personal productivity.

✔ ***Streetwise Time Management: Get More Done with Less Stress by Efficiently Managing Your Time*** by Marshall Cook (Adams Media). In this book, Marshall Cook, Professor of Journalism and Communications at the University of Wisconsin, guides you through the steps necessary to reduce stress and become more productive by effectively managing your time.

Online Resources

The Internet is a great resource for information on personal productivity. The online resources listed here include companion Web sites for many of the productivity titles listed in the preceding "Print Resource" section. I also include a Lifehack Web page dedicated to personal productivity. Visit these Web sites to find up-to-date information on the authors, books, and the principles of personal productivity.

- ✔ **Dr. Greg's Stress-Free Productivity and Collaboration Strategies** at www.harveyproductivity.com. This is my companion Web site for *Manage Your Life with Outlook For Dummies*. Visit this site to get more information about personal productivity and team collaboration as well as to give me your feedback about the book.

- ✔ **FranklinCovey** at www.franklincovey.com. This is the place to go for FranklinCovey items of any type, including day planners and planning software. It's also an excellent resource for more information about the FranklinCovey Planning System.

- ✔ **David Allen** at www.davidco.com. This is David Allen's official Web site as well as the companion site for his bestselling book, *Getting Things Done*. Visit this Web site to get more information about David Allen's philosophy and principles of productivity as well as to order any of the many productivity products he offers for sale.

- ✔ **McGhee Productivity Solutions** at www.mcgheeproductivity.com. This is Sally McGhee's official Web site as well as the companion site for her book, *Take Back Your Life*. Visit this site to get more information about her Integrated Management Productivity system and various consulting services.

- ✔ **Workday Control** at www.workdaycontrol.com. This is New Academy Publisher's companion Web site for Michael Linenberger's book, *Total Workday Control*. Visit this Web site to get more information about Linenberger's principles for efficient task and e-mail management and to sign up for a free Outlook Productivity E-Mail Newsletter.

- ✔ **Productivity: Stepcase Lifehack** at www.lifehack.org/productivity. This is the productivity page of the LifeHack.org blog site that features all sorts of articles and posts following the latest ideas and trends in personal productivity. If you're using Outlook 2007, you can subscribe to the posts from this blog as an RSS feed and have the articles automatically delivered to your Outlook Inbox. (Click the RSS Feeds folder in the Outlook Navigation Pane in the Mail module to display instructions on how to subscribe to an RSS feed.)

Appendix B

Personal Productivity Self-Assessment

. . . .

*1*dentifying where you're at with personal productivity currently as well as where you want to be, both in the near future and in the long term, are very important aspects in the process of realizing greater work/life balance. For this reason, I've included this appendix to enable you to assess your current situation and personal productivity goals.

By taking time to reflect upon your attitudes and feelings about work/life balance and to record your personal productivity goals, you're actually making the first change and taking the necessary first step in the process of actualizing those goals.

Envisioning Work/Life Balance

What's your image of work/life balance? What does this balance look like and what advantages do you expect it to bring? Does attaining it simply mean doing less work and having more free time? Or does it also mean becoming more competent in your professional and personal roles so that you can reduce stress as you get more done in less time? Finally, how does work/life balance relate to your vision of being a happy and fulfilled individual?

Go ahead and jot down every idea, thought, and feeling you have about work/ life balance and the benefits you hope it will bring into your life:

_____

_____

_____

_____

_____

_____

_____

_____

_____

_____

_____

_____

_____

_____

_____

Beliefs about Personal Productivity

Your beliefs about personal productivity and attitudes about what it takes to achieve it have a great effect on your ability to reach your goals and make the necessary changes. For example, some folks believe that attaining peak personal productivity is primarily the result of possessing innate personality characteristics such as being naturally organized and self-directed. Others, like me, believe that achieving peak personal productivity is mainly a matter of getting proper training and developing appropriate new habits.

So, where you do you fall in the debate on the effects of nature versus nurture in terms of personal productivity? Take the time here to state your beliefs about personal productivity and what it takes to attain it:

_____

_____

_____

_____

_____

_____

_____

_____

_____

_____

_____

_____

_____

_____

Short-Term Productivity Goals

The goals you set for yourself in the pursuit of increased personal productivity and greater work/life balance are both short term (to be achieved anywhere from tomorrow to next week to the next few months) and long term (to be achieved in at least six months or longer).

Begin by recording your immediate productivity goals and then follow those with the goals you have in the near term. These short-term goals can include anything from re-organizing your desk and physical files to cleaning up and organizing your Outlook e-mail Inbox and increasing your competency using all the program's various modules.

_____

_____

_____

_____

_____

_____

_____

_____

_____

_____

_____

_____

_____

Long-Term Productivity Goals

Achieving peak personal productivity isn't just about taking immediate
steps to organize your life and better manage your time. It's also about
developing new habits that enable you to achieve long-term goals. Long-term
productivity goals can include such things as keeping your e-mail Inbox
empty (or as near as possible to empty), keeping your to-do lists up-to-date,
and taking steps to enhance certain professional and personal skills.

Go ahead and write down your long-term productivity goals here:

_____

_____

_____

_____

_____

_____

_____

_____

_____

_____

_____

_____

_____

Personal Productivity Strengths

Each person begins the process of improving his or her productivity with certain natural strengths or proclivities. By relying on these strengths, you can accelerate and greatly enhance the process. These strengths can run the gamut from being an organized person to having little or no trouble making decisions about prioritizing the things you need to do.

Write down your personal productivity strengths on the following lines:

_____

_____

_____

_____

_____

_____

_____

_____

_____

_____

_____

_____

_____

_____

_____

Personal Productivity Improvements

Natural strengths in the personal productivity arena are often offset by those areas which need improvement. These areas can be anything from organizational skills to decisiveness and the shouldering of more responsibility on your own.

On the following lines, write down the areas in personal productivity where you could stand to make some improvements:

_____

_____

_____

_____

_____

_____

_____

_____

_____

_____

_____

_____

_____

_____

Time Traps

Time traps are the natural enemy of personal productivity. They comprise all the activities you find yourself naturally indulging in that tend to make you less productive. They include all manner of interruptions and behaviors that take you away from the task at hand and disrupt your concentration.

Jot down the time traps you need to be aware of and try to avoid:

_____

_____

_____

_____

_____

_____

_____

_____

_____

_____

_____

_____

_____

_____

Index

Notes

Notes

Notes

BUSINESS, CAREERS & PERSONAL FINANCE

Accounting For Dummies, 4th Edition*
978-0-470-24600-9

Bookkeeping Workbook For Dummies†
978-0-470-16983-4

Commodities For Dummies
978-0-470-04928-0

Doing Business in China For Dummies
978-0-470-04929-7

E-Mail Marketing For Dummies
978-0-470-19087-6

Job Interviews For Dummies, 3rd Edition*†
978-0-470-17748-8

Personal Finance Workbook For Dummies*†
978-0-470-09933-9

Real Estate License Exams For Dummies
978-0-7645-7623-2

Six Sigma For Dummies
978-0-7645-6798-8

Small Business Kit For Dummies, 2nd Edition*†
978-0-7645-5984-6

Telephone Sales For Dummies
978-0-470-16836-3

BUSINESS PRODUCTIVITY & MICROSOFT OFFICE

Access 2007 For Dummies
978-0-470-03649-5

Excel 2007 For Dummies
978-0-470-03737-9

Office 2007 For Dummies
978-0-470-00923-9

Outlook 2007 For Dummies
978-0-470-03830-7

PowerPoint 2007 For Dummies
978-0-470-04059-1

Project 2007 For Dummies
978-0-470-03651-8

QuickBooks 2008 For Dummies
978-0-470-18470-7

Quicken 2008 For Dummies
978-0-470-17473-9

Salesforce.com For Dummies, 2nd Edition
978-0-470-04893-1

Word 2007 For Dummies
978-0-470-03658-7

EDUCATION, HISTORY, REFERENCE & TEST PREPARATION

African American History For Dummies
978-0-7645-5469-8

Algebra For Dummies
978-0-7645-5325-7

Algebra Workbook For Dummies
978-0-7645-8467-1

Art History For Dummies
978-0-470-09910-0

ASVAB For Dummies, 2nd Edition
978-0-470-10671-6

British Military History For Dummies
978-0-470-03213-8

Calculus For Dummies
978-0-7645-2498-1

Canadian History For Dummies, 2nd Edition
978-0-470-83656-9

Geometry Workbook For Dummies
978-0-471-79940-5

The SAT I For Dummies, 6th Edition
978-0-7645-7193-0

Series 7 Exam For Dummies
978-0-470-09932-2

World History For Dummies
978-0-7645-5242-7

FOOD, GARDEN, HOBBIES & HOME

Bridge For Dummies, 2nd Edition
978-0-471-92426-5

Coin Collecting For Dummies, 2nd Edition
978-0-470-22275-1

Cooking Basics For Dummies, 3rd Edition
978-0-7645-7206-7

Drawing For Dummies
978-0-7645-5476-6

Etiquette For Dummies, 2nd Edition
978-0-470-10672-3

Gardening Basics For Dummies*†
978-0-470-03749-2

Knitting Patterns For Dummies
978-0-470-04556-5

Living Gluten-Free For Dummies†
978-0-471-77383-2

Painting Do-It-Yourself For Dummies
978-0-470-17533-0

HEALTH, SELF HELP, PARENTING & PETS

Anger Management For Dummies
978-0-470-03715-7

Anxiety & Depression Workbook For Dummies
978-0-7645-9793-0

Dieting For Dummies, 2nd Edition
978-0-7645-4149-0

Dog Training For Dummies, 2nd Edition
978-0-7645-8418-3

Horseback Riding For Dummies
978-0-470-09719-9

Infertility For Dummies†
978-0-470-11518-3

Meditation For Dummies with CD-ROM, 2nd Edition
978-0-471-77774-8

Post-Traumatic Stress Disorder For Dummies
978-0-470-04922-8

Puppies For Dummies, 2nd Edition
978-0-470-03717-1

Thyroid For Dummies, 2nd Edition†
978-0-471-78755-6

Type 1 Diabetes For Dummies*†
978-0-470-17811-9

* Separate Canadian edition also available
† Separate U.K. edition also available

INTERNET & DIGITAL MEDIA

AdWords For Dummies
978-0-470-15252-2

Blogging For Dummies, 2nd Edition
978-0-470-23017-6

**Digital Photography All-in-One
Desk Reference For Dummies, 3rd Edition**
978-0-470-03743-0

Digital Photography For Dummies, 5th Edition
978-0-7645-9802-9

**Digital SLR Cameras & Photography
For Dummies, 2nd Edition**
978-0-470-14927-0

**eBay Business All-in-One Desk Reference
For Dummies**
978-0-7645-8438-1

eBay For Dummies, 5th Edition*
978-0-470-04529-9

eBay Listings That Sell For Dummies
978-0-471-78912-3

Facebook For Dummies
978-0-470-26273-3

The Internet For Dummies, 11th Edition
978-0-470-12174-0

Investing Online For Dummies, 5th Edition
978-0-7645-8456-5

iPod & iTunes For Dummies, 5th Editie
978-0-470-17474-6

MySpace For Dummies
978-0-470-09529-4

Podcasting For Dummies
978-0-471-74898-4

**Search Engine Optimization
For Dummies, 2nd Edition**
978-0-471-97998-2

Second Life For Dummies
978-0-470-18025-9

**Starting an eBay Business For Dummi
3rd Edition†**
978-0-470-14924-9

GRAPHICS, DESIGN & WEB DEVELOPMENT

**Adobe Creative Suite 3 Design Premium
All-in-One Desk Reference For Dummies**
978-0-470-11724-8

**Adobe Web Suite CS3 All-in-One Desk
Reference For Dummies**
978-0-470-12099-6

AutoCAD 2008 For Dummies
978-0-470-11650-0

**Building a Web Site For Dummies,
3rd Edition**
978-0-470-14928-7

**Creating Web Pages All-in-One Desk
Reference For Dummies, 3rd Edition**
978-0-470-09629-1

**Creating Web Pages For Dummies,
8th Edition**
978-0-470-08030-6

Dreamweaver CS3 For Dummies
978-0-470-11490-2

Flash CS3 For Dummies
978-0-470-12100-9

Google SketchUp For Dummies
978-0-470-13744-4

InDesign CS3 For Dummies
978-0-470-11865-8

**Photoshop CS3 All-in-One
Desk Reference For Dummies**
978-0-470-11195-6

Photoshop CS3 For Dummies
978-0-470-11193-2

Photoshop Elements 5 For Dummies
978-0-470-09810-3

SolidWorks For Dummies
978-0-7645-9555-4

Visio 2007 For Dummies
978-0-470-08983-5

Web Design For Dummies, 2nd Editi
978-0-471-78117-2

Web Sites Do-It-Yourself For Dummi
978-0-470-16903-2

Web Stores Do-It-Yourself For Dummi
978-0-470-17443-2

LANGUAGES, RELIGION & SPIRITUALITY

Arabic For Dummies
978-0-471-77270-5

Chinese For Dummies, Audio Set
978-0-470-12766-7

French For Dummies
978-0-7645-5193-2

German For Dummies
978-0-7645-5195-6

Hebrew For Dummies
978-0-7645-5489-6

Ingles Para Dummies
978-0-7645-5427-8

Italian For Dummies, Audio Set
978-0-470-09586-7

Italian Verbs For Dummies
978-0-471-77389-4

Japanese For Dummies
978-0-7645-5429-2

Latin For Dummies
978-0-7645-5431-5

Portuguese For Dummies
978-0-471-78738-9

Russian For Dummies
978-0-471-78001-4

Spanish Phrases For Dummies
978-0-7645-7204-3

Spanish For Dummies
978-0-7645-5194-9

Spanish For Dummies, Audio Set
978-0-470-09585-0

The Bible For Dummies
978-0-7645-5296-0

Catholicism For Dummies
978-0-7645-5391-2

The Historical Jesus For Dummies
978-0-470-16785-4

Islam For Dummies
978-0-7645-5503-9

**Spirituality For Dummies,
2nd Edition**
978-0-470-19142-2

NETWORKING AND PROGRAMMING

ASP.NET 3.5 For Dummies
978-0-470-19592-5

C# 2008 For Dummies
978-0-470-19109-5

Hacking For Dummies, 2nd Edition
978-0-470-05235-8

Home Networking For Dummies, 4th Edition
978-0-470-11806-1

Java For Dummies, 4th Edition
978-0-470-08716-9

**Microsoft® SQL Server™ 2008 All-in-One
Desk Reference For Dummies**
978-0-470-17954-3

**Networking All-in-One Desk Reference
For Dummies, 2nd Edition**
978-0-7645-9939-2

**Networking For Dummies,
8th Edition**
978-0-470-05620-2

SharePoint 2007 For Dummies
978-0-470-09941-4

**Wireless Home Networking
For Dummies, 2nd Edition**
978-0-471-74940-0

OPERATING SYSTEMS & COMPUTER BASICS

Mac For Dummies, 5th Edition
978-0-7645-8458-9

Laptops For Dummies, 2nd Edition
978-0-470-05432-1

Linux For Dummies, 8th Edition
978-0-470-11649-4

MacBook For Dummies
978-0-470-04859-7

Mac OS X Leopard All-in-One Desk Reference For Dummies
978-0-470-05434-5

Mac OS X Leopard For Dummies
978-0-470-05433-8

Macs For Dummies, 9th Edition
978-0-470-04849-8

PCs For Dummies, 11th Edition
978-0-470-13728-4

Windows® Home Server For Dummies
978-0-470-18592-6

Windows Server 2008 For Dummies
978-0-470-18043-3

Windows Vista All-in-One Desk Reference For Dummies
978-0-471-74941-7

Windows Vista For Dummies
978-0-471-75421-3

Windows Vista Security For Dummies
978-0-470-11805-4

SPORTS, FITNESS & MUSIC

Coaching Hockey For Dummies
978-0-470-83685-9

Coaching Soccer For Dummies
978-0-471-77381-8

Fitness For Dummies, 3rd Edition
978-0-7645-7851-9

Football For Dummies, 3rd Edition
978-0-470-12536-6

GarageBand For Dummies
978-0-7645-7323-1

Golf For Dummies, 3rd Edition
978-0-471-76871-5

Guitar For Dummies, 2nd Edition
978-0-7645-9904-0

Home Recording For Musicians For Dummies, 2nd Edition
978-0-7645-8884-6

iPod & iTunes For Dummies, 5th Edition
978-0-470-17474-6

Music Theory For Dummies
978-0-7645-7838-0

Stretching For Dummies
978-0-470-06741-3

Get smart @ dummies.com®

- Find a full list of Dummies titles
- Look into loads of FREE on-site articles
- Sign up for FREE eTips e-mailed to you weekly
- See what other products carry the Dummies name
- Shop directly from the Dummies bookstore
- Enter to win new prizes every month!

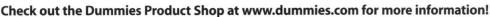